Animal Rights Without Liberation

Critical Perspectives on Animals: Theory, Culture, Science, and Law

CRITICAL PERSPECTIVES ON ANIMALS
Series Editors: Gary L. Francione and Gary Steiner

The emerging interdisciplinary field of animal studies seeks to shed light on the nature of animal experience and the moral status of animals in ways that overcome the limitations of traditional approaches to animals. Recent work on animals has been characterized by an increasing recognition of the importance of crossing disciplinary boundaries and exploring the affinities as well as the differences among the approaches of fields such as philosophy, law, sociology, political theory, ethology, and literary studies to questions pertaining to animals. This recognition has brought with it an openness to a rethinking of the very terms of critical inquiry and of traditional assumptions about human being and its relationship to the animal world. The books published in this series seek to contribute to contemporary reflections on the basic terms and methods of critical inquiry, to do so by focusing on fundamental questions arising out of the relationships and confrontations between humans and nonhuman animals, and ultimately to enrich our appreciation of the nature and ethical significance of nonhuman animals by providing a forum for the interdisciplinary exploration of questions and problems that have traditionally been confined within narrowly circumscribed disciplinary boundaries.

Animal Rights Without Liberation

APPLIED ETHICS AND HUMAN OBLIGATIONS

Alasdair Cochrane

COLUMBIA UNIVERSITY PRESS

NEW YORK

Columbia University Press
Publishers Since 1893
New York   Chichester, West Sussex
cup.columbia.edu
Copyright © 2012 Columbia University Press
All rights reserved

Library of Congress Cataloging-in-Publication Data

Cochrane, Alasdair, 1978–
Animal rights without liberation : applied ethics and human
obligations / Alasdair Cochrane.
p. cm.—(Critical perspectives on animals)
Includes bibliographical references and index.
ISBN 978-0-231-15826-8 (cloth : alk. paper)—ISBN 978-0-231-15827-5
(pbk. : alk. paper)—ISBN 978-0-231-50443-0 (ebook)
1. Animal rights. 2. Animal welfare. I. Title.

HV4708.C627 2012
179′.3–dc23
2012011701

∞
Columbia University Press books are printed on permanent and
durable acid-free paper.
This book is printed on paper with recycled content.
Printed in the United States of America
c 10 9 8 7 6 5 4 3 2 1
p 10 9 8 7 6 5 4 3 2 1

COVER IMAGE: Photo by D-BASE © Getty Images

References to Internet Web sites (URLs) were accurate at the time of writing.
Neither the author nor Columbia University Press is responsible for URLs that
may have expired or changed since the manuscript was prepared.

Contents

Acknowledgments

This book began life as my Ph.D. thesis, completed in the Department of Government at the London School of Economics. While what is presented here differs markedly from that thesis, the central arguments were conceived while I was studying at the LSE. As such, special thanks go to my supervisor, Cécile Fabre. Without her encouragement and enthusiasm for the project, as well as her dedicated and diligent reading and rereading of drafts, the thesis would never have been completed. I also thank my adviser, Paul Kelly, and examiners Anne Phillips and Albert Weale, whose comments and advice led to important refinements of the arguments. (Thanks also to Anne for allowing me to steal the title idea!) I am grateful to the Political Theory Group at the LSE for extensive comments on many of the ideas presented in the book. Of particular help were comments from and discussion with Garrett Brown, Phil Cook, Katrin Flikschuh, James Gledhill, Muriel Kahane, Andrej Keba, Camillia Kong, Chandran Kukathas, Alex Leveringhaus, Christian List, Fintan McCullagh, Panos Papoulias, Matt Sleat, Kai Spiekermann, Laura Valentini, Philipa Walker, and Jeremy Williams.

In the process of rewriting the manuscript, I have drawn on the important advice of a number of individuals. For discussion and critique, I thank especially Paula Casal, Alejandro Chehtman, Steve Cooke, Conor Gearty, John Hadley, Emily Jackson, Siobhan O'Sullivan, Thomas Poole, Krithika Srinivasan, Kim Stallwood, Martin Whiting, and Dita Wickins-Drazilova. Special thanks also go to Robert Garner, who read and commented on the entire manuscript (and received some strange phone calls concerning crop cultivation and the death of field animals).

My appreciation goes to the editorial team at Columbia University Press for handling the transition of the manuscript into a published book with such care: Wendy Lochner, Christine Mortlock, Roy Thomas, and Anita O'Brien have all been invaluable in this process.

An earlier version of chapter 3 appeared as "Animal Interests and Animal Experiments: An Interest-Based Approach," *Res Publica* 13, no. 3 (2007): 293–318. I am grateful to Springer and to the editors of that journal for permission to use it.

Finally, I thank all the friends and family who provide me with the reason to meet my deadlines—and not to work evenings and weekends. Most crucially, I thank Susie, without whom none of this would be worthwhile.

Animal Rights Without Liberation

One

Introduction

The question of what we owe to nonhuman animals is rightfully considered an important and serious question for academics and policy makers alike. Animal ethics is a well-established topic of inquiry in academia, drawing the attention of scholars from disciplines as diverse as philosophy, political science, sociology, anthropology, and zoology. Animal protection is also a settled policy goal of most contemporary societies, with increasingly stringent animal welfare laws being passed in countries on every continent. But although the question of what we owe to animals is considered important and serious, that does not mean there is any agreement concerning the answers. While it is reasonable to suggest that there is a loose consensus that political communities can and ought to do much more for the well-being of both domesticated and wild animals, precisely what that "more" requires is a subject of heated debate.

One of the greatest sources of debate arises over the issue of animal rights. On the one hand, for many people the idea of animal rights is simply nonsense.[1] It is nonsense, these animal rights skeptics claim, because animals are unable to respect the rights of others or claim rights for themselves, two supposedly necessary conditions for possessing rights. For these thinkers, we may have good reason to treat animals better, but those reasons are not and cannot be based on anything like the rights of animals. On this view, then, animal rights are a ludicrous impossibility. For most proponents of animal rights, on the other hand, recognizing the rights of animals is not only possible but is also necessary to making their lives better.[2] According to these thinkers, animal rights are a necessity because they, and they alone, demand an end to all the ways in which animals are used, owned, and exploited for human purposes. In other words, animal rights are a necessary condition of animal liberation.

This book argues that neither the skeptics nor the proponents of animal rights have got it quite right. Contrary to the skeptics, rights can indeed be sensibly ascribed to animals. After all, it does not matter that animals themselves cannot respect or claim rights; all that matters is that they possess basic interests that ground certain duties on our part. Furthermore, and contrary to the proponents, animal rights do not necessarily demand animal liberation. That is, animal rights do not require all animals to be set free from being used, owned, and exploited by human beings.[3] Indeed, the book argues that a properly constructed theory of animal rights—while including many powerful and demanding rights—does not include an animal right to be liberated.

In response to both the skeptics and the proponents, this book puts forward and defends an alternative view: a theory of animal rights without liberation. Such a theory can be viewed as embodying a much more qualified—mundane even—view of rights than that adopted by the skeptics or the proponents of animal rights. For under this theory, the possession of rights does not depend on their holders having complex mental powers related to moral and rational agency; nor do rights require that their holders be set free to lead lives of their own choosing. Rights possession simply means that their holders have certain important, basic interests that impose duties on others. Such an understanding of rights leads to a theory of animal rights without liberation.

This introductory chapter provides a brief outline of the theory of animal rights that the book will defend and apply. First the chapter explores how the link between animal rights and animal liberation came to be established in debates concerning our obligations to animals. The second section briefly explains why animal rights and animal liberation should be decoupled. It argues that given a proper understanding of why animals possess rights, and given a proper understanding of their interests, a theory of animal rights without liberation follows. The final section sketches how this theory of the *moral* rights of animals relates to the real-world obligations of contemporary political communities.

The Coupling of Animal Rights and Animal Liberation

A key assumption within the animal ethics literature is that all theories of animal rights necessarily endorse a specific ethical position: a position that is concerned not simply with animal welfare but with animal exploitation.[4] According to this view, what makes animal rights theories distinctive is that they are not concerned with *regulating* the use of animals in zoos, circuses, laboratories, farms, pet keeping, and so on. Instead, rights theories require that all such uses be *abolished* and the animals involved *liberated*. The assumption is that once it is acknowledged that animals possess certain rights, it must also be acknowledged that they possess the right not to be used for certain purposes. In this sense, then, animal rights are often considered to be analogous to human rights. For human rights do not demand that we stop beating our slaves, or that we regulate the ways women are trafficked more humanely; instead, they demand that such forms of exploitation be abolished and the victims liberated. Many animal ethicists believe that animal rights have similar implications. For example, Gary Francione writes: "Animal rights ensure that relevant animal interests are absolutely protected and may not be sacrificed simply to benefit humans, no matter how 'humane' the exploitation or how stringent the safeguards from 'unnecessary' suffering. Animal rights theory rejects the regulation of atrocities and calls unambiguously and unequivocally for their abolition."[5]

To understand why theories of animal rights have come to be intrinsically linked to demands for abolition and liberation, it is necessary to consider the evolution of thinking in animal ethics over the past forty years or so. In particular it is necessary to understand the work of the influential animal ethicist Peter Singer and the ways in which a number of animal protection scholars have sought to distance their theories from his work.

In 1975 Singer published his justly celebrated book *Animal Liberation* and transformed the way we think about the treatment of animals in contemporary society.[6] Singer exposed the realities of the ways in which animals are used on modern farms and in laboratories, revealing previously hidden cruelties that shocked his readers. Singer's book was not a mere exposé, however: the book also developed a sophisticated philosophical framework to explain why such uses of animals are wrong and should be stopped. The most striking claim that Singer makes in the book is that humans and sentient nonhuman animals are moral equals.[7] Obviously Singer does not mean that humans and animals are equal in terms of their abilities or capacities. Rather, he means that humans and animals have equal moral status and should have their interests considered equally when we are deciding on our actions and policies. This, of course, was and remains an incredibly radical proposal. Mainstream Western social, political, and moral thought simply takes for granted that human beings possess a greater moral worth than nonhuman creatures. So how does Singer justify such a controversial position?

Singer refers to the changes in thought and policy developed by such social movements as women's liberation, black liberation, and gay liberation and points out that we now consider all humans to be of equal moral worth. This is not, Singer claims, because of any factual equality about their strength, rationality, virtue, or other capacity, for obviously humans differ radically in their possession of such qualities. Instead Singer argues that human beings are of equal moral worth because, at bottom, we can all suffer. Because we can all suffer—because we are all "sentient"—we also possess morally significant interests. That is, as sentient beings who can experience ourselves in the world, we necessarily have interests in how our lives fare. Because of this shared capacity among humans, Singer argues, it is only right to consider the interests of all humans equally when deliberating about how we ought to treat one another. So while I might be more intelligent than my newborn baby, while my wife might be more virtuous than I am, and while my neighbor might be stronger than all of us, at bottom each of us is a sentient being with morally significant interests. On this simple basis we should each have our interests considered equally when decisions are made about what we are owed. Crucially, of course, human beings are not the only creatures that can experience joy and suffering in their lives: many species of nonhuman animal are also sentient. As such Singer argues that because sentience provides the basis for the equality of human beings, to be consistent we must extend this moral equality to all sentient creatures.

It is important to be clear, however, about what moral equality entails. It certainly does not mean, for example, that animals are entitled to exactly the same treatment as human beings. Equality for animals does not require us to give pigs the vote. For Singer, equality does not require equal treatment, but equal consideration. More precisely, equality demands that we grant equal consideration to the interests of all sentient creatures. In other words, it demands that we weigh and consider interests on their own merits, not on the basis of to whom they belong. For just as privileging the interests of one ethnic group is racist and privileging the interests of one gender is sexist, so for Singer privileging the interests of one species is *speciesist*.[8] Crucially, Singer ties this principle of equal consideration to the utilitarian goal of maximizing overall welfare. That is, he argues that we ought to consider the interests of all sentient individuals equally while formulating actions and policies that aim to maximize overall levels of interest satisfaction. Importantly, when these twin principles of equal consideration and utility maximization are applied, policies that treat individuals differently will often emerge—but such differential treatment will be fair.

So, under these principles, it is perfectly legitimate to grant adult humans the vote while denying it to pigs. Crucially, this is not because pigs' interests are of less moral concern, but simply because, unlike humans, pigs have no interest in voting. When we consider all interests equally and seek to maximize overall interest satisfaction, there is clearly no need to give the vote to pigs. According to these principles, however, it is not legitimate to permit, for example, agricultural systems that inflict routine forms of suffering on pigs. This is because pigs, just like humans, have a clear and strong interest in not suffering. Equal consideration and utility maximization demand an end to agricultural practices that inflict gross sufferings on pigs. As such, Singer's principles of equal consideration and of utility maximization provide a simple means by which to condemn many of the ways we treat animals in modern societies as unfair, discriminatory, and wrong.

From the moment of its publication, Singer's book and theory faced a number of critics. Many were appalled by the radical nature of its proposals. Treating animals as the moral equals of human beings was too much for many to swallow, notwithstanding the clarity and logic of Singer's reasoning. Critics of this kind chastised Singer for breaking down the moral divide between humans and animals and condemned his arguments as implausible and dangerous. Interestingly for our purposes, however, another set of critics did not think that Singer went far enough. For the latter thinkers, in spite of the name he had given it, Singer's proposal was not really a theory of animal *liberation* at all. These writers claimed that Singer's theory was not a call to liberate animals from their oppressive and exploitative relationships with humans but simply one to improve their lot. After all, Singer never categorically rules out the human use of animals. Instead he argues that we ought to consider their interests equally when formulating our actions and policies. Moreover, as a utilitarian philosopher, he argues that our actions and policies should serve to maximize utility—the overall satisfaction of interests. As such, under Singer's theory, it is possible to use animals for certain human purposes so long as their interests have been considered equally, and so long as such uses maximize overall utility. As many thinkers pointed out, this type of reasoning can be used to justify all sorts of terrible harms to individual animals, so long as such harms increase aggregate welfare. For example, if a painful experiment on a handful of animals leads to a drug that benefits many more, then under Singer's reasoning such use would be legitimate. For some critics, a theory that condones these kinds of uses and sacrifices of animals is far too permissive. In particular, Tom Regan's book, *The Case for Animal Rights*, published in the early 1980s, provided a powerful challenge to Singer's philosophical framework and practical conclusions.[9]

Regan argues that to achieve justice for animals, we need to recognize that they possess *moral rights*. Moreover, according to Regan, the possession of rights implies something more than equal moral worth or the entitlement to equal consideration of one's interests. Instead, it means that some uses of animals are ruled out categorically, irrespective of how they affect levels of interest satisfaction. For according to Regan, the most basic of rights is the right to respectful treatment, and being treated respectfully means that one must never be used merely as a means to secure the best overall consequences.[10] Regan claims that sentient animals possess this right to respectful treatment because essentially they are individuals whose value cannot be reduced to their usefulness to others; that is, they possess "inherent value." Sentient animals possess this inherent value for Regan because they are "subjects-of-a-life": beings with beliefs, desires, a sense of themselves over time, interests in their own fate, and so on.[11] Regan is thus arguing that entities with these sorts of mental attributes possess a value all of their own—a value that is independent of how they are valued by others. As such, they have a right to respectful treatment; that is, a right to be treated in accordance with their inherent value.

When it comes to applying this theory to the use of animals, Regan's rights-based position is clearly very restrictive. Singer's theory permits the human use of animals if their interests are considered equally and if such use increases aggregate welfare. Regan's theory, on the other hand, condemns every form of exploitation of animals that treats them solely as tools, instruments, or a means to improve overall consequences. On this basis Regan writes: *"The rights view will not be satisfied with anything less than the total dissolution of the animal industry as we know it."*[12] Francione develops Regan's rights-based theory to argue that this rules out *all* human uses of animals: "The use of animals for food, sport, entertainment, or research involves treating animals merely as means to ends, and this constitutes a violation of the respect principle."[13] For Regan and his followers, then, only a rights-based theory can properly be called a theory of animal liberation, for a rights-based theory condemns all the ways in which animals are used as tools to serve human ends.

The theories of Peter Singer and Tom Regan have been the most influential contributions to animal ethics: *Animal Liberation* and *The Case for Animal Rights* have provided a reference point for all subsequent scholarly works on debates about our obligations to nonhuman animals. This is not to say that all have aligned themselves as either pro-Singer or pro-Regan. Indeed, it is not even to say that all subsequent contributions have aligned themselves along the spectrum that these positions mark out. After all, many scholars with feminist, postmodern, and ecocentric inclinations have rejected not only the specific arguments of Singer and Regan but also the traditional philosophical frameworks through which they are made.[14] Nevertheless, even those theories that have attempted to transcend Singer and Regan acknowledge their importance by that very attempt. Crucially, an explanation of the dichotomy between a Singer-influenced "welfarism" and a Regan-influenced "rights position" has now become a necessary ingredient in any textbook, research monograph, course, or lecture on animal ethics. What has followed as result of this influence, however, is the entrenchment of this perceived dichotomy. Moreover, it is now often assumed that any animal rights theory must necessarily be a theory with the same reasoning and implications as Tom Regan's. There is now a rarely questioned assumption within animal ethics that an animal rights position necessarily entails the abolition of animal use and the liberation of used animals. The next section explains why that assumption should be abandoned.

Decoupling Animal Rights from Animal Liberation

This book challenges the idea that a theory of animal rights must necessarily be a theory of animal liberation. It also challenges the idea that a theory of animal rights has to follow the reasoning and implications of Regan's type of animal rights theory. Indeed this book claims that if a properly nuanced understanding of what it means to possess rights is accepted, and if a properly nuanced understanding of the interests of animals is adopted, then a theory of animal rights without liberation logically follows. This section briefly explains why this is the case.

First it is necessary to make it clear that what rights are, how they are justified, and what they entail are all extremely contested questions in rights theory. Sometimes scholars working in animal ethics neglect this fact. As we have seen, Regan's view is that all animal rights are essentially derivatives of the basic right to respectful treatment, which all entities with inherent value possess. But there is no need for all theories of animal rights to follow this line of reasoning; in fact, there is good reason for them not to. Regan's theory of rights employs a Kantian type of moral reasoning. For Immanuel Kant, ultimate value resides in those entities with "dignity." Individuals with dignity are moral and autonomous agents: they have the capacity to reason about and act on moral principles, as well as the capacity to fashion, to some extent, their own destiny. According to Kant, all entities with such agency can legitimately be described as "ends-in-themselves," should always be treated as such, and thus should never be used exclusively as a means. Entities without such dignity are for Kant mere "things" that can legitimately be treated simply as means.[15] Regan's line of argument is extremely similar. Kant grounds dignity in the self-governing agency of individuals, which demands that such individuals never be used solely as a means. Regan, on the other hand, grounds inherent value in being a subject-of-a-life, which demands that such individuals never be used solely as a means.

The problem here, though, is that being a subject-of-a-life is not the same as being a self-governing agent, an end-in-oneself. It is possible for a creature to have desires, a memory, a sense of oneself over time, interests in one's fate, and so on, without also having the capacities of moral and autonomous agency. Most of us would recognize that while the majority of human beings can legitimately be described as moral and autonomous agents, the majority of nonhuman creatures cannot. Sentient animals may have phenomenal consciousness and possess desires, but most, if not all, certainly do not have the capacities to reason, reflect, and act on self-chosen moral principles or life goals.

The fact that the characteristics for being a subject-of-a-life are different from those necessary for being an end-in-oneself poses a big problem for Regan's argument. Regan might be correct that subjects-of-a-life possess inherent value. However, he does not provide convincing grounds for the claim that they necessarily possess a basic right to respectful treatment. After all, many subjects-of-a-life do not have the capacities of moral and autonomous agency and so are not "ends-in-themselves" as Kant uses the term. Crucially, it is unclear why creatures who are not ends-in-themselves must always be treated as ends-in-themselves. Thus Regan's argument that animals possess a basic right to respectful treatment—a right not to be used only as a means—is extremely dubious. Since for Regan all animal rights are derivatives of this basic right, his entire theory of animal rights rests on rather uncertain foundations.

So does this mean that the very idea of animal rights is nonsensical? Do the problems with Regan's theory reveal that the notion of animal rights is an absurdity, as claimed by the skeptics mentioned at the outset of this chapter? Certainly not. Just because Regan attempts to ground animal rights via this Kantian reasoning does not mean that it is the only way it might be done. A much more plausible and straightforward means of establishing a theory of animal rights is not through an appeal to dignity or inherent value, but through interests. The interest-based rights approach that this book employs is outlined and defended in much greater depth in the next chapter. However, it will be useful to sketch the approach in general terms here so that its differences from Regan's account of animal rights can be fully appreciated.

The idea of basing animal rights—and indeed human rights—in the interests of individuals is not unique to this book. For example, Joel Feinberg, Bernard Rollin, and James Rachels have all claimed that animal rights derive from animals' interests.[16] As such they have offered theories of animal rights that have a more tangible and concrete grounding than any that relies on such notions as dignity or inherent value. What differentiates the theory of animal rights proposed in this book, however, is the comprehensive way in which it engages with interests—identifying them, evaluating their strength, and balancing them—in order to establish the rights of animals. In so doing, the book employs Joseph Raz's famous formulation of what it means to have a right. Raz argued that an individual has a right when that individual has an interest that is sufficient for holding someone else under a duty.[17] This analysis can be used to understand the types of things that rights are: it states, after all, that rights are protections of certain important interests. Crucially, however, the formulation can also be used as a method with which to *assign* rights. For we can use this framework to assign a right to an individual when we have good reason to judge one of his or her interests to be sufficiently strong, all things considered, to impose a duty on someone else.

Of course, judging whether an interest is indeed "sufficiently strong" requires a good deal of normative argument. Interests have to be identified, strengths of interests must be established, interests must be balanced against competing interests and values, and the burdens any putative right claim places on any potential duty-bearer must be assessed. The bulk of this book engages in precisely this kind of argumentation—justifying rights through careful assessment of these factors. It is certainly true to say that this type of framework requires a lot of work in order to establish any list of rights. Under this scheme, rights cannot be considered "self-evident" or "natural"—labels that are often attributed to theories of moral rights. For according to interest-based approaches, rights are not metaphysically mysterious entities with dubious foundations. Rather, they are justified by reference to something tangible and concrete—the well-being of individuals—via a process that is clear and systematic. Indeed, the interest-based approach does not even regard rights as fundamental or basic to morality. Instead it views them as second-order moral principles that require justification through ordinary normative reasoning. Crucially, then, the interest-based approach demystifies rights.[18]

Importantly for our purposes, this theory of rights also leaves open the precise content of rights. This is quite different from the theories of rights that Regan and his followers propose. After all, under Regan's type of rights theory, the very fact that animals possess rights necessarily means that we have specific obligations with respect to them. Regan argues that it means that animals must never be used solely to secure the best consequences, ruling out all sorts of uses and exploitation of animals. Gary Francione elaborates on this idea, arguing that acknowledging that animals possess rights necessarily means that we cannot class animals or treat them as the *property* of human beings.[19] However, the interest-based account of rights is quite different. Recognizing that animals possess interest-based rights does not by itself tell us *which* rights animals possess. Contrary to Regan, it might be that animals have some rights but have no right not to be used and exploited by human beings. Contrary to Francione, it might be that animals have some rights but have no right not to be owned by humans. The argument of this book is that when we have a proper understanding of the interests of sentient animals, there is no reason to grant animals a right never to be used, owned, and exploited by human beings. Because the vast majority of sentient animals have no intrinsic interest in liberty, they possess no fundamental right to be free, and no fundamental right to be liberated.

How can such a claim be justified? What is the basis for the claim that the vast majority of sentient animals have no intrinsic interest in liberty?[20] Most sentient animals have no intrinsic interest in liberty, the book claims, because they lack the capacities of autonomous agency. That is, the majority of sentient animals lack the ability to frame, revise, and pursue their own conception of the good.[21] Lacking such capacities, these animals are not necessarily harmed when they have their freedom curtailed and are prevented from leading their own chosen lives. Lacking autonomous agency, sentient animals are not necessarily harmed when they are interfered with, used for particular purposes, or even have their desires shaped and molded by others. In other words, there is an important difference between the interests of sentient nonhuman animals and most human beings in this respect. Because most humans possess the ability to frame, revise, and pursue their own conceptions of the good, they have an intrinsic interest in governing their own lives. As such, interfering with them, using them against their will, and molding their desires are usually incredibly harmful to human beings. As a result of this difference, then, some practices that are objectionable when done to humans are not objectionable when done to animals: keeping an animal as a pet is quite unlike keeping a human as a slave; using animals to undertake certain types of work is quite unlike coercing human beings to labor; buying and selling animals is quite unlike trading human beings; and so on. Since the vast majority of animals have no intrinsic interest in liberty, they have no fundamental right to freedom and to liberation.

It is important, however, to make two clarifications at this point. First, the claim is not that *all* nonhuman animals possess no intrinsic interest in liberty; rather, it is that the vast majority of them do not. This qualification is important because although it is evident that most sentient animals cannot frame, revise, and pursue a conception of the good, there may be a few exceptions. It might be that some nonhuman animals are autonomous agents with an interest in leading their own freely chosen lives. For example, evidence concerning the complex cognitive capacities of the great apes and cetaceans is increasing all the time and has led several scholars to declare that these animals are "persons," in the sense that they are rational, goal-pursuing agents.[22] This book remains agnostic on this issue and does not attempt to conclude whether any nonhumans can be described as autonomous in this way. However, given that there is a possibility that such creatures might have these capacities, and given that the evidence is changing all the time and usually changes to attribute greater and more complex attributes to these animals, a precautionary principle is probably wise. That is, in the face of this changing evidence, it would seem only sensible to treat the great apes and cetaceans as if they are autonomous agents with an intrinsic interest in liberty. None of this, however, undermines the key central and clear point: the vast majority of sentient animals do not have the kinds of mental capacities to frame, revise, and pursue their own conceptions of the good, and they thus have no intrinsic interest in liberty.

The second clarification is that this book does not deny the obvious point that all kinds of uses, exploitation, and ownership of animals cause harm to animals. Depriving animals of liberty through confining them in cages and stalls, or through using them to model painful and deadly diseases, obviously inflicts serious harm on them. However, the claim of this book is that it is the pain, suffering, and death that cause the harm in such instances, not the use itself. As such, we can say that sentient animals possess an instrumental, rather than intrinsic, interest in liberty. For autonomous beings, on the other hand, curtailing their freedom in such ways is harmful irrespective of whether it causes pain and suffering: their interest in liberty is intrinsic. Consider the case of Truman Burbank in the movie *The Truman Show*.[23] In that movie Truman leads an extremely happy life: he has a good job, good friends, and a loving wife. Little does Truman know, however, that this life of his is being filmed for a television show, and that his colleagues, friends, and wife are all actors. In spite of the fact that Truman leads a life of happiness, most of us consider this not to be a good life for him to lead. That is because we think that there is something impoverished about the fact that Truman is unable to forge and pursue his *own* goals and his *own* relationships. His life is happy but inauthentic, and, as a rational and autonomous agent, he is harmed by this.

This book claims that the interests of most sentient animals are quite different in this respect. For example, the lives of many dogs who work in the theater, on television, or in film might be said to be somehow inauthentic. Think, for example, of the various dogs who have unwittingly played Toto over the years. Clearly the animals who are used in these ways do not understand that their training and work is being utilized for human entertainment in plays, TV shows, and movies. However, it would be odd to regard such inauthentic lives as necessarily harmful to these dogs, all else being equal. If the dogs are well looked after, happy, and fulfilled, it is difficult to identify what harm is being done to them. This is precisely because dogs are not rational autonomous agents with an interest in leading their own freely chosen lives, and as such their interests are quite different from those of humans in this respect.

In sum, this book claims that sentient animals have strong and compelling rights, but have no right to be liberated. It is important to remind ourselves of the first of these two claims. For while this book does not assign to animals a fundamental right to be free, it does assign to them other rights that impose extremely demanding obligations on us. Indeed, as we shall see, the book claims that animals possess prima facie moral rights not to be made to suffer and not to be killed. Undoubtedly the recognition of such rights forces us to reevaluate and transform many of the practices of contemporary societies. This book outlines the transformations that these rights demand by systematically evaluating current practices in the contexts of experimentation, agriculture, genetic engineering, entertainment, environmental protection, and culture. In each case the claim of this book is that while there is no obligation to liberate *all* animals from *all* these contexts, such uses of animals need to be completely transformed if they are to be compatible with the rights of animals. Of course, the transformation of our uses of animals brings up the question of how far this theory of animal rights relates to the real-world practices of existing political communities. This relationship between the theory and practice of animal rights is taken up in more detail in the next section.

Animals' Moral and Legal Rights

It is important to bear in mind that the theory of animal rights presented in this book is a theory of *moral rights*. In other words, it is a theory about the types of rights and obligations that can be derived from moral reasoning and principles. However, this does not mean that it is a completely abstract or purely theoretical endeavor. Indeed, the theory of moral rights provided in this book has an intrinsic relationship to both law and politics. After all, by providing an account of the moral *rights* of animals, the book is not merely saying that it would be permissible or desirable for animals to be treated in this way or that. Instead the language of rights immediately implies that this treatment of animals is a matter of *justice*. That is, it is a matter that pertains to what individuals can be legitimately coerced to comply with.[24] To say that animals have some moral right to some good means, then, that we expect political communities to protect and uphold those rights through their legal rules. The account of the moral rights of animals provided in this book thus proposes what the legal rights of animals *ought to be*. While it is certainly a theoretical endeavor, the theory is intimately connected to the practice of both law and politics.

To be clear, this book does not aim to capture or account for all our moral relations with animals. Rather, it provides an account of those that the state can legitimately make individuals comply with. It is undoubtedly the case that individuals have moral duties with respect to animals that it may not be appropriate for the state to enforce, such as those duties grounded in benevolence, generosity, or charity. As such, it is important to remember that this book has a more limited remit. It attempts to provide an account of the moral rights of animals that political communities ought to recognize and enforce.

However, this should not be taken to mean that the book is claiming that all moral rights ought to be enforced as legal rights.[25] For it is important to acknowledge that there are some moral rights—particularly those pertaining to personal relationships and the like—that states should not enforce. For example, if I have promised to stay at home and cook my partner her favorite meal for her birthday, it is plausible to say that she has a moral right (an interest that is sufficient to impose a duty on me) that I fulfill my promise. And yet there are good reasons, based on practical problems of enforcement and moral problems to do with its impact on trust, that count against states' enforcing such rights. And this is just as true when it comes to the moral rights of animals. Animals may have certain rights against us that states ought not to enforce. For example, it is not unreasonable to suggest that my cat has an interest that is sufficient to impose a duty on me that I consider his reduced mobility and arthritis (he has only three legs) when choosing somewhere new to live. But it certainly seems inappropriate and impractical for the state to enforce this kind of right—to *make* me select a home, say, without steep staircases. With all this in mind, while there are certainly *some* moral rights that states ought not to enforce, this book is concerned to examine and establish only those rights of animals that ought to become legal rights. Its aim is to come up with a moral theory of rights that is focused on the legal and political domains.

Moreover, although the book does claim that political communities ought to protect these animal rights, that is not the same thing as calling for states to implement these rights in their totality and with immediate effect.[26] The book does not call for such immediate and wholesale implementation for two main reasons, one practical and one normative. The practical reason simply recognizes that how rights are best upheld and protected is an extremely complex and demanding question. For example, there is considerable debate concerning whether the rights of *humans* are more robustly protected by constitutional protection combined with judicial enforcement or through legislative change via elected representatives.[27] The same debate applies to animals: should those rights be protected in some kind of bill of animal rights or through ordinary legislative acts? It is also unclear whether there ought to be the same answer to such a question in different political communities. After all, the political culture, history, and institutions of a community all seem relevant to successful rights protection. Importantly, these types of question cannot be answered easily or quickly but demand the close attention of social scientists, lawyers, historians, social movement theorists, activists, and others. It is crucial, then, that this kind of social scientific work is undertaken before the rights and obligations of the theory are translated into policy.

The second reason why the book does not demand that these rights be implemented with immediate effect and in their totality has a more normative basis. For to institutionalize these animal rights immediately and in their totality has a worrying implication in terms of democratic procedures. It seems to suggest that such procedures can and ought to be overridden. But while this book aims to provide a theory of animal rights that is compelling, urgent, and important, that does not mean that it has to be institutionalized at any cost. The effort of this book is part of what Adam Swift and Stuart White have referred to as "democratic underlabouring."[28] That is, the aim is to improve the public's and policy makers' understanding of our obligations to animals, and also to persuade them of the presented theory of animal rights.[29] As such the book does not seek to circumvent the democratic process when enacting these protections for animals. Rather it seeks to contribute to the democratic process by informing and persuading others of their compelling force.

This introduction has briefly outlined the theory of animal rights without liberation that is to be defended and applied throughout the remainder of this book. The theory denies the claim of animal rights skeptics that it is necessary to be able to respect rights or claim them for oneself in order to possess rights. Instead, it argues that all one needs in order to possess rights is to have certain interests that are sufficient to impose duties on others. The book claims that sentient nonhuman animals satisfy that condition. Crucially, the theory also denies that a theory of animal rights must necessarily be a theory of animal liberation. That is, it refutes the widely held assumption that once we recognize that animals possess rights, we must also acknowledge that it is impermissible to use, own, or exploit them for certain purposes. The assumption that animal rights theories must have this implication is, at least in part, an unfortunate consequence of the deeply embedded dichotomy between Peter Singer's utilitarianism and Tom Regan's rights-based theory in the animal ethics literature. Not all theories of animal rights have to follow Regan's theory of rights—alternative and more qualified theories of animal rights are available. Moreover, given the serious flaws with Regan's theory, finding and using such an alternative is preferable. As such, this book uses Joseph Raz's account of rights to ground and assign rights to animals: an animal possesses a right when it has an interest that is sufficient, all things considered, to impose a duty on another. The theory defended here argues that because most animals are not autonomous agents who can frame, revise, and pursue their own conceptions of the good, they have no intrinsic interest in liberty and thus no basic right to be liberated. We can respect the rights of animals, the theory claims, while still using, owning, and exploiting animals for certain purposes. Once again, this is obviously not to condone all uses of animals—many of which cause them severe forms of suffering and result in their death—but simply to recognize that it is the suffering and killing that are harmful in such instances, not the use itself.

In sum, the theory proposed in this book calls for profound changes in many of the ways in which we use and treat animals, but not for all such uses to be abolished. Ultimately this theory of animal rights is directed at the political realm—to be enforced as legal rights by political communities. However, just because the theory proposes rights and obligations that are compelling and urgent does not mean that it ought to be implemented in its totality with immediate effect in all contexts.

The remainder of the book develops, defends, and applies the theory of animal rights that has been sketched in this introduction. Chapter 2 explains and defends the interest-based rights approach in more detail. It first explains why it is meaningful and appropriate to acknowledge that we have moral obligations to sentient animals. It then defends the view that sentient animals can also possess rights, arguing that the possession of interests is the necessary and sufficient condition for holding rights. Finally it explains why the interest-based rights approach is the best means of delineating our obligations to animals.

Chapter 3 applies this interest-based rights framework to the most controversial issue in animal ethics: animal experimentation. The chapter begins by defending the claim that nonhuman animals possess prima facie rights not to be killed and not to be made to suffer. Crucially, the chapter argues that these rights are maintained even when they conflict with the human interest in realizing the benefits of animal experimentation. Finally, however, it argues that these rights do not require the abolition of all animal experimentation: experiments where animals are not killed or made to suffer are permissible, all else being equal.

Chapter 4 moves from the most controversial issue to the one that affects the largest number of animals: agriculture. The chapter examines the implications of this theory of animal rights for the farming of animals. It argues that the theory requires a total transformation of agricultural systems, including an end to all means of intensively farming animals and an end to raising animals for their meat. The chapter examines a number of objections to this proposal, including the idea that animals are better off for being raised to be killed, and finds them all to be wanting.

One of the ways in which animals are used in experimentation and in agriculture is as the subjects of genetic engineering: to model particular diseases, and to possess certain traits desirable to farmers. However, because genetic engineering raises extremely complicated ethical issues in and of itself, chapter 5 is devoted exclusively to this issue. Given the rights of animals, the chapter argues that engineering animals who end up with diseases, disabilities, or other reduced opportunities for well-being is impermissible. However, it claims that there is usually nothing wrong with engineering animals who end up with opportunities for well-being similar to ordinary members of the species, even if they are altered in quite dramatic ways.

Chapter 6 evaluates the ways in which we use animals to entertain us: in zoos, in sport, in circuses, and as pets. Its claims are in stark contrast to those of other proponents of animal rights. For it is argued that none of these practices—including displaying animals in zoos and circuses—is harmful in and of itself. This is not to sanction the status quo and the various harmful ways that animals are currently used to entertain us. The point is that the obligation of political communities lies in radically transforming the ways in which they use animals, not in liberating all animals from all such uses.

In chapter 7 the book moves on to consider the question of our environmental obligations in light of this theory of animal rights without liberation. The chapter argues against assigning moral status or rights to the nonsentient environment, on the basis that sentience is a necessary condition for the possession of interests. This does not mean, however, that this theory of animal rights offers a weak environmental ethic, for strict environmental obligations derive from a welfare-centric ethic that grounds our environmental obligations in our duties to sentient animal life. The chapter also considers issues surrounding therapeutic hunting and argues that policies of killing abundant animals should not be followed, but that interfering with those animals, through contraception for example, is perfectly permissible.

Chapter 8 addresses an area of animal use that has been underexplored in animal ethics: the use of animals by cultural groups. In recent years there has been controversy over such practices as religious slaughter, religious animal sacrifice, and indigenous hunting. Do the rights of animals not to be made to suffer and not to be killed still stand even when they clash with the human rights to religious freedom and cultural expression? This book claims that they do.

The concluding chapter has two main aims: to summarize the various animal rights defended in the book and to reflect further on what this means for the policies and actions of political communities. This second objective returns the book to the issue of how these rights ought to be implemented and protected, allowing for further discussion of the merits of the approach of democratic underlaboring.

Two

Animals, Interests, and Rights

This book argues that while sentient animals can and do possess certain moral rights, we are under no obligation to liberate them. So while sentient animals have particular interests that impose strict duties on us in a whole variety of contexts, those duties do not include having to refrain from using, keeping, and owning them. Separating animal rights from animal liberation in this way will strike some readers as odd. After all, as was seen in the previous chapter, there is a widely held assumption within animal ethics that a theory of animal rights must also be a theory of animal liberation. One of the fundamental aims of this book is to decouple animal rights from animal liberation: it claims that animals possess rights but have no right to be liberated. These claims are made through an application of what can be called an interest-based rights approach. More details as to the particular elements of this approach are provided later in the chapter. However, the essential idea is as follows: we work out the rights of animals by considering whether they possess any interests that are sufficient, all things considered, to impose duties on us. Because sentient animals ordinarily have clear and discernible interests in not suffering and in continued life, animals possess prima facie rights not to be made to suffer and not to be killed. But because most animals possess no interest in leading freely chosen lives, they possess no prima facie right to be liberated. As such, while we often have an obligation not to commit acts that kill animals or cause them to suffer, the theory of animal rights defended in this book claims that we are under no obligation to always refrain from using, keeping, and owning them.

The aim of this chapter is to outline and defend the interest-based rights approach that will be applied in the subsequent chapters. The approach depends on two important assumptions that require justification: first, that it is meaningful to talk of moral obligations to animals;

and second, that it is meaningful to talk of animal rights. Because recognizing that we have obligations to sentient animals is less controversial than acknowledging that they possess rights, more time is devoted here to the defense of the latter claim than to the defense of the former. The first section explores and defends the claim that sentient animals are the types of beings to whom we have moral obligations. The second section asks whether sentient animals can also be meaningfully considered to possess rights. It argues that they can and refutes a number of important objections to the very idea of animal rights. In the final section the interest-based right approach is defended as the most appropriate framework with which to delineate our moral obligations toward animals.

Sentient Animals and Moral Status

This book assumes that sentient animals have moral status. The concept of moral status is quite simply "a means of specifying those entities towards which we believe ourselves to have moral obligations."[1] So the ascription of moral status to sentient animals is just another way of saying that we have certain moral obligations to them. Importantly, this ascription is something more than the acknowledgment that we have obligations *regarding* sentient animals. This point is important because it is perfectly possible to have obligations *regarding* something without necessarily having obligations *to* that thing. For example, imagine that I have an obligation not to kick your dog; on what basis might that obligation be founded? On the one hand, the obligation might be based solely on the fact that you own the dog and do not want him to be kicked. In this case my obligation relates to the dog but is ultimately owed to you; we need not consider the dog to have moral status of his own. Alternatively, my obligation not to kick your dog might persist even if you encourage me to kick him. This might be because my obligation is based on the fact that kicking the dog will cause him pain and make his life worse. Here my obligation is owed to the dog himself, and so the dog *is* considered to have moral status. Moral status, then, is a means of delineating the entities to whom we have direct moral obligations.

Neither this chapter nor the book as a whole will provide a full defense of the claim that sentient animals possess moral status. It will not delve in any great detail into questions concerning animals' value or the nature of their minds. For this book is concerned to get on with outlining *what* obligations we have to animals, rather than becoming entangled with the intricacies of *whether* we have any at all. After all, it is a reasonable assumption that most people are quite happy to accept that sentient animals are worthy of *some* ethical consideration.[2] Nevertheless, something needs to be said about the ascription of moral status to sentient animals; not least because the answer to why sentient animals possess moral status affects both the nature of our obligations to them and the reasons for assigning them rights. As such, a brief defense and examination of the claim that sentient animals have moral status is necessary as a starting point.

In fact the notion that sentient animals possess moral status involves at least two separate assumptions. The first is that there *are* some animals with sentience. The second is that those animals with sentience have the necessary characteristic for moral status. In what follows, each assumption is examined in turn.

ANIMALS AND SENTIENCE

This book takes sentience to be equivalent to the capacity for phenomenal consciousness: the qualitative, subjective, experiential, or phenomenological aspects of conscious experience.[3] In other words, to be sentient is to be able to *feel* and to *experience* the world. As such, sentience has a close relationship with the ability to feel pain and pleasure. Indeed, by definition things that feel pain and pleasure must be sentient. Of course, it will be obvious to anyone who has had any contact with animals that many of them are sentient in the sense described. Nevertheless, philosophers and scientists have commonly provided three reasons to bolster the commonsense belief that many animals are indeed sentient.[4]

First, many animals *behave* as if they have sentience. This is illustrated by the fact that animals sometimes cry out, recoil, or grimace when in pain. The reason that we can take such actions to be more than some unfeeling reflex response is based on the fact that such action will often be accompanied by the adaptation of behavior. For example, many animals will tend to avoid those things that have caused them pain and will protect injured body parts. Clearly such behaviors are extremely good evidence of an animal's ability to feel and have experiences.

Second, while there are obvious differences between humans and other species of animal, it is important to bear in mind that we are all essentially made of the same stuff. For example, zoologist Donald R. Griffin writes:

> As mental experiences are directly linked to neurophysiological processes—or absolutely identical with them, according to strict behaviorists—our best evidence by which to compare them across species stems from comparative neurophysiology. To the extent that basic properties of neurons, synapses, and neuroendocrine mechanisms are similar, we might expect to find comparably similar mental experiences. It is well known that basic neurophysiological functions are very similar indeed in all multicellular animals.[5]

Humans share very similar neural mechanisms with other animals, and this in itself makes it likely that our experiences are to some extent alike.

The third reason for supposing that many animals do have some mental experience is that it makes sense from an evolutionary perspective. The ability to feel pain and experience comfort makes it likely that mobile creatures will avoid the former and pursue the latter. The effect of such experiences on behavior is of course vital for survival and successful reproduction. One would thus expect many successful species of roaming animal to have the capacity for some subjective experience.

But while the question of whether any animals possess sentience is relatively clear-cut, the question of *which ones* has proven much trickier to answer definitively. Our convictions concerning animal sentience are quite firm in relation to mammals: cats, dogs, cows, pigs, and so on. For most of us, however, those convictions become quite shaky as we move around the animal kingdom. Do birds, fish, insects, or reptiles have sentience, for example? Most writers on the topic—and many animal welfare laws—agree that a significant line can be drawn between vertebrates, who possess complex central nervous systems, and invertebrates, who do not. Thus the physiological structure and behavior of animals such as mammals, birds, reptiles, amphibians, and fish strongly suggest that they have the capacity for conscious experience, whereas those of insects, molluscs, crustaceans, arachnids, and so on suggest that they do not. For example, mammals are considered to be sufficiently similar to humans (remembering of course, that humans *are* mammals) in so many ways that they are regarded as extremely useful in cosmetic and medical experiments.[6] It is extremely likely, owing to their similar neural structures and nervous systems, that such similarities extend to the capacity to have experiences. The case for sentience in birds is also strong. For example, studies on factory-farmed chickens have shown that given a choice of two feeds, one with and one without painkillers, lame chickens choose the feed with painkiller more often than fit birds, and as levels of lameness increase, so too does consumption of the painkiller feed.[7] More controversial, however, is the case of fish. Two studies in 2003 provided different accounts of whether fish can feel pain. In the first, James D. Rose argued that fish brains are not sufficiently developed to experience pain. He claimed that other studies that have put forward evidence of fish pain have in fact only provided evidence of nociception, the unfelt reflex reaction to threatening and injurious stimuli.[8] However, a later study also in 2003, this time by the Roslin Institute in Edinburgh, found evidence in trout of nociception and the experience of pain. In the later study the fish were initially found to have nociceptors on their heads and mouths. Some fish then had bee venom injected into their mouths, which caused them to express anomalous behavior. For example, the trout went into a rocking motion similar to that exhibited by stressed mammals, rubbed their lips onto the gravel and walls of the fish tank, and took three times as long to resume feeding compared to the fish who were not injected.[9] Such behavior appears to be more than simple reflex reaction and seems to provide compelling evidence that fish can and do feel pain. Moreover, if fish have the capacity for phenomenal consciousness, it is also likely that amphibians and reptiles have the capacity to experience the world. This is because fish, amphibians, and reptiles possess similar neurophysiology and behavioral patterns.

When we turn to invertebrates, however, the evidence for phenomenal consciousness is much weaker. Taking insects, for example, there is no strong evidence for the existence of the capacity for phenomenal consciousness. It is true that insects do possess sophisticated apparatus to sense their environment, including sensory hairs to detect touch, tympanal organs to detect sound, and chemoreceptors to detect chemical signals.[10] Moreover, recent studies with insects have shown the presence of quite complex brain functions, including sleep, learning, memory, and attention.[11] All this provides good evidence of the ability to access the world and respond to it. However, proof of the ability to *experience* that world is limited. While endogenous opiates are present in many insects, their central nervous system is greatly limited when compared to that of other animals, and there is little behavioral evidence to suggest the ability to feel states such as pain. For example, insects continue with their normal behavior even after severe injury or loss of limb, and sometimes even while being devoured.[12] More evidence is needed, but there is little reason at present to believe that insects can feel pain and are phenomenally conscious.

The same is true with other invertebrate animals: behavioral and physiological evidence suggests that the majority are not phenomenally conscious. Caution is necessary here, however, for invertebrates are a wide group containing a diverse variety of species, and the evidence is changing all the time. For example, while we can be reasonably sure that creatures such as amoebas and oysters lack the capacity for consciousness, there is some debate over such animals as lobsters, prawns, and cephalods (octopi and squid). It is widely reported that when a live lobster is plunged into boiling water (this is the way some people cook them), it thrashes about seemingly in pain. However, a 2005 Norwegian study declared that lobsters' nervous systems are too simple to feel pain, and that their thrashing when boiled alive is merely muscle contraction.[13] And yet a more recent study conducted in the UK found convincing evidence of the experience of pain in lobsters and prawns. In this study, when the animals were dabbed on their antennae with an irritant, they engaged in specific and prolonged rubbing of the affected area, much like sentient vertebrates.[14] The case of octopi and squid is more difficult still, as their nervous systems are the most advanced of all invertebrates, but still much simpler than those of vertebrates. What is needed is more evidence, and no doubt this will come. At present, however, it is probably most reasonable to conclude, given the evidence available, that all vertebrates (mammals, birds, fish, reptiles, amphibians) are phenomenally conscious, while most invertebrates (insects, molluscs, crustaceans, arachnids, and so on) are not. What is most important for our purposes, however, is that the group "sentient animals" is a meaningful category. The relevant question is not whether *any* animals have sentience, but how many.[15]

SENTIENCE, WELL-BEING, AND MORAL STATUS

But even if it is accepted that some animals are indeed sentient, why then should it also be accepted that we have moral obligations to those animals? Why does sentience lead to the possession of moral status? For many philosophers, it is not sentience itself that qualifies these animals for moral status, but what sentience signifies. Sentience signifies that an entity has the capacity for well-being. The capacity for well-being is synonymous with the possession of a welfare, a good of one's own, and interests. Having a life that goes well or badly for oneself is considered to qualify an entity for moral status because of the incredibly important role that well-being plays in ethics and normative reasoning. After all, much of ethics concerns deliberating on how to make the lives of individuals go better and how to avoid making them go worse. Some philosophers, known as "welfarists," would go further than this and claim that well-being is the *only* concern of ethics. However, whether we take a full-blown welfarist approach or recognize other values to be of ethical importance, there is no doubting the centrality of well-being to ethics. To put it crudely, well-being is what gets our ethical juices flowing. Improving and protecting lives is the raison d'être of debating and outlining our moral obligations. As such, it really is little wonder that sentient animals are owed ethical consideration in their own right. Sentient animals are quite unlike entities such as rocks, soil, tables, and chairs. Sentient animals have lives that can go better or worse for themselves: the very subject that is so central to normative reasoning.

Of course, it is possible to acknowledge that well-being is crucial for ethics but also to maintain that it is only *human* well-being that matters. Perhaps, then, moral status should be reserved exclusively for human beings. Indeed, the history of Western philosophy has been dominated by just such a view. But given the straightforward connection between well-being and ethical consideration, and the clear existence of the capacity for well-being in some nonhuman entities, just how can such human exclusivity be justified? Broadly, three rationales have been offered, each of which will be examined in turn.

Perhaps the traditional basis for reserving moral status exclusively for human beings is religious. The Judeo-Christian notion that human beings are made in the image of God and are touched by the divine through their possession of a soul has had a huge influence on Western philosophy. This idea has served to separate humans from the animals, putting "us" in the domain of the divine and the moral, and "them" in the domain of the earthly and the amoral. There are two important problems with this argument, however. First, to exclude animals from the possession of moral status on the basis of an article of faith from a controversial religious doctrine is to ask too much. There is no way of proving that humans are made in the image of God or that they possess a soul that animals lack. Many of us have no religious belief, and many of us have religious beliefs that do not separate the human and animal worlds in quite such stark contrast. If animals are to be shown not to have moral status, a philosophical argument that we can all potentially engage with needs to be provided. Second, even if we do accept that human beings are made in the image of God, possessing a soul that animals lack, that still does not show that animals have no moral status. For it is perfectly plausible to derive an account of moral obligations owed to animals from Judeo-Christian foundations.[16] For example, it might be claimed that we have such obligations because God has made us stewards of Earth and all its creatures.

Perhaps a more plausible basis for reserving moral status only for human beings can be derived from the unique capacities that humans possess. The capacities that have been put forward by philosophers as morally relevant in this way are often referred to as the capacities for personhood or dignity: moral agency and autonomy. As we saw in the previous chapter, moral agency is the ability to reason and act on moral principles, while autonomy is the ability to frame, revise, and pursue a conception of the good life. Some philosophers argue that to be part of the moral community, an entity needs to possess these moral and autonomous capacities.[17] Such arguments owe a debt to Immanuel Kant, who argued that rational beings like humans are ends-in-themselves: individuals who can exercise moral judgment and free will, and who are not bound by instinct and emotion. Because rational beings are ends-in-themselves, Kant claimed that they have dignity and moral status. However, by virtue of the fact that animals are not rational in this way, Kant argued that they are mere "things" to whom no obligations are owed.[18]

Of course, for this argument to work, it must be shown that these relevant capacities are unique to human beings. Can only human beings be "persons"?[19] For the vast majority of species of animal, there is no evidence to suggest that they possess the capacities for moral agency and autonomy. Sentient animals may well have the capacity for conscious experience, but for most there is little in their physiology or behavior to suggest that they have the ability to act on moral principles and pursue their own considered goals. For some species of animal, however, the issue is not quite so clear-cut. Some philosophers and scientists have maintained that the great apes (chimpanzees, bonobos, and gorillas) and cetaceans (whales and dolphins) do have the capacities for personhood. Such capacities have been attributed to these animals on the basis of their apparent ability to master sign language or other forms of communication.[20] And clearly there is ample evidence of these species of animal using various symbols to communicate information and their desires.

We must be cautious here, however. For while the ability to communicate in this way is indeed remarkable, it does not necessarily reveal the presence of moral agency or autonomy. For one, it seems perfectly plausible that an animal might be able to use signs to communicate desires or feelings without necessarily being able to ruminate on those desires and feelings or adjust them in relation to moral principles or a conception of the good. Nevertheless, using such signs to express *particular types* of feeling could indicate the presence of such capacities. For example, consider the communication of a feeling of regret. Regret certainly seems to convey a reflective capability: it involves both deliberation over past actions and critical judgment based on certain values. Interestingly, there is some anecdotal evidence that indicates the expression of regret in gorillas.[21] Of course, anecdotal evidence is one thing, while hard evidence from scientific experiments is quite another. And some scientists have interpreted evidence from experiments with great apes to state that even they lack the ability to inhibit and modify their first-order desires.[22] As things currently stand, I do not think that we can be certain that any nonhumans do have the capacities for personhood. However, nor can we be certain that they do not. So even if we agree with Kant that only persons possess moral status, it may well be the case that some nonhumans also qualify.

Having said all this, there is good reason *not* to agree with Kant that these capacities for personhood are necessary for moral status. Quite simply, many uncontroversial possessors of moral status lack these moral and autonomous capacities. For example, young infants and some individuals with severe mental disabilities are not able to understand and act on moral rules, nor can they frame, revise, and pursue their own conceptions of the good. If the capacities for personhood are what confer moral status, then it must be the case that these individuals lack moral status. This is problematic because most of us believe that such individuals do have moral status: that they are owed ethical consideration in their own right, and that we have a range of moral obligations to them. For example, if I were to torture an infant, I would surely be doing more than just failing in some duty to her family, to my potential future adult victims, or to society. Because that infant can experience pain, and because my torturing her would cause her excruciating and unnecessary pain, then it seems obvious that I would be violating an obligation owed directly to her. If this is correct, an entity's moral status seems not to depend on its ability to exercise moral agency or autonomous choice.

Carl Cohen and Michael Fox have accepted the claim that some nonpersons have moral status. However, they claim that only *human* nonpersons have moral status. They argue that it is unimportant that particular humans lack the usual necessary characteristics for inclusion in the moral community because "the issue is one of kind," and that what is important "are the characteristics that a certain class of beings share in general, even if not universally."[23] For Fox and Cohen, then, human nonpersons possess moral status because they belong to a group whose members ordinarily possess the characteristics required for inclusion. Nonhuman animals are excluded, on the other hand, because they belong to a group whose members generally lack such capacities.

Nathan Nobis has pointed out, however, that even if we accept that we should base an individual's moral status on the characteristics of the group to which it belongs (which is extremely dubious), many animal nonpersons still warrant entry into the moral community. After all, many animal nonpersons belong to groups that human persons belong to. For example, both are living organisms, both are sentient, both have the capacity for well-being, both have desires, and so on. Since such animal nonpersons belong to these groups whose members have the capacities required for moral status, it remains unclear why animals must be excluded from the moral community even on Fox's and Cohen's own terms.[24]

All these attempts to limit the possession of moral status to human beings fail. And it is little wonder that they fail. If ethical reasoning has as its focus the well-being of individuals, it is completely arbitrary to restrict ethical consideration to just one species. As we have seen, the evidence strongly suggests that many types of nonhuman animal have lives that can go better or worse for themselves. As such, all these entities merit ethical consideration in their own right. In light of all this, the interesting question is not *whether* we have obligations to sentient nonhuman animals, but just *what* obligations we have to them.

Can Sentient Animals Have Rights?

Of course, just because sentient nonhuman animals possess moral status, that does not mean that they thus also possess rights. And the idea that animals can possess rights is extremely controversial. So what is it that makes an entity a putative right-holder? The argument of this book is that just as well-being is the necessary and sufficient condition for the possession of moral status, so it is the necessary and sufficient condition for the possession of rights. That is, all those entities that have a life that can go well or badly for themselves—all those entities who possess interests—are also the types of entities we have moral obligations toward, and also the types of entities who can possess rights.

Such an argument is by no means novel. It was most famously proposed and defended in a classic early paper on animal rights by Joel Feinberg.[25] In that paper Feinberg considered the popular idea that in order to possess rights, one must be the kind of entity that can claim one's rights for oneself: in other words, one must be a moral agent. Feinberg refutes this argument, pointing out that if moral agency of this kind were a necessary condition for having rights, then individuals like small children and people with serious mental disabilities would not be able to possess them. Feinberg argues that such individuals are capable of holding rights because they can have their rights claimed by representatives on their behalf. Furthermore, he suggests that it is plausible for children, individuals who are seriously mentally disabled, *and animals* to have their rights claimed by others because they all possess *interests* that can be represented. Entities such as inanimate objects and plants, on the other hand, have no interests that can be represented on their behalf and thus cannot hold rights. As such, Feinberg argues that the possession of interests is both a necessary and sufficient condition for being a right-holder.

Despite Feinberg's argument, many philosophers have resisted the claims that animals can possess rights, and possess them on the basis of their interests. This section examines four important objections to the idea that animals can possess rights on the basis of their interests. The first two objections question the interest-requirement itself: that is, they deny the fundamental premise that all and only interest-holders possess rights. The final two objections deal with the nature of interests and the question of which entities can possess them. I argue that all these objections fail and thus they do not disprove the argument that animals can possess rights on the basis of their interests.

MAINTAINING MORAL AGENCY AS A NECESSARY CONDITION FOR RIGHTS

Perhaps the most common objection to the idea of animals being potential right-holders is made by those philosophers who see moral agency as the necessary and sufficient condition for holding rights. Moral agency is generally considered to be crucial to the ascription of rights for two different reasons. First, it has been argued that reciprocity is a vital feature of rights.[26] The importance of reciprocity is usually advanced by "contractarian" political and moral philosophers. These philosophers regard the rights and responsibilities we possess as the result of some kind of hypothetical agreement between parties, usually based on mutual benefit.[27] Thus the idea is that I would choose to agree to constrain my behavior toward you on the basis that you would do the same for me. As such, the benefits, burdens, rights, and duties we hold as individuals are justified to the extent that we would choose them in the formulation of this contract. Lacking moral agency—the ability to deliberate and act on moral reasons—animals are incapable of deciding to constrain their behavior and are incapable of consenting to any contract. According to this reasoning, animals are not the type of beings that can benefit from the possession of rights.

As Feinberg and many others have pointed out, animals are not the only types of beings that lack moral agency. So if we exclude animals from possessing rights on the grounds that they cannot reciprocate, we will also have to exclude children and those who are severely mentally disabled. However, the vast majority of us do not want to exclude such humans from the class of potential right-holders. This is because we want to protect the important interests of such individuals in the same way that we protect those of adults. For most of us, withholding a right not to be tortured from a young child on the basis that he cannot reciprocate, while awarding it to his father on the grounds that he can, makes little sense. For what seems to be important in terms of awarding this right is not whether the individual can act morally himself, but the simple question of whether the individual has an interest in not suffering terribly that justifies placing others under a duty not to torture him.

As mentioned above, however, there is another reason why moral agency is thought to be crucial for the possession of rights. Under the choice or will theory of rights, the essential feature of a right is the presence of choice in the right-holder. To be more specific, it is claimed under this theory that when an individual has a right to something, that individual is able to demand or waive enforcement of the relevant corresponding duty.[28] Take, for example, the case of a loan: I have lent you some money, and you have promised to pay me back. It is clear that in this situation you have a duty to repay me. Moreover, it is perfectly legitimate for me to demand repayment from you, or, if I so choose, I can waive your duty to repay, thereby canceling the debt. Here it is possible to talk of my having a right to repayment because of my moral agency: I have a degree of choice over the repayment. Under this account, then, rights demarcate spheres of personal jurisdiction for individuals, recognizing and protecting the autonomous capacities of persons. The implication of this understanding of rights is that those individuals who lack the capacity for moral agency—and thus lack the ability to exercise choice in this way—cannot possess rights.

At first sight this account of rights seems to face exactly the same problem as that which faced the understanding based on reciprocity: namely, it excludes children and mentally disabled people from the class of potential right-holders. However, Hillel Steiner has provided an intriguing proposal for a way around this problem. Steiner argues that the interests of children and animals *do* merit protection in the form of rights, even under the will theory. But interestingly, Steiner claims that the right lies not with the child and animal themselves, but with some other individual capable of demanding or waiving the relevant duties on their behalf.[29] For example, a child has an interest in not being beaten, and that interest is so important that it should be protected by a right. But that right lies not with the child herself, but with someone else, someone who can exercise the right by waiving or demanding enforcement of the relevant duty. Such an individual could plausibly be one of her parents, a guardian, a member of the police, a state official, or some other relevant individual. In this way, it seems possible to protect the important interests of children, severely mentally disabled individuals, and animals via the ascription of rights while maintaining that such individuals themselves are incapable of possessing rights owing to their lack of moral agency.

This approach is unsatisfactory for two reasons. First, ordinarily in right claims, the right-holder and the object of our moral concern co-incide. Under Steiner's scheme, however, the individual who possesses the right and our object of moral concern are different people. This seems strange because we are used to conferring rights on individuals on the basis of what they are owed, rather than on the basis of what someone else is owed. Of course, this point does not defeat Steiner's argument: he might simply respond that we should adjust our ordinary understanding of rights to fall into line with his approach. However, there is a second and more devastating objection to Steiner's scheme. For Steiner, a right can exist only when there is someone with the ability to exercise choice over the right: to waive or demand enforce-ment of the relevant duty. However, this is implausible. For example, it is evident that no one can legitimately waive our moral duty not to torture children. Such a duty is unwaivable. Thus for Steiner it must be the case that not only do children have no moral right not to be tortured, but *no* one—not a parent, a policeman, a state official, or anyone—has a moral right against child torture. So we are left in a situation where children's important interests remain unprotected by rights, the very situation that Steiner himself hoped to avoid.

Given these arguments, it seems correct to abandon moral agency as a necessary condition for the possession of rights. If we want to award pro-tection to children and those who have severe mental disabilities in the form of rights, we can do so straightforwardly on the basis of interests. But if we do recognize that the possession of interests is the necessary and sufficient condition for having rights, then to be consistent we must also acknowledge that sentient animals are potential right-holders.

RELATIONAL ACCOUNTS OF RIGHTS

However, there is another objection to the link between interests and rights. This objection maintains that rights are properly assigned not through the intrinsic characteristics of individuals—such as the pos-session of interests or the capacity for moral agency—but through our *relations* with the potential right-holder. To assign rights outside of the context of meaningful social relations, it is argued, is implausible. For example, Elizabeth Anderson argues that rights "do not flow im-mediately from a creature's capacities, but make sense only within a complex system of social relations and meanings."[30]

To explain her point, Anderson gives two examples. First, she gives the example of a group of wild creatures on the brink of starvation, such as a pod of dolphins. Anderson argues that these dolphins clearly have an interest in having food. However, she claims that in spite of this fact, these creatures do not have any right to be provided with food by us. This, she argues, is because rights to the provision of goods are based on and only make sense in relation to membership of a shared society: individuals have no rights to positive provision outside of a societal context.[31] Second, Anderson gives the example of vermin, such as rats, who have invaded a human house. She argues that these rats clearly have an interest in not being exterminated or evicted by the householder. However, in spite of this fact, these creatures have no *rights* not to be exterminated or evicted by us. This, she argues, is because rights require the putative right- and duty-bearers to have interests that can be accommodated. That is, Anderson argues that rights possession requires not only that an individual has an interest in some good, but that one can have peaceable relations with the individual with that interest.[32] In both examples given above, Anderson is arguing that the possession of an interest in something, even if extremely strong, is not a sufficient condition for holding a right to that thing: the social relations and context of the interests in question are also fundamental.

We might then use this argument of Anderson's to claim that because rights are necessarily relational, and since not all sentient animals are or can be in the relevant types of relationship with human beings, not all sentient animals can hold moral rights against us. However, I think that such a claim not only would be mistaken in and of itself, but would also be an incorrect interpretation of Anderson's own argument. After all, it is important to note that Anderson is claiming that social relations and context are crucial to the *content* of individuals' rights, not to the question of whether they can possess any rights at all. Anderson herself acknowledges that even wild dolphins and rats possess some rights, but far fewer than held by those animals that can live peaceably within human communities. For example, Anderson recognizes that the former possess, at the very least, the right not to be treated with wanton cruelty.[33] Anderson is surely correct not to make close relations a prerequisite for the possession of basic rights. After all, many of us recognize the existence of a set of basic universal *human* rights, even in the absence of a global social relationship between all human beings. Moreover, this recognition is based on the reasonable suggestion that as beings who can lead minimally decent lives, there are some entitlements that all humans share, irrespective of where they happen to reside.[34] Clearly a similar argument can be made with respect to animals and their rights. Close social relations may provide the basis for individuals to have more and stronger claims against others, but they are not a necessary condition for the possession of rights per se.

ANIMALS CANNOT POSSESS INTERESTS

Even if it is accepted that possessing interests is the necessary and sufficient condition for being a right-holder, that still does not show that *sentient animals* are putative right-holders. For maybe animals cannot possess interests. So far in this chapter I have been making the assumption that the capacity for well-being and the possession of interests are equivalent: to have interests is to have well-being and vice versa. Because sentient animals obviously have lives that can go well or badly, they seem to be the types of thing that can have interests. Because rocks, tables, and chairs are inanimate and have no such lives, they have no well-being and thus no interests.

However, some philosophers have questioned this welfarist account of interests. Both H. J. McCloskey and R. G. Frey, for example, have argued that to have interests entails something more than mere welfare.[35] As McCloskey writes: "They [interests] suggest that which is or ought to be or which would be of *concern* to the person/being. It is partly for this reason—because the concept of interests has this evaluative-prescriptive overtone—that we decline to speak of the interests of animals, and speak rather of their welfare."[36] As an initial response to McCloskey's remarks, it is perhaps worth pointing out that as a matter of fact we do not ordinarily decline to speak of the interests of animals. To most of us, talking about the interests of animals is uncontroversial. Nevertheless, McCloskey clearly wants to limit such talk because animals, while in possession of a welfare, cannot be *concerned* about their welfare. Such concern seems to be important for him because of its "evaluative-prescriptive" overtones. So just what does this mean?

Tom Regan has helpfully attempted to put some flesh on these bones. Regan sees the "evaluative" overtone of interests referred to by Mc-Closkey as relating to a judgment about what is good for an individual. If correct, this sees interests as corresponding to welfare and so does not bar animals from the possession of interests. However, Regan sees the "prescriptive" overtone of McCloskey's conception of interests as an action-guiding component. Thus to say that A has an interest in X is also to say that A does or should want X and does or should act so as to get X.[37] This prescriptive element of McCloskey's account seems to be something over and above mere welfare. To this extent it is in keeping with Frey's understanding of interests, who connects interests to desires.[38] Importantly for both thinkers, their accounts of interests provide them with a reason to say that animals cannot possess interests: animals can neither want nor pursue what is good for them.

But the claim that animals can neither want nor pursue what is good for them is an empirical claim that appears at odds with common sense and everyday observation. For example, we can legitimately say that it is good for my cat to eat well, to move around freely, to see off encroachers on his territory, to have love and affection, and so on and so forth. All these things manifestly contribute to his well-being. Additionally, and of crucial import to my inquiry, these goods also appear to be *of concern* to him: he wants these goods and acts so as to achieve them. My saying this is not based on some kind of anthropomorphic fantasy, but simply on my observations of what he does: he begs for food; he scratches at doors that prevent him from getting to where he wants to; he chases cats that come into his garden; he jumps on my lap for a cuddle when I come home from work; and so on. Given such simple evidence, the burden of proof must lie with Frey and McCloskey to show why animals cannot want or be concerned about what is good for them. In the absence of such proof, it is surely legitimate to assume that even if interests do require a degree of actual concern on the part of the potential interest-holder, many animals still possess interests.

However, McCloskey's understanding of interests does not focus solely on what *is* of concern to individuals, but also what *ought to* or *should be* of concern to individuals. Here, then, might be an important difference between animals and humans, which counts against assigning interests to the former. For suppose that a human and a dog have both been involved in accidents, and both require stitches. Clearly it would contribute to the welfare of both individuals if they went to the hospital and got those stitches. Now imagine that the human individual is unaware of the extent of her injuries and makes no effort to go to the hospital. In spite of her attitude, it still makes sense, under McCloskey's account, to say that she has an interest in going to the hospital. After all, she "ought to be concerned" and undoubtedly "would be concerned" if she had all the relevant information. However, when we consider the case of the dog, things are quite different. Not only is the dog unconcerned about going to the animal hospital for stitches, but she *cannot* be concerned about going to the hospital. This is because dogs are not the type of being who can take themselves off to the hospital, nor are they the type of being who can conceive of themselves as either going to the hospital or receiving stitches. In sum, it makes no sense to say that the dog "ought to be concerned" or "would be concerned about this particular good" because she simply *cannot* be concerned about that good.

Of course, the objection does not prove that animals have no interests whatsoever. All it can show—if correct—is that animals, and humans, have no interest in a good that they cannot be concerned about.

But there are good reasons to reject this entire conception of interests, based as it is on actual or hypothetical concern. For accepting such an understanding of interests would lead us to make some very odd distinctions about what is and is not in the interests of individuals. For example, according to this view we could say that a baby has an interest in being fed, but we could not say that a baby has an interest in being vaccinated against measles. We could say that individuals in the nineteenth century had an interest in employment, but we could not say that smoking tobacco ran contrary to their interests. We could say that a bleeding dog has an interest in his pain coming to an end, but we could not say that he has an interest in being treated by a veterinarian. But such distinctions seem extremely odd and a long way from our ordinary understanding of interests. As such, there seems to be good grounds for maintaining a straightforward welfarist account of interests: that is, understanding interests simply as those things that make life go well for individuals themselves. But *even if* we adopt the view that real or hypothetical concern about a good is necessary to possess an interest in that good, it is still perfectly evident that sentient animals possess many interests. All in all, then, the claim that sentient animals cannot possess rights based on their interests because they have no interests is unfounded.

THE INTERESTS AND RIGHTS OF PLANTS AND INANIMATE ENTITIES

If, as suggested, the more plausible understanding of interests is that they correspond with welfare and well-being, then that raises the question of which entities possess the capacity for well-being. The chapter so far has been following Feinberg's line of reasoning in assuming that the possession of sentience is both necessary and sufficient for well-being, and hence interests. But perhaps this is not the case. Perhaps nonsentient entities like plants and even inanimate objects have the capacity for well-being; perhaps plants and inanimate objects also possess interests. Some philosophers have explicitly endorsed the view that they do.[39] For instance, Matthew H. Kramer writes: "to say that some interest(s) of X will be advanced through the occurrence of an event or the emergence of a state of affairs is to say that X will benefit in some way(s) from the specified event or state of affairs. That is, the event or state of affairs will improve X's condition or will avert a deterioration therein. By adopting this expansive conception of the matter, I am allowing that interests can be ascribed not only to all animals and plants but also to many inanimate entities."[40]

When this understanding of interests is combined with the interest requirement for the possession of rights, it leads us to conclude that not only are animals putative right-holders, but so too are plants and inanimate entities, such as books and bicycles.[41] For some, such a conclusion is absurd and undermines the interest requirement for the possession of rights. In a nutshell, the objection would be that the possession of interests cannot be the crucial criterion for rights possession because it would lead to a ludicrously inflated set of rights possessors.

This section leaves aside the issue of whether it is ludicrous to assign rights to plants and inanimate objects. That question is immaterial because quite simply it is a serious mistake to see plants and inanimate objects as possessors of interests. To explain, note in the quotation cited above that Kramer actually uses two very different understandings of interests. The first comes when he claims that in order for a state of affairs to be in X's interests, it must *improve X's condition*. This understanding of interests is extremely liberal and would allow for an enormous number of entities to be described as possessors of interests. For if all that is required in order to have interests is that one's *condition* be improved (or deteriorated), then quite clearly interests belong to a huge number of entities. Animals would have interests, plants would have interests, but so too would vases, books, bicycles, and much besides.

Kramer, however, uses a quite different understanding of interests earlier in the quotation. There he argues that for states of affairs to be in X's interests, they must *benefit X*. This understanding is the familiar welfarist account of interests: interests are those things that, when satisfied, make life better for that individual. Importantly, this understanding narrows the class of interest-holders to those with their own well-being: to those who can be benefited or harmed by actions themselves. So while sentient animals can obviously be benefited and harmed themselves by states of affairs, plants and inanimate objects cannot. It is of no benefit to a vase to be in one piece; it is of no benefit to my bicycle to be well-oiled; and it is of no benefit to your book to have all its pages bound inside. Such objects cannot themselves be benefited or harmed. This is because they have no well-being. Yes, their condition can deteriorate or improve, but they themselves receive nothing from such states of affairs—and they thus possess no interests.

This fact alerts us to an important feature of well-being: it is a *prudential value*. That is, it concerns what is good for the individual whose life it is. In this sense, it can be contrasted with *perfectionist value*, which concerns what makes an individual a good example of its kind.[42] States of affairs may well make a plant a better plant, but they can never make things better *for* the plant itself. States of affairs may improve or deteriorate such things as plants, but lacking conscious life, no state of affairs can actually make things better or worse for plants themselves. Because they lack sentience, plants and inanimate objects possess no well-being and possess no interests. As such, recognizing that animals possess rights because of their interests does not require us to recognize rights for such entities as plants, vases, books, and bicycles.

In this section I have examined four important objections to the claim that sentient animals can possess rights based on their interests: that only moral agents can possess rights; that rights are relational; that sentient animals possess no interests; and that recognizing interest-based animal rights inevitably leads to rights for plants, books, and vases. These objections are certainly diverse and derive from a range of philosophical traditions. Nevertheless, they all fail. Sentient animals, as phenomenally conscious entities whose lives can go well or badly for themselves, can meaningfully be said to possess rights that derive from their interests.

The Interest-Based Rights Approach

So far this chapter has argued that sentient animals possess moral status and are the types of entities that can possess rights. However, the case has not yet been made for a theory of animal rights. That is, while animals clearly *can* possess rights, it has not yet been shown that animals *do* have rights or that rights are the appropriate means by which to formulate our obligations to them. It could well be that animals possess moral status and are putative right-holders, but it might still be inappropriate to use rights as the means by which to frame our ethical and political relations with them.

The first part of this section examines a non-rights-based means of delineating our obligations to animals—one that is in keeping with the prominence given to well-being in the arguments made so far in this book. That alternative theory is utilitarianism. While utilitarianism has considerable appeal by virtue of its simplicity and clarity, this book rejects it as the means by which to formulate our obligations to animals. Utilitarianism is rejected quite simply because it fails to take individual well-being seriously enough. In the next section, the interest-based rights approach is proposed and defended as a useful corrective to utilitarian reasoning. Like utilitarianism, it provides a straightforward and systematic means of delineating our obligations, but unlike utilitarianism, it does not reduce all judgments of policy and action to their effects on aggregate well-being. Finally, two critiques of this interest-based rights approach—that it is inflationary and overly rationalistic—are anticipated and rejected.

MAXIMIZING ANIMAL WELL-BEING

If sentient animals are owed ethical consideration on the basis of their well-being, then perhaps our obligations to them ought to be based not around rights, but on the goal of *maximizing* their well-being. After all, if well-being is of such crucial importance to ethical reasoning, as this chapter has suggested, then surely the more of it the better. Utilitarianism is the ethical theory that condones this kind of maximizing strategy, and there is no doubt that utilitarian philosophers have been at the forefront of campaigns calling for the better treatment of animals. As the previous chapter described, Peter Singer in his groundbreaking book *Animal Liberation* argued that we should aim to maximize the interest-satisfaction (well-being) of all sentient beings, irrespective of their species.[43]

The appeal of using a principle of utility such as this to formulate our obligations is certainly strong. For one, it is worth reminding ourselves of the crucial importance that well-being has in ethical reasoning. As discussed previously, deliberating on how to make the lives of individuals better, and how to prevent them from faring badly, really is the fundamental basis of normative reasoning in the realms of morality, society, politics, and law. Second, using well-being as a guide to moral and political action has clear advantages over other concepts such as "natural rights" or "universalizable maxims" because it is tangible and can be measured. Of course, this does not mean that there are no controversies over what constitutes well-being: debates rage within utilitarianism over whether well-being is best measured by feelings of pleasure, preference-satisfaction, the capability to achieve valuable functions, and so on. But in each case well-being is something that can be measured and thus can serve as a concrete tool to guide action. Finally, having a single principle to follow when deliberating over actions and policies provides clarity and focus. Indeed, such clarity is particularly beneficial when considering difficult normative issues where deeply embedded norms, customs, and prejudices are at stake. Utilitarians are unafraid to propose new and radical policy prescriptions even when they clash with traditional customs. It is no surprise, then, that utilitarians were and continue to be at the forefront of campaigns to enfranchise the working class, end the oppression of women, extend civil rights across races and sexualities, and award far stronger forms of protection to sentient nonhuman animals.

Despite the good work of philosophers like Singer, however, and despite the appeal of this kind of reasoning, this book rejects utilitarianism as the means of delineating our obligations to animals. In fact adopting utilitarianism as the theoretical framework of this project would be self-contradictory, for it would be at direct odds with the account of moral status offered earlier in the chapter. Utilitarianism is aggregative, seeking to produce the best overall balance of good over bad consequences for all under consideration. While every individual counts under an aggregative theory, the individual is neither the prime focus nor the prime source of value. Instead, individuals are merely receptacles of value, with ultimate value residing in what is deemed good: well-being.[44] This means that *individual* well-being can and ought to be sacrificed should it lead to higher *aggregate* well-being. Hence opponents of utilitarianism claim that it can have certain unpalatable results: the conviction of an innocent man simply to appease a baying crowd; the killing of a healthy patient to provide organs for the numerous sick; the enslavement of a minority group for the happiness of the master majority; and so on.

But the account of moral status put forward in this book counts against treating individuals as mere receptacles of value. Entities with moral status have a certain standing, meaning that they merit ethical consideration in their own right and are not valuable simply because of their contribution to some other goal, such as aggregate well-being. To be specific, nonhuman animals are valuable in themselves—possess moral status—because they have lives that can go well or badly for themselves. So well-being is crucial for our obligations, but well-being that is possessed by individuals. As such, the theoretical framework that is required is one that recognizes the value of well-being but is also able to *individuate* entities, and not be purely aggregative.

THE INTEREST-BASED RIGHTS APPROACH

The framework that can meet this need is the interest-based rights approach. Using rights immediately recognizes that there are limits to what can be done to the individual in the name of aggregate well-being. Some philosophers have argued that this is precisely what rights do: they act as trumps or side-constraints on the pursuit of overall utility.[45] However, if we are to use rights, we face the difficult problem of explaining where they come from and justifying how they are assigned. The previous chapter explained that Tom Regan grounds animal rights in the inherent value of individual subjects-of-a-life. For Regan, all individuals with a certain complexity of conscious life have a value that cannot be reduced to their usefulness to others. As such, Regan argues that such individuals have a basic right to respectful treatment, entailing that they cannot be used simply as a means to securing the best overall consequences.

However, we saw in the previous chapter that there are important problems with Regan's theory of animal rights. There it was argued that Regan fails to establish his basic animal right to respectful treatment because he fails to explain why creatures who are not ends-in-themselves must always be treated as ends-in-themselves. But this is by no means the only critique of Regan's theory. Philosophers such as Mary Anne Warren and Mark Rowlands have also complained that Regan's notion of inherent value is too mysterious and ethereal to be an effective means by which to ground moral rights.[46] Some theorists would argue that Regan's theory is symptomatic of a fault that is inevitable in all theories of moral rights. Quite simply, these critics claim, there is no plausible means of explaining where moral rights come from and how they are justified.[47]

But under the theory advanced in this book, rights are not mysterious at all. As the previous chapter briefly discussed, the interest-based rights approach derives rights from the concrete interests of individuals. This method utilizes Joseph Raz's famous analysis of rights: "'X has a right' if and only if X can have rights, and, other things being equal, an aspect of X's well-being (his interest) is a sufficient reason for holding some other person(s) to be under a duty."[48] This interest-based understanding of rights provides an effective answer to those critics who argue that rights are necessarily mysterious. For under this conception, rights are both explained and justified by an appeal to the well-being of individuals. There is nothing strange or metaphysically controversial about rights in this understanding: we justify rights by identifying interests and evaluating whether they are sufficient, all things considered, to impose duties on another. The great advantage of this interest-based rights theory, then, is that we have a theory that takes individuals and their interests seriously while also having plausible and tangible foundations.

Before proceeding to an examination of some challenges to this interest-based rights approach, it is probably valuable to explain in a little more detail just what it entails. First, it is worth emphasizing that under this account, having an interest in something does not mean that one automatically has a right to that thing. Instead, in order to have a right the interest must be *sufficient* to give grounds for holding another to be under a duty. Thus while we might recognize some interest of an individual, it may well be that it is insufficient to impose a duty on anyone, and therefore that no relevant right exists. For example, if I do not like the look of my face, I might have an interest in being provided with a face-lift. However, given the expense of face-lifts, and given the strength and nature of my interest, it may be that no one is under a duty to provide me with one, and thus that I have no right to be provided with a face-lift.

To determine whether an interest is indeed sufficient to ground a right, several considerations are relevant. First, the strength of an interest must be taken into account. Trivial interests in things like face-lifts ordinarily seem too weak to ground a duty in others to fulfill them. But also "all other relevant considerations" must be evaluated. An assessment of all other considerations will involve examining any competing interests at stake, and their strength, as well as the burdens on the potential duty-bearers. So while I might have a very strong interest in something, all other relevant considerations might mean that the interest is insufficient to impose a duty on anyone else, and thus that no right is established. For example, I have an extremely strong interest in free expression—an interest that is often sufficient to impose on others a duty not to interfere with my exercise of it. However, if the kind of free expression I enjoy most is the dissemination of lies to ruin the reputation of my neighbor, that kind of interest does not seem worthy of protection "all things considered." The interest of my neighbor in not having his reputation falsely ruined seems to outweigh my interest in free expression in this particular case. From this, we can see that for this interest-based rights approach *context* is crucial to the recognition of rights. This is because in different contexts there are always different "other relevant considerations" to take into account.

The final important feature of this approach is that it is a scheme in which *moral rights* are established. That is, it is an approach that uses moral reasoning to come up with a set of legal rules that political communities ought to enforce. This book does not seek to come up with a theory of all our moral duties with respect to animals, or indeed all their moral rights. Rather its aim is to delineate a more limited set of duties and rights: those that political communities ought to enforce as legal rights. Furthermore, just because the moral rights that the book establishes are urgent and pressing, that does not mean that they must be enacted in their totality and with immediate effect. For as has already been discussed, the effective and legitimate enactment of such rights relies on their having some kind of accordance with the wishes and values of the political community that is to live by them. This theory of animal rights thus serves as a form of "democratic underlaboring" to inform and persuade political communities and policy makers of their validity.[49]

Taken together, these aspects of the interest-based rights approach reveal the methodology that will be employed throughout this book. That is, what political communities owe to animals is worked out by establishing an account of the moral rights of animals, which in turn is worked out by careful consideration of their interests in particular contexts. Crucially the interest-based rights approach does not provide a definitive list of animals' rights in the abstract. Instead, the concrete rights of animals are worked out in context: the interests of animals need to be identified; their strength needs to be evaluated; those interests need to be weighed against any competing interests; and they also need to be balanced against the burdens they impose on the putative duty-bearers. As such, the remaining chapters—on experimentation, agriculture, genetic engineering, entertainment, the environment, and culture—are not simple applications of this theory of rights, but are integral to the determination of the rights themselves. Before that determination takes place, however, it is necessary to examine two objections to the interest-based rights approach that can be anticipated.

RIGHTS INFLATION AND RIGHTS CONFLICTS

The first objection might claim that the interest-based rights approach necessarily leads to an inflation of rights. For if rights can coherently be assigned to anything with interests, and on the basis of any of their interests, it can reasonably be assumed that this will lead to huge numbers of rights claimants and claims. The proliferation of rights is sometimes argued to be problematic not merely because it can lead to a cheapening of rights discourse, but because it inevitably leads to irresolvable conflicts between rights.[50] As Tibor R. Machan puts it: "One problem with this view is that it violates the universalizability condition for ascribing basic rights. Inasmuch as some beings have an interest in benefits that others also have an interest in, it would be impossible to respect the rights of both beings if having interests conferred on them rights, too. Both the United States and Iraq have an interest in Kuwait's oil. To ascribe to both countries the right to the oil would result in peacefully unresolvable conflict."[51]

If the interest-based rights approach does lead to the kinds of irresolvable clashes Machan describes, then the approach is fatally undermined. This is because most rights-theorists believe that rights should have what Joseph Raz has described as "peremptory force."[52] The peremptoriness of rights is generally taken to mean that rights are not simply important considerations to be weighed and balanced against other considerations in our moral deliberations. Instead, rights *end* such balancing by delineating what ought to be done.[53] However, if an interest-based account of rights inevitably leads to endless conflicts of rights, rights lose their special force in our moral deliberations and simply become just one moral consideration among many.

I believe that this criticism of the interest-based approach fails. First and crucially, it must be reemphasized that under the interest-based rights approach not all of an individual's interests translate into rights. If the method were to do this it would lead to bizarre consequences where countless individuals have innumerable rights to all sorts of different goods, as illustrated by Machan in his example of Kuwaiti oil. However, the approach advocated in this book maintains that all rights are based on interests, not that all interests translate into rights. As has been discussed already, under the interest-based approach, in order to have a right, an interest must be sufficient to give grounds for holding another to be under a duty, all things considered. Thus while we might recognize that an individual has a particular interest, other considerations might mean that no one is under a duty with respect to it, and therefore that no relevant right exists. So, returning to Machan's example of Kuwaiti oil, we can acknowledge that both the United States and Iraq have an interest in possessing the oil without also recognizing that both have the *right* to possess the oil. For it is clear that in this situation the interests of the Kuwaiti people over their own natural resources are somewhat weightier and more compelling than the interests of the United States. Because the interest-based approach has sophisticated means of discriminating between interests, worries about it leading to absurdly inflated sets of rights are unfounded. The approach does not force us to assign rights to all that is if of value to interest-bearers but offers us the opportunity to examine an interest of an individual, take all the relevant factors into account, and evaluate whether it merits being translated into a right.

But while the interest-based approach does not lead to absurdly inflated sets of rights, that still does not resolve the problem of rights conflicts. For it seems to be the case that with any type of theory where rights are grounded in interests, there will inevitably be occasions when rights conflict. After all, in a world of scarce resources, not all the pressing and urgent interests of all individuals can be satisfied at once. Is the inevitability of clashes of right fatal to the interest-based rights approach? Not necessarily. An interest-based approach can deal effectively with conflicts of rights if it employs the distinction between prima facie and concrete rights.[54] Prima facie rights are those rights that exist at a more abstract level outside of specific circumstances. In effect, then, prima facie rights are not "all things considered" rights, but rights that are established via a more general judgment about whether an interest is sufficient to impose a duty on another. Crucially for our purposes, prima facie rights can meaningfully conflict and will inevitably conflict. Concrete rights, on the other hand, do not conflict. Concrete rights are "all things considered" rights and are established by close attention to specific circumstances of any particular case. These rights consider every detail of a situation to judge whether an interest is sufficient to impose a duty on another. Concrete rights resolve conflicts between prima facie rights and have peremptory force—finally determining what ought to be done.

So, to take an example, it can legitimately be argued that both you and I have a prima facie right to health care. After all, in general terms, both you and I have an interest in health care that is ordinarily sufficient to impose duties on others. However, now suppose that I require a pill to cure my mild skin complaint that is astronomically expensive, so expensive in fact that its provision to me would divert resources away from the medical care you need for your more serious and debilitating condition. In this situation it is plausible to state that you and I have prima facie rights to health care that clash. However, this does not mean that we have no means of determining what finally ought to be done using the interest-based approach. For we can use a careful analysis of interests in this particular context to determine who has a concrete right. In the situation described above, it is clear that your interests are far weightier and more pressing than mine. All things considered, then, it seems sensible to see your interest as sufficient to ground a duty in others to provide you with health care, whereas mine is not. Put simply, we can say that you have a concrete right to health care and I do not. Our prima facie rights may have clashed, but your concrete right determined what finally ought to be done.

Importantly, this distinction between prima facie and concrete rights accords closely with how rights function in most legal regimes. Rights to health care, privacy, free speech, free association, and so on have to be regarded as prima facie to make sense. It may be possible and useful to write these rights into the law in general terms, but to make sense of them we need legal and political procedures to work out what the protection and promotion of our prima facie rights actually entail. That is, we need those procedures to establish our concrete rights. The following chapter puts forward the claim that animals possess prima facie rights not to be made to suffer and not to be killed. The remainder of the book examines whether these rights lead to concrete rights in the contexts of experimentation, agriculture, genetic engineering, entertainment, the environment, and culture.

RIGHTS AS OVERLY RATIONALISTIC

Before proceeding with this investigation, however, it is worth examining one final possible objection to the type of interest-based theory of rights proposed in this chapter. This critique argues that a rights-based approach is an inappropriate means by which to delineate our political obligations to animals because it is overly rationalistic. A number of different claims are often involved when this charge is made. For example, some communitarian, feminist, and postmodern thinkers would argue that the kind of rights-based approach proposed in this book employs forms of reasoning that are antagonistic, essentialist, and hierarchical. What unites all these claims is the idea that the use of abstract reasoning to establish a set of rules, principles, and rights is a flawed means by which to formulate our proper relations with animals.

To evaluate this critique, it will be useful to consider the different components of it in turn. The ecofeminist scholar Marti Kheel has charged that rights are necessarily antagonistic: "The notion of rights can, in fact, be conceived of only within an antagonistic or competitive environment. The concept of competition is inherent in the very definition of rights."[55] The reason Kheel and others believe that rights are competitive in this way is that they are claims against other individuals: that is, they are individual demands to the performance of duties on the part of others. Thinkers like Kheel claim that a concept with this kind of competition at its heart is no way to build improved relations within a community. Critics of this sort sometimes point to selfish, antagonistic, and atomized modern societies as evidence of the effects of a strident rights discourse.[56] As an alternative, these critics claim that instead of basing their policies on rights, political communities should look to build more caring and harmonious societies: societies where the demand and enforcement of rights will cease to be necessary.

The problem with this argument is not that its goals are misplaced: a more caring and harmonious society where rights are unnecessary is certainly something worth aiming for. No, the problem is that such a society is either hopelessly utopian or at least a very long way off from present circumstances. Throughout the history of human societies, some individuals have sought to disrupt harmonious societal living through the promotion of their own interests at the expense of others. Given this, a set of rights can serve to protect individuals from the harmful actions of others. After all, when properly conceived, rights should act not as tools to further trivial interests, but as safety nets to protect us from serious harms. Moreover, rights necessarily entail correlative duties that helpfully make explicit the limits of what individuals can do to one another. As such, then, rather than viewing rights as things that promote antagonisms, it is more plausible to view rights as things that protect us from the inevitable antagonisms within society.

The second possible charge that forms part of this critique is that the kind of interest-based rights approach proposed in this book is "essentialist." That is, it reduces all animals and their experiences to a stripped-down bundle of interests.[57] This essentialism is claimed to be problematic for two reasons: first, it fails to recognize that animals are individuals with their own particular needs; and second, it ignores the fact that our obligations to animals depend not merely on their interests but also on the context of the relations we have with them. In both cases, the claim is that rights are too abstract a way of formulating our obligations to animals, and that we need a more contextual and relational approach.

In response to this objection, however, it is worth reminding ourselves that the goal of this theory is to come up with a set of moral rights that political communities ought to enforce and protect. Given that it is attempting to inform policies that govern large societies, some degree of abstraction and generalization seems only necessary. Just as political communities cannot make policies tailored precisely to the needs and well-being of specific humans in society, nor can they tailor policy to the needs and well-being of particular individual animals. Furthermore, while it is true that relations and context are vital to our obligations, the interest-based rights approach does recognize this. Rather than coming up with a set of absolute rights in the abstract and applying them wholesale to different policy areas, the interest-based rights approach recognizes that animals' rights must be justified contextually. So while we might be able to argue in general terms that animals possess a prima facie right to life, the question of whether a concrete animal right to life can be justified in relation to experimentation, agriculture, religious sacrifice, and so on requires careful assessment of the salient normative issues of the particular context under scrutiny.

The final objection that forms part of the rationalist critique is that the kind of interest-based rights theory proposed in this book is hierarchical. This objection takes issue with the proposed method of assigning rights and balancing conflicts between them. For under the interest-based rights theory, those with more and stronger interests are elevated above those with fewer and weaker interests.[58] Moreover, the very notions of "stronger" and "weaker" are judged purely in anthropocentric terms, taking human well-being as the ultimate basis of comparison. So while the theory of this book aims to transform communities' relations with animals in quite radical and profound ways, this objection states that it uses the very same methodologies that have served to entrench human superiority over animals, and as a result can have only limited efficacy.

While it is true that the interest-based approach prioritizes stronger interests over weaker ones, this should not be taken to mean that it advocates any kind of hierarchy among those with stronger or weaker interests. It is possible to acknowledge that all creatures with sentience possess moral status equally while also recognizing that some of the claims of those with moral status are more compelling than others. So, to return to the example given above, just because your right to health care is more compelling than mine in that context, that does not mean that you are morally superior to me or have greater moral worth than I have. The fact that your interests win out in that particular situation in no way implies that your interests will win out in other situations. When justifying rights and adjudicating rights disputes, favoring those interests that are the most compelling provides us with a fair and sensible methodology. It certainly does not entrench arbitrary hierarchies among sentient creatures.

Of course, that still leaves the charge that in this process interests and their strength can be judged only by human beings, rendering this whole process necessarily anthropocentric and biased toward human beings.[59] Such a criticism is, in my opinion, wrongheaded. Ethical enquiry must begin with human judgments and human experiences because human beings are the only types of creatures that we know of who can engage in such an enterprise. Quite simply, we have no means of transcending our humanity. As such, if we are to make normative judgments about social and political life, we have to begin somewhere, and that somewhere must always be with human beings. However, that does not mean that the theory will inevitably privilege human beings when working out what ought to be done. Under the framework outlined in this book, human interests can and do lose out when they are faced with certain nonhuman interests. After all, when we judge interests on their own merits and not on the basis of to whom they belong, humans are bound to sometimes lose out.

This chapter has introduced and defended the interest-based rights approach in three stages. First, the claim that sentient animals possess moral status was outlined and justified. It argued that there are compelling grounds for believing that some species of nonhuman animal possess the ability to experience the world and themselves in it. This capacity for experiences means that sentient animals have lives that can go well or badly for themselves. In other words, these sentient creatures have well-being and interests. Since normative inquiry is so focused on how the lives of individuals fare, it is only sensible to recognize that sentient animals are the proper concern of normative enquiry—that sentient animals possess moral status.

But can sentient animals possess rights? The second section argued that they can, using Feinberg's interest-based model for rights possession. The crucial claim put forward by Feinberg is that an entity does not need to be able to claim rights for itself in order to have rights, for if it has interests, then those interests can be represented and claimed by others on its behalf. The section examined a number of important critiques of this interest requirement for rights and found them all wanting.

Finally, the chapter defended the interest-based rights approach as the appropriate means by which to formulate our obligations to animals in political communities. By justifying rights through assessing whether interests are sufficient to impose duties, all things considered, this approach has two big advantages: it recognizes the importance of individual over aggregate well-being, and it grounds rights in something tangible and concrete. The section claimed that complaints that this method leads to an overinflation of rights, or that it is overly rationalistic, are misplaced.

Now that we have a grasp of the method to be used in this book, we are in a position to apply it. In other words, we are in a position to ask what rights animals possess. To do so, we have to answer the following important question: which interests of animals, if any, are sufficient to impose duties on us, all things considered? This task is taken up in the next chapter, by asking whether animals have any interests that are sufficient to establish animal rights not to be made to suffer, killed, or used in experimentation.

Three

Animal Experimentation

So far the book has argued that political communities have certain obligations to sentient nonhuman animals, and that these obligations can
be delineated using an interest-based rights approach. The first context
in which this framework will be applied is the most politically heated:
animal experimentation. To examine this issue, it is necessary to briefly
outline what I mean by animal experimentation. After all, animals are
experimented on across the globe for a vast number of aims and goals.
To simplify, it is helpful to distinguish between two different types of
animal experimentation: therapeutic and nontherapeutic.[1] The former
is often also referred to as "medical experimentation" and includes those
procedures that are carried out to research diseases and biological processes, to develop new drugs, and to test drugs for safety. While most of
these experiments are designed to bring improvements to *human* health,
it should not be overlooked that experiments for animal medicines also
fall under this therapeutic umbrella. The second class of experimentation, nontherapeutic, includes those procedures that are carried out for
general biological research, for educational purposes, and for the testing
household products and cosmetics. While the EU now bans the testing
of toiletries and cosmetics on animals, most countries do currently permit nontherapeutic experimentation. Since it is also claimed to confer
considerable benefits to humans, it is worthy of being included in the
analysis of this chapter.[2] One type of experimentation that I will not
consider here is the genetic engineering of animals. Because the genetic
engineering of animals also takes place in contexts outside of animal
experimentation, and because it raises its own difficult ethical issues,
chapter 4 is devoted to a full analysis of that topic.

Whenever animal experimentation is debated—whether it be therapeutic, nontherapeutic, or that which involves genetic engineering—
it usually generates passionate responses. For some, such as Colin

Blakemore, the former chief executive of the Medical Research Council in the UK, animal experimentation is possibly "the most noble thing we do to animals."[3] For others, like the vocal antivivisection lobby, animal experimentation is backward, barbaric, and a straightforward example of the powerful abusing the vulnerable.[4] The polarization of the debate over animal experimentation can be explained in part by the intuitive appeal of each of the opposing views. On the one hand, proponents of animal experimentation point to the incredible benefits that humans are claimed to receive from experimenting on animals and conclude that such experiments are absolutely essential for human well-being. Those opposed to animal experiments, on the other hand, point to the enormous levels of suffering that such experiments inflict on animals and provide gruesome details of practices within the laboratory that create incredible distress to millions of sentient beings.

This chapter enters the debate by exploring whether animals have a moral right not to be experimented on. To determine this, and following the interest-based rights approach that was outlined in chapter 2, the chapter examines whether animals possess an interest that is sufficient, all things considered, to impose a moral duty on us not to experiment on them. First, a means of assessing the strength of an individual's interests is proposed and defended. Next, three potential interests of animals that might ground an animal right not to be experimented on are examined and evaluated: the interest in not suffering, the interest in continued life, and the interest in being free. The chapter argues that the first two interests are sufficient to ground concrete animal rights not to be made to suffer and not to be killed in experimentation. However, it also claims that because animals possess no intrinsic interest in being free, they have no right not to be used in any and all forms of experimentation. In sum, then, the chapter claims that animal experiments that result in pain or death are morally illegitimate, while painless experiments in which the animal does not die are permissible, all else being equal.

Establishing the Strength of an Interest

To establish whether animals have a right not to be experimented on, we need to assess whether they have any interests that are sufficient to impose duties on others. Part of determining whether an interest is sufficient must involve an assessment of the strength of that interest. That is, it involves coming up with a judgment about how crucial that good is for the well-being of the individual in question. Obviously, determining the strengths of interests is a complex task. So just how are we to go about this process? This section proposes two broad criteria that determine the strength of an interest: the value of the particular good to the well-being of the individual; and the level of psychological continuity between the individual now and when the good or goods will occur.[5]

The first obvious way in which we can determine the strength of an interest is to consider its value to the individual in question. While determining the value of a good to an individual is sometimes a difficult task, it is by no means impossible. For example, I have an interest in both having enough to eat and receiving a paid holiday. However, the value of having enough to eat is greater to me than receiving holiday pay. This is simply because I could live a life of high quality without a paid holiday but would find it hard to do so without having enough to eat. It therefore makes sense to say that my interest in having sufficient food is stronger than my interest in receiving holiday pay.

It should not be taken from this understanding of interests that they are purely subjective. The point is that the strength of an interest must relate to the value of the good *for* the individual concerned. However, individuals themselves can be wrong about both what is good for them and the relative value of a good. For example, an individual may strongly desire to injure himself, but that does not mean that he has an *interest* in injuring himself. Similarly, an individual may place great value in seeing her family eat, so much so that she herself goes without food, thereby suffering malnutrition. However, it would be wrong to say that this individual has only a weak interest in eating—her life would clearly go much better if she ate, even if she believes otherwise. So although the strength of an interest is partly determined by the value of the good for the individual concerned, the individual is not necessarily the final arbiter of the value of that good.

As well as the value of the good for the individual, there is also a second important factor for determining the strength of an interest. This criterion concerns the relationship between the individual at the time when we attribute the interest and the individual when that interest will be satisfied. Jeff McMahan calls this the "psychological continuity" of the individual between now and when the future good or goods will occur.[6] By psychological continuity McMahan means those psychological connections that link us over time. Examples of such connections include the relation between an experience and the memory of it; a desire and the later experience of its satisfaction or frustration; and the earlier and later manifestation of a character trait, value, or belief.[7] Without doubt, not everything and everyone has equal levels of psychological continuity over time. For example, ordinarily a human toddler has negligible levels of psychological continuity with his future self at age twenty-one, while a twenty-one-year-old has strong continuity with himself as a twenty-five-year-old. McMahan's claim is that an individual's interest in a future good varies with the strength of this psychological continuity. So if the level of psychological continuity between the individual now and the time when the goods occur is strong, then the interest in that good becomes stronger. However, if the level of psychological continuity is weak, then the corresponding interest becomes weaker.

Psychological continuity is important to determining the strength of an interest because, as was explained in the previous chapter, well-being is a prudential value. That is, well-being concerns how life goes *for the individual whose life it is.* So when we are judging the strength of an interest, we cannot just assess the net value of the good that the interest protects. Instead, we must judge the value of that good *for the individual whose interest it is.* Since we ought to be concerned with the value individuals themselves receive from the good, the psychological continuity of those individuals must be important when evaluating interests that span across time. For quite straightforwardly, a future good will provide more value to an individual the more that he or she can identify with the future self who receives that good.

A Right Not to Be Subject to Painful Experimentation?

Given this account of the strength of interests, it is now necessary to consider whether animals possess any interests that are sufficient to establish an animal right not to be experimented on. First, it will be useful to consider the animal interest in not suffering. After all, it is evident that most experiments carried out on animals *necessitate* the infliction of pain: experiments are usually designed to model particular diseases, to assess the effects of drugs, and to test how much of a particular product can be administered before it becomes dangerous. Furthermore, the animal subjects are often kept in caged, cramped conditions that cause considerable suffering. Given these points, we need to ask whether animals have an interest in not suffering that is sufficient to establish an animal right not to be subjected to painful experimentation. The first step in coming up with an answer to this question involves judging the strength of the animal interest in not suffering.

How valuable is being free from suffering to nonhuman animals? While a definitive answer to this question is difficult to provide—much of course depends on context—some general points can be made and are useful to establish. After all, as phenomenally conscious beings ourselves, we do all know what suffering is: by its nature it is a bad experience. And just as it is a bad experience for you or me, we can also be confident that it is bad for any creature capable of conscious experience. Might we then say that the interest that sentient creatures have in avoiding pain is equivalently strong? Is pain pain, no matter to whom it belongs?

Some would no doubt want to deny this claim and argue that the suffering of those beings with richer and more complex cognitive abilities— like humans—is worse. To illustrate, imagine that my dog and I suffer in some accident that causes both of us to break a leg. It is possible to claim in such an instance that this suffering is worse for me because of my extra cognitive capacities. For instance, I might dwell on and become obsessed by the pain, thus spiraling into a depression. Also, as a person I have certain aims and projects I wish to fulfill that might be frustrated by my broken leg, exacerbating my suffering. Both capacities are lacking in my dog, perhaps making the break less bad for him. As such, it might be argued that the more cognitively complex a being, the greater the strength of its interest in avoiding pain.

And yet similar arguments referring to the extra capacities of individuals can also be used to support the idea that my dog suffers *more* from his leg being broken. For example, perhaps my additional capacities allow me to rationalize my pain, understanding that it will come to an end. My dog, on the other hand, might be totally consumed by his suffering. Similarly, it might be that my plans and projects actually lessen the effects of my pain, helping me to enjoy a decent quality of life in spite of the break.

It seems to me that there is little chance of coming up with any definitive resolution to this kind of problem. It is impossible to say that the suffering of those with greater cognitive complexity is always worse, or indeed that the suffering of those with reduced cognitive complexity is always worse. Instead much will depend on the circumstances of each case. As such, it is preferable to take account of those circumstances and recognize that suffering is sometimes worse for humans, sometimes worse for sentient animals, and sometimes equivalent. Nevertheless, and most importantly, we can confidently say that avoiding suffering is extremely valuable for all sentient creatures, whether human or not. Obviously both I and my dog have a very strong interest in not suffering from a broken leg.

But what about the other factor relating to the strength of an interest: psychological continuity? It seems clear that animals possess weaker psychological continuity with their future selves when compared to most human beings. This is simply because animals have fewer earlier and later mental states that refer to one another.[8] While it would be a mistake to suggest that animals are entirely "trapped in the present," it is perfectly reasonable to recognize that given their more limited cognitive abilities, animals have fewer psychological connections over time than most adult humans. Does this make the animal interest in not suffering weaker than that of humans? Not necessarily. For the interest individuals have in not suffering does not always refer to some future good, to be obtained by some future self; in fact, it usually relates to an immediate good to be received by one's present self. In light of this, we can acknowledge that their differing levels of psychological continuity give adult humans a stronger interest than animals in, say, not contracting arthritis when they reach old age. However, we must also recognize that it does not give them any stronger interest in not contracting arthritis *now*.

Clearly there are difficulties with measuring the relative strength of the animal interest in avoiding suffering. However, there is no difficulty in recognizing that suffering is ordinarily a serious harm for animals, just like it is ordinarily a serious harm for humans. Because of the strength of this interest, there is good reason to acknowledge that animals, like humans, have a prima facie right not to be made to suffer. What I mean by this is that sentient animals can be considered to possess a *general* right not to be made to suffer. But whether a concrete right is established in any particular context will depend on the circumstances of the situation. So in those situations where there are no competing interests at stake, and there are no other overriding relevant considerations, animals can plausibly be said to have a concrete right not to be made to suffer. For example, the interest of my dog in not suffering is surely sufficient, all things considered, to impose a duty on me not to beat him simply for my own amusement. My dog has an obvious concrete right in this case because of the absence of any important competing interests. However, the context of animal experimentation is quite different. In experimentation, there are weighty competing interests to consider, and there are other relevant, important factors at stake. So perhaps because of these other considerations, the animal interest in not suffering from experimentation is insufficient to ground a duty in another. In other words, perhaps a concrete animal right not to be made to suffer from experimentation cannot be established.

It is possible to think of three separate arguments that might be employed to claim that the animal interest in not suffering is insufficient to establish an animal right not to be made to suffer in experiments. First, the great benefits provided by animal experimentation can be pointed to, with the accompanying claim that such benefits override animals' interests in avoiding pain. Second, some might argue that we have special obligations to our fellow human beings that override the consideration we ought to give to the interests of individuals from different species. Finally, it can be claimed that human life is worth more than animal life. Such an assertion can be used to argue that while humans have a right not to be made to suffer in experimentation, non-human animals hold no such equivalent right. Each of these claims is examined and evaluated in the remainder of this section.

THE BENEFITS OF EXPERIMENTATION JUSTIFY ITS CONTINUATION

The most common argument put forward by those in favor of animal experimentation is what we might deem the "argument from benefit." This argument conducts a simple cost-benefit analysis and concludes that the interests of animals in avoiding pain are outweighed by humans' interests in the results of animal experimentation. Put in the terms of the interest-based rights framework employed in this book, it could be argued that the interest of animals in being free from suffering is insufficient to establish an animal right not to be subjected to painful experimentation—and it is insufficient because of the weighty benefits that human beings receive from such experimentation. In other words, when all things are considered, the argument might be that the benefits of animal experimentation are simply too great to warrant any thought of its discontinuance.

Of course, the type of argument outlined above can only have plausibility when it comes to *therapeutic* experiments on animals. The benefits that human beings receive from experiments that test cosmetics, toiletries, and the like are certainly rather trivial when compared to the interest that sentient beings have in not suffering. That is, human beings can lead lives of extremely high quality even without the opportunity to use new and different shampoos and oven cleaners. Animals' well-being, on the other hand, is necessarily limited when subjected to routine forms of painful experimentation. This is not to say that nontherapeutic experimentation provides no benefits; it is simply to recognize that those benefits are difficult to view as weightier and more compelling than the basic interest in being free of suffering.

Therapeutic animal experimentation, of course, is another matter entirely. In this case, the alleged benefits to humans cannot be regarded as trivial: "proponents cite progress in the area of Alzheimer's disease, AIDS, basic genetics, cancer, cardiovascular disease, haemophilia, malaria, organ transplantation, treatment of spinal cord injuries and countless others."[9] Moreover, it is claimed that this progress has not just been to the benefit of humans: animal experimentation has also generated improved treatment for sick and injured animals. The argument suggests that all future progress in these areas would be lost should painful experimentation on animals be stopped. In light of these important benefits, can we conclude that the animal interest in avoiding pain is insufficient to establish an animal right not to be subjected to painful experimentation?

To defeat this argument from benefit, many proponents of animal rights deny its fundamental premise. They argue that animal experiments not only are unnecessary given the availability of alternatives, but are actually a hindrance to medical progress because of the differences in physiology between species.[10] What are we to make of such arguments? This is a large and difficult topic, which I lack the space to explore fully here. Moreover, an assessment of the scientific validity of using animal models in experiments is best conducted by those with much greater scientific expertise than I have. However, this by no means entails that there is nothing left to say in relation to the normative issue at hand. For without doubt, an empirically based cost-benefit analysis of animal experimentation will not definitively decide the moral question. For example, animal experiments may provide wide-ranging therapeutic benefits *and* be morally impermissible. It is this possibility that I now wish to explore.

The rest of this section will assume, for the sake of argument, that painful experimentation on animals can and does provide some contribution to medical progress. This assumption, however, cannot by itself legitimate painful experimentation on animals. For if political communities were concerned *solely* with the benefits afforded by medical progress, then they should begin wholesale programs of experiments on human beings. This is because human subjects provide the best experimental models for researching human diseases and for testing the effects of drugs on humans. While an experiment on a rat may provide clues as to the effect of a particular drug on humans, an experiment on a human being will provide much harder and more reliable evidence. This is precisely why clinical trials on humans are conducted. Importantly, however, such trials always require consent and very rarely involve the kind of invasive and painful experimentation that takes place on animals. So if we consider nonconsensual painful experiments on sentient animals to be justified on the basis of the wide-ranging benefits that they confer, then we will also have to regard nonconsensual experiments on human beings to be justified. This is simply because human experiments would confer even greater benefits.

Most of us believe—quite rightly—that such programs of painful human experimentation would be impermissible, even in the face of such potentially enormous gains. Since rights are meant to act as brakes on the untrammeled pursuit of aggregate welfare, many would consider programs of painful and nonconsensual human experimentation as violations of important human rights, irrespective of the overall benefits they might produce. The Nuremburg Code, the Helsinki Declaration, and the Universal Declaration on Bioethics and Human Rights all explicitly state that such forms of human experimentation are violations of human rights.[11] Of course, this raises a crucial question: given that nonhuman animals also possess an interest in avoiding suffering, why do they not possess equivalent rights? Why is the human interest in avoiding pain sufficient to ground a human right not to be subject to painful experimentation, while the animal interest is not?

SPECIES MEMBERSHIP IS ETHICALLY SIGNIFICANT

Perhaps there is a relevant difference between the human and the animal interest in not being subject to painful experiments—and perhaps it comes down to species membership. Some argue, for instance, that it is legitimate for humans to grant extra weight to the interests of fellow humans. This is because it is claimed that species membership itself is morally relevant, and that it is normally justifiable for individuals to favor the interests of the species to which they belong. It might thus be argued that, as humans, it is legitimate for us to give extra weight to the human interest in not suffering and translate this into a right not to be subject to painful experimentation, while denying an equivalent right to nonhumans. To make this kind of claim plausible, the argument needs to provide an explanation of why it is permissible and not prejudicial to favor our own species at the expense of others in this way.

Lewis Petrinovich has put forward one of the most comprehensive attempts to offer such an explanation.[12] Petrinovich first argues that speciesism (favoring one's own species) is a natural fact of life: "Humans, as well as all other social animals, are speciesists. Animals of all species show a clear preference for their own kind: They associate and mate with their own species; they fight alongside their own kind against members of a foreign species to secure resources; and they defend the young of their own species. Any species that did not show preference for its own kind would become extinct."[13]

Petrinovich then asserts that favoring our species can be likened to favoring our kin members: both "moral feelings" have evolved in order to protect the replication of genes. Furthermore, he argues, both are justified as ethical positions because we have stronger emotional bonds to our kin and fellow species members.[14] In light of this, subordinating the interests of other species can be justified, a position directly relevant for the case of animal experimentation: "I maintain that, when push comes to shove, the interests of members of our species should triumph over comparable interests of members of other species. This position does not imply that any human whim should take precedence over essential needs and deep welfare interests of nonhuman animals. It only means that human interests should be read as high cards in any game where costs and benefits are taken into consideration."[15]

Unfortunately, Petrinovich's argument has clear and obvious problems. First, one can question the rather simplistic model of species solidarity that Petrinovich presents. He claims in the quote above that members of a species breed with one another, defend themselves against other species, and protect one another's young. Of course, none of these traits is without significant exceptions. Individuals can and do breed with mates outside of their species, fight and kill members of their own species, and kill and eat each other's young.

Even if we accept Petrinovich's flawed picture of nature, however, that still does not show that we should preserve it. Indeed, Petrinovich appears to commit the naturalistic fallacy of deriving an *ought* from an *is*. His argument suggests that we *do* favor our own species, that evolution explains *why* we favor our own species, and thus that we *should* favor our own species. But the question of what is right can be decoupled from the question of what is natural. For example, it is no doubt natural for humans to rape and murder one another. Clearly, however, the fact that rape and murder are natural does not make them right.

In light of such arguments, Petrinovich argues that compatibility with the laws of biology is a *necessary but insufficient* condition for a valid moral claim. Thus in his view an ethical position must also be consistent with the "basic freedoms of human beings".[16] This would seem to get around my examples of rape and murder, where clear violations of basic freedoms take place. Essentially, then, Petrinovich permits a degree of rational thinking to supplement his biological thesis. But once a degree of rationality is allowed in, it is unclear why we must stop at basic human freedoms. After all, if rational thinking is allowed to supplement the basic biological argument, then one could provide a rationally based defense of *nonhuman* freedoms. Or rather one could offer a rational defense of nonhuman well-being and claim that animals' interests should not always be trumped by those of humans. Without doubt Petrinovich owes us an argument for why some supplementary rational arguments are acceptable and others are not.

There remains a further problem with the claim that species membership is ethically relevant: of all the classes and types of living organisms, why is species membership the relevant one? After all, we all belong to a wide variety of groups and classes. In light of this, it might be deemed arbitrary to choose species membership as ethically relevant instead of, say, biological class, biological order, race, gender, or religion.[17] For it is no doubt the case that many of us have closer emotional bonds to some of these groups than to our species.

Putting the boot on the other foot also highlights the difficulty with claiming that it is justifiable to favor the interests of one's own species. Imagine, for example, a situation in which human beings were not the most powerful species on the planet. Thanks to science fiction, it does not take much effort to conjure up scenarios where Earth has been visited—or invaded—by aliens from other worlds. In effect, arguments using species solidarity such as that put forward by Petrinovich must claim that it would be legitimate for an alien species to experiment on human beings in order to further its own interests. To most this will not seem like a very palatable conclusion. Indeed, the example works well to highlight the fundamental prejudice inherent in theories that justify privileging one's own group: they end up favoring the strong at the expense of the vulnerable.

In conclusion, it is not enough to say that we can subordinate the interest of animals in not suffering just because they belong to a different species. Individuals belong to a wide variety of groups and classes, and it is unclear why favoring the interests of our own species is any different from favoring the interests of our own race, gender, or religious community. Of course, sometimes showing partiality to particular groups—friends, family, and the like—can be acceptable in certain situations. But recall that this book is concerned with outlining a system of rights and obligations that can be enforced by political communities. And while showing partiality toward friends and family is undoubtedly acceptable in aspects of our everyday lives, such partiality is of course seriously problematic when used as a basis to distribute the benefits and burdens of large-scale communities.[18] Impartiality across individuals is crucial when formulating principles to guide the policies of political communities. This does not require that all groups be treated exactly alike, but it does mean that if extra weight is to be granted to the interests of any group, justifiable reasons must be given for so doing. As such, if subordinating the animal interest in avoiding pain is to be justified, species solidarity cannot simply be invoked—instead, a morally relevant difference between humans and animals must be proposed. Perhaps, for example, human life is worth more. This is the issue that is examined in the next section.

HUMAN LIFE IS WORTH MORE THAN ANIMAL LIFE

Many philosophers seem to accept the claim that human lives are worth more than animal lives. Perhaps, then, an animal's interest in avoiding pain can be overridden, but the equivalent human interest cannot, because of the simple fact that human lives are worth more. To make such a claim stand up, it is necessary to point to those particular characteristics that humans possess that make their lives more valuable. This section examines one such attempt to do this.

Bonnie Steinbock has proposed that animal experimentation is justified, and she bases her argument on the fact that humans possess what in chapter 2 I referred to as the characteristics of personhood: moral agency and autonomy. "Both rats and human beings dislike pain, and so we have a prima facie reason not to inflict pain on either. But if we can free human beings from crippling diseases, pain and death through experimentation which involves making animals suffer, and if this is the only way to achieve such results, then I think that such experimentation is justified because human lives are more valuable than animal lives."[19]

Upon reading Steinbock's position, however, a problem immediately becomes obvious. For as was pointed out in chapter 2, not all human beings possess the capacities for autonomy and moral agency: young infants and those who are severely mentally disabled do not possess these capacities of personhood. So do human nonpersons such as newborn infants and those who are mentally disabled also have less valuable lives than persons, making painful experiments on them permissible?[20]

Steinbock addresses this problem directly and argues that it is not justifiable to experiment on such humans. In her view, humans that lack such autonomy cannot survive in the world without our special care, whereas nonhuman animals survive very well despite having fewer capacities than ordinary humans. Because of this difference Steinbock argues that it is justifiable to experiment on animals but not on so-called marginal humans.[21] However, even if we concede the premise that there is this difference between nonhuman animals and non-autonomous humans, this does not appear to lead to the conclusion Steinbock wants it to. What is needed, but not provided, is a case to be made for the moral relevance of being able to survive with or without special care. After all, and as Angus Taylor points out, Steinbock first wanted to subordinate the interests of animals because they possess fewer capacities than humans, and yet now she wants to subordinate them because they possess greater capacities.[22]

In reality Steinbock's argument concerning special care is a red herring. Her fundamental argument for why we should experiment on animals but not on humans essentially comes down once again to the assumption that species membership is ethically relevant. Her real argument is based on our ability to identify with members of our own species and to empathize with others. She writes that "when we consider the severely retarded, we think, 'That could be me.' It makes sense to think that one might have been born retarded, but not to think that one might have been born a monkey."[23] It is hard to know what to make of such an argument. Importantly, *why* does it make sense to think that one might have been born disabled, but not to think that one might have been born a monkey? Surely, considering being born as someone or as something else are equally far-fetched imaginative flights of fancy. In any case, determining whether lives are more valuable than others solely on our capacity for empathy with them is both dubious and dangerous. As pointed out above, people have variously strong sympathies with different groups: does this mean that the suffering of our fellow nationals, religious believers, or gender counts more in each case? It is difficult to come up with a rational basis to explain why.

I wish to end this long section with the claim that animals have a concrete right not to be subjected to painful experimentation. The interest that animals have in avoiding pain is fundamental to their well-being. If we are to take animal well-being seriously, as has been suggested, then those who claim that we can subordinate animal interests by conducting painful experimentation on them need to provide convincing arguments to support their case. However, none of the arguments presented by proponents of animal experimentation do the work that their advocates want them to: the arguments from benefit, species membership, and the value of human life all fail. In sum, we must conclude that the nonhuman animal interest in avoiding pain is sufficient to impose a duty on us not to subject sentient creatures to painful experimentation.

A Right Not to Be Killed by Experimentation?

If sentient animals have a right not to be subjected to painful experimentation, it might seem fairly obvious that they also have a right not to be killed by experimentation. However, on reflection this is not obvious at all. First, one can conceive of experiments whereby animals are anesthetized, experimented on, and then killed painlessly. That is, not all experiments that end in death need also involve pain. Second, the interest that an animal has in avoiding pain is clearly different from the interest that an animal has in continued life. In fact, while an animal's interest in avoiding pain is relatively clear, it is uncertain whether animals even possess an interest in continued life. In light of this, to determine whether animals have a right not to be killed by experimentation, we must first determine whether they even have an interest in continued life.

DO ANIMALS HAVE AN INTEREST IN CONTINUED LIFE?

Some might argue that if causing animals to suffer harms them (as I have claimed), then so too does killing them. Such a judgment would presumably be based on the assumption that being killed is a greater misfortune than being made to suffer. However, the claim that an entity has an interest in not suffering does not entail that it also has an interest in continued life; nor can we take it for granted that death is a greater misfortune than suffering. There is one obvious and important difference between death and suffering: it feels like something for an animal to be in pain, while it clearly does not feel like anything for an animal (or anyone else) to be dead. This considerable difference between suffering and being dead is reason enough to warrant a separate justification for the claim that animals have an interest in continued life.

It must be pointed out that in the discussion that follows I will be concerned only with *painless* death and killing. For it is clear from the argument above that a painful death necessarily harms an animal because animals have an interest in avoiding pain. However, what we are concerned with here is assessing whether death and killing are *in themselves* harmful to animals.

As a reminder, interests should be regarded as components of well-being. In light of this, to ascertain whether sentient animals have an interest in continued life, we must ask whether continued life makes their lives go better. The most obvious way of arguing that it does is to point to the opportunities that continued life affords for pleasant experiences. After all, it seems only reasonable to claim that if suffering is bad for animals, then pleasant experiences are good for them. Consequently we might say that an animal has more well-being overall in her life the more pleasurable experiences she has in that life. Clearly when an animal dies or is killed, the amount of possible pleasure in her life is ended. We can thus conclude that ordinarily animals have an interest in continued life so that they may have more pleasant experiences and greater overall well-being in their lives.[24]

THE STRENGTH OF THE INTEREST IN CONTINUED LIFE

Several other proponents of animal rights agree with this conclusion that sentient animals have an interest in continued life. In similar arguments, these philosophers tend to argue that death harms sentient animals because it forecloses their opportunities for future valuable experiences.[25] However, most of these philosophers regard the interest in continued life as one of the strongest that animals possess. Thus the move from an interest in continued life to a moral right to life would be easy for such philosophers to make. But is the animal interest in continued life as strong as such philosophers tend to assume?

Remember that two factors determine the strength of an interest: the value of the good in question for the individual whose life it is, and the psychological continuity between the individual now and when the good will occur. Let us take the value of continued life first. It might be useful to judge the strength of the value of continued life for animals by comparing it to that of humans. Is the good of continued life more valuable for humans than it is for animals? Part of a human's interest in continued life has similar foundations to that of an animal's interest: continued life permits future valuable experiences. However, continued life provides more value to the well-being of human persons in at least two other related respects. For one, continued life contributes to most humans' *immediate* well-being because they have the capacity to reflect on those future valuable experiences. For example, it makes me now happy to think of my plans for this coming weekend and the visit of some friends. I can imagine being with my friends and having a good time, and such a thought makes me happy now. While many animals must surely have certain short-term desires about their immediate future, their capacities are unlikely to extend to the ability to picture themselves in the future and reflect on what it might be like.

Furthermore, as autonomous beings, human persons have certain projects and goals that they wish to fulfill. Continued life provides them with the opportunity to pursue such ambitions, change them, and hopefully eventually to realize them. Once again, then, the prospect of continued life provides persons with the present satisfaction that they can continue pursuing these goals and take pleasure from so doing. While it is true that animals possess certain short-term desires and aims, these do not equate to the self-chosen life goals of an autonomous agent. Accordingly, the animal interest in continued life is not supported by life's contribution to the shaping and fulfillment of goals. Because of these two related factors, it is reasonable to state that ordinarily continued life is more valuable for most humans than it is for most nonhuman animals.

However, it might be pointed out that this account of the strength of the interest in continued life has a rather odd implication. For it seems to imply that individuals who are depressed, or who merely possess a pessimistic frame of mind, have a weaker interest in continued life than those without depression and with a cheery outlook. After all, there are some individuals who do not take satisfaction from the prospect of future goods and possess no projects that they look forward to pursuing in the future. Does this mean that such individuals have only a very weak interest in continued life? No, it does not. Recall from the earlier discussion of what it means to have an interest the claim that interests are not wholly subjective. I argued that part of the strength of an interest is determined by the value of the good for the individual in question, but also that the individual can be wrong about what is good for him or her, and the strength of the value of that good. As such, we ought not to judge the strength of the interest in continued life simply on the basis of the individual's own assessment of his or her future projects and goals. Rather, we should make a more general judgment about what human beings can possibly achieve in their future lives. In so doing, we can reasonably say that depressed and pessimistic individuals ordinarily do have an extremely strong interest in continued life on the basis that they have the prospect of achieving future goods and have the capacity to pursue valuable projects in the future.[26]

Finally, we must remember that the value to the individual is not the sole determining factor of the strength of an interest: the level of psychological continuity between the individual now and when the goods will occur is also relevant. This provides a further reason to consider the animal interest in continued life to be weaker than that of human persons. For unlike the absence of suffering, continued life necessarily relates to a future good. And since most animals have lower levels of psychological continuity with their future selves than do persons, their interest in that future good is weaker.

In sum, we can recognize that animals possess an interest in continued life based on the overall amount of good in their lives. However, we must recognize that the animal interest in continued life is weaker than that of human persons for three reasons: animals lack the capacity to take immediate satisfaction from the prospect of continued life; they do not possess future self-chosen goals and projects to pursue; and they possess weaker psychological continuity with their future selves.

A MORAL RIGHT NOT TO BE KILLED BY EXPERIMENTATION?

What does all this mean for an animal's putative right not to be killed by experimentation? Remember that in order for an animal to possess a right, an animal's interest must be sufficiently important to impose a duty on us. Perhaps because an animal's interest in continued life is only weak, it is insufficient to impose a duty on us not to kill her. However, such a claim is too hasty. After all, the interest that animals have in continued life exists and cannot simply be ignored. Moreover, in some circumstances there may be an absence of competing interests, providing good grounds for acknowledging an animal's right to life. For example, my cat's interest in continued life certainly seems sufficient to ground a duty in me not to kill him, say, because I am going on holiday and cannot be bothered to organize feeding him while I am away. So in light of their interests, there seems to be good reason for acknowledging that sentient animals possess a prima facie right to life.

However, we must remember that if an animal's interest in continued life is weak, then the basis of his subsequent right to life is also weak. Thus it might be correct not to assign it in cases where there are sufficiently strong and pressing competing interests at stake. Some would argue that the case of therapeutic animal experimentation is one context in which such sufficiently strong and pressing interests exist. For while it might be acknowledged that the interest we have in cosmetics or detergents is insufficient to trump the animal interest in continued life, the interests that are promoted by therapeutic experimentation, such as basic human health, are sufficiently strong.

But there is a serious problem with this line of argument. I have proposed that, for most animals, their interest in continued life is weak for three reasons: they do not immediately benefit from the prospect of continued life; they do not have goals and projects to pursue; and they have weak psychological continuity with their future selves. But these factors also apply to human nonpersons. So human babies and severely mentally disabled individuals must also have a weaker interest in continued life. This is a problem for thinkers who claim that an animal's interest in continued life is too weak to ground a right not to be killed by therapeutic experimentation, for they must also acknowledge that these humans' interest is too weak to ground such a right. Put simply, if it is legitimate to thwart an animal's interest by killing that animal painlessly in a therapeutic experiment, it must also be legitimate to do the same to human babies and individuals who are seriously mentally disabled.

We are thus effectively left with two choices. First, we could simply conclude that it is legitimate to conduct painless but deadly experiments on *both* animals and humans who lack these capacities. However, even utilitarians, aiming to maximize overall welfare, balk at embracing such conclusions.[27] And no doubt almost all of us would regard this option as too costly to embrace. Alternatively, then, we might have to conclude that the interest in continued life of both humans and nonhumans is sufficiently strong to ground in us a duty not to kill them by experimentation.

And yet perhaps there is a third option that has not been considered. It might be possible to make the case that these nonautonomous humans have a *greater* interest in continued life than animals do. If this case can be made, it will be just a short step to arguing that the interest of human nonpersons is sufficient to impose on us a duty not to kill them, while that of animals is not.

One way of constructing such an argument is to return to the account of the relevant factors in determining the strength of an interest. Recall that part of the strength of an interest depends on the levels of psychological connectedness between the individual now and the individual later when the goods will occur, and part depends on the value of the good for the individual in question. However, Jeff McMahan presents the latter factor in a slightly different way. He claims that the second determinant of the strength of an interest is the "net amount of good" that will occur from the satisfaction of that interest.[28] In keeping with this account, many would make the reasonable claim that the net amount of good a human nonperson will receive from future life will be greater than that which an animal will receive. For the added richness of experience that human beings are capable of could be pointed to as evidence of this greater level of good. For example, McMahan himself writes: "Because of their limited cognitive and emotional capacities, most animals lack the capacity for many of the forms of experience and action that give the lives of persons their special richness and meaning, and without which our lives would be greatly impoverished."[29] One might claim, then, that the interest of human nonpersons in continued life is greater than that of nonhumans because the former will attain more net good than the latter in the future. If we accept such an argument, perhaps it does now make sense to say that human nonpersons have a right not to be killed by therapeutic experimentation, but that nonhumans do not.

Unfortunately this extra-goodness argument has some important problems. First, it assumes that the lives of *all* human nonpersons will be capable of such richness in the future. However, while most babies and infants will come to have such capacities, those with permanent mental disabilities and those with degenerative conditions will not. The logic of this extra-goodness argument thus suggests that the interest in continued life of human nonpersons with permanent or degenerative disabilities is insufficient to ground a duty on us not to kill them in therapeutic experiments. This jars against our intuitions, making it a very unappealing conclusion.

However, I think there is another problem with the extra-goodness argument that does not rely on an appeal to our intuitions. For when we talk about the "net amount of good" in a life, this raises the question, good for whom? In McMahan's account, when the strength of an interest is being determined, the value of the good *for the individual whose life it is* does not matter; all that matters is that there is more net good. But this takes us away from the notion of interests and well-being as prudential values. If, as I claimed in the previous chapter, the interests of an individual relate to how well life goes for the individual whose life it is, then an interest must be stronger only if it relates to a good that is of more value *for that individual*.

For example, a baby usually has the opportunity to realize more good through continued life than a dog does. All being well, the baby will grow up to be able to act morally, have loving relationships, worship gods, write poetry, appreciate art, and so on. A dog, on the other hand, while able to realize some goods, such as eating, exercising, and companionship, is likely to produce less net good compared to the human. These goods, we might concede for the sake of argument, are straightforwardly less valuable than those of the human. However, none of this says anything about the value of these goods *for* the human and the dog. The goods the dog receives may be less valuable than those of the human, but the value of these goods for the dog will be equivalent to the value of the other goods for the human. After all, both the dog and human have lives that can go well or badly, so each possesses, from their point of view, an equivalent stake that they go well. If interests relate to how life goes for the individual whose life it is, the fact that babies can produce more net good does not by itself make their interest in continued life any stronger than that of nonhumans.

To sum up this section, I want to claim that nonhuman animals possess a concrete right not to be killed by experimentation. Most animals have an interest in continued life. While it is true that the animal interest in continued life is weaker than that of human persons, that does not mean that it is too weak to ground in us a duty not to kill animals in experiments, all things considered. After all, many *human* nonpersons have an interest in continued life that is equivalent in strength to that of animal nonpersons. Finally, then, we have to make a judgment. Either we regard the interest in continued life of both human and nonhuman nonpersons as insufficient to ground the right, making permissible deadly experiments on animals, infants, and individuals who are severely mentally disabled, or we regard the interests of both as sufficient to ground the right, making such deadly experimentation impermissible. In keeping with most people who consider such a choice, my judgment is in favor of the latter. As such, I claim that animals have a moral right not to be killed by experimentation.

A Right Not to Be Used in Experimentation?

So far this chapter has argued that animals' interests in not suffering and in not being killed are both sufficient to ground in us a duty not to conduct experiments on animals that cause them pain or result in their death. However, perhaps animals have a more general interest in not being experimented upon: perhaps they have an interest in not being *used* in experimentation. That is, perhaps animals have a right not be used as experimental tools, irrespective of whether such use causes them pain or death. Such an interest in not being used could be founded on the interest animals might have in *being free.*

The claim that animals have an interest in being free can take one of two forms, each relative to the particular conception of freedom that is used. First, one might take a negative conception of freedom and argue that animals have an interest in not being interfered with. Alternatively, one might take a positive conception of freedom and argue that animals have an interest in being in control of their own lives.[30] Whichever conception of freedom is adopted, it is clear that experimenting on animals imposes on that freedom, because it both interferes with them and inhibits their ability to control their own lives. Importantly, if animals do have an interest in freedom, and if that interest is sufficient to ground a duty in us not to impose on their freedom, then we can say that *all* forms of experimentation on animals are morally illegitimate. For even if an experiment causes an animal no pain and does not result in death, we can be almost certain that by using an animal in an experiment we are *necessarily* interfering with the animal and inhibiting that individual's ability to control his own life.[31] Thus it is imperative to discover at the outset whether animals do have this interest in freedom.

DO ANIMALS HAVE AN INTEREST IN NEGATIVE FREEDOM?

When philosophers talk of negative freedom they are referring to those times when we consider individuals to be free from constraints and interference.[32] Without doubt there are numerous ways in which experimentation interferes with an animal. First, an experiment might involve removing an animal from his natural habitat in order to take him to the laboratory for experimentation. This is a clear and obvious case of interference. However, it also makes sense to say that those animals that are bred in captivity for experimentation are interfered with and constrained. Being held in cages is a fairly obvious form of constraint, while being injected or force-fed are clear cases of interference. What needs to be considered is whether this interference necessarily harms animals.

A difficulty in answering this question relates to the fact that the interferences and constraints of experimentation almost always involve suffering. For example, taking animals from their natural habitat is usually traumatic for both the animals involved and often—if they are social animals—those animals that are left behind. Keeping animals in cages can inhibit movement, causing cramp and sores, as well as boredom, frustration, and other forms of suffering. Finally, forcing animals to take particular substances by injection or other means is often distressing for the animal subjects. So while we can say that in these examples the animals are being harmed by being interfered with and by being constrained, this is based on their fundamental interest in not suffering. To discover whether interference and constraint are *in themselves* harmful to animals, we need to consider those instances when such impositions do not involve the infliction of pain.

To help ascertain whether interference and constraint are in themselves harmful to animals, it is useful to look at why interference with human persons is usually considered harmful, and to see if the same applies to animals. By way of an example, then, imagine experimenting on a human person against her will. As was discussed above, most of us consider such an experiment to be morally illegitimate. However, imagine that the individual is drugged so that she is caused no pain by the experiment and will have no memory of it (perhaps she is anesthetized without her knowledge while asleep). Finally, suppose that we can somehow guarantee that the experiment will not affect that individual's health in any way throughout the remainder of her life. Even with these provisos, most of us still regard this experiment to be morally wrong. And I believe that such a judgment is correct. The reason this experiment would be wrong comes down to the fact that human persons have an interest in leading freely chosen lives, as self-governing autonomous agents. Clearly, using individuals in nonconsensual experimentation, even when it causes no suffering or distress, violates this important interest of human persons.

However, the same is not true with regard to most nonhuman animals. Most animals are not autonomous agents with the capacity to reflect on, choose, and pursue their own goals.[33] They thus have no interest in leading their own freely chosen lives. Sentient animals can make choices and act on those choices, but that is something quite different. Without the capacity to reflect on their choices, or on the reasons for their choices, animals are locked into their ends and goals in a way that most adult humans are not. In light of this, nonconsensual interference, constraint, and use are not *in themselves* harmful to animal nonpersons, as they are for human persons. This, of course, has important implications for using animals in experiments. If a sentient animal born in captivity is drugged and anesthetized so that he is caused no distress, and if that animal is not killed, then, all else being equal, that animal is not harmed.

DO ANIMALS HAVE AN INTEREST IN POSITIVE FREEDOM?

The previous section argued that most animals have no intrinsic interest in avoiding being interfered with. This is based on the fact that most animals are not autonomous beings and do not possess an interest in leading a freely chosen life. In light of this, the question of an animal's interest in positive freedom—being in control of one's own life—might seem obvious. That is, if most animals are not autonomous beings, it would be extremely unlikely that they have an interest in being in control of their own lives; that is, in framing, revising, and pursuing their own freely chosen ends. And indeed, most nonhuman animals have no such interest. However, a slightly different understanding of positive freedom is often put forward in relation to animals and is worth considering. This understanding of positive freedom is not so much about individuals having control of their own lives as about individuals being able to pursue their biological ends.

One such argument might be based on arguments put forward by Paul W. Taylor. Taylor argues that one plausible conception of freedom is the ability to pursue one's ends. Moreover, although most animals (and other living things) cannot choose their own ends, they nevertheless have their own biological ends that are valuable to them. According to Taylor, being free to pursue these ends is thus in the interests of animals.[34] Can we then say that using animals in experimentation harms animals because it prevents them from freely pursuing their biological ends?

The first awkward problem for this argument is determining what the biological ends of animals are. For example, what are the biological ends of an individual laboratory mouse? This is a hugely difficult question and poses an enormous problem for Taylor's argument. However, let us for the sake of argument assume that the true biological ends of creatures can in fact be determined. One reasonable proposal as to the biological end of mice is that they are gene replicators. In other words, we might say that a mouse's ultimate purpose is to produce as many healthy offspring as possible. Does this explain why it would harm a lab mouse to keep him in captivity or to use him for certain purposes? Unfortunately it does not. For it would be quite possible to allow a mouse to breed while in captivity or while being used for some other purpose. Indeed, keeping the animal in captivity might allow for an increased opportunity for the mouse to fulfill his ends, by facilitating breeding programs and engineering conditions so that his offspring have good survival chances.[35]

In response it might be objected that captive mice can never really fulfill their biological ends. For it might be claimed that as captives, their lives are necessarily artificial, and so too are any of their activities, such as breeding. As such, it might be argued that animals have an interest in positive freedom, where freedom is defined as the ability to pursue their biological ends *in the wild*. Using animals in experimentation might thus be claimed to necessarily harm animals insofar as it infringes on their freedom conceived of in this sense. The problem with this argument, however, is that it imposes aesthetic and perfectionist judgments on what makes animals' lives go well. Well-being, you will recall, is a prudential value and so concerns how life goes for the individual whose life it is. So while some people might find it distasteful to keep animals in captivity and prefer to see them in their natural habitats, that does not mean that living in their natural habitats always improves the quality of life for those animals themselves. It is simply a mistake to believe that individuals' lives *necessarily* go better when they fulfill their biological ends in the wild. For example, an animal may be a better specimen of her kind if she engages in species traits like fighting with her rivals. However, if such fighting leads to painful injury, it is unclear how that fighting makes life better for the individual whose life it is. And we must remember that when determining interests, we should remain focused on how life goes for the individual whose life it is. So even when we conceive of freedom as the ability to pursue one's natural biological ends, animals still possess no intrinsic interest in freedom.

Essentially, the conclusion that most animals possess no intrinsic interest in freedom comes down to the fact that most animals are not persons: they are not creatures with the capacity for rational and moral agency, who can frame, revise, and pursue their own ends. Only autonomous persons of this sort have an interest in governing their own lives without interference from others. Only autonomous persons have an interest in freedom that is intrinsic.

At this stage of the argument, the assumption that sentient animals lack autonomy might be questioned. For example, Tom Regan has claimed that the sort of definition of autonomy that I give (the ability to frame, revise, and pursue a conception of the good) is not the only legitimate one. In fact he labels definitions like that given in this book as "Kantian" and contrasts it with what he calls "preference autonomy." Regan argues that this latter type of autonomy resides in all those creatures who have preferences and who are able to act in order to attempt to satisfy them.[36] It might then be possible to use this understanding of autonomy to make a case for an animal interest in liberty. For example, just as it is good for humans to be free so that they can realize their own autonomous lives in the form of pursuing their own conceptions of the good, perhaps it is good for animals to be free so that they can realize their autonomous lives in the form of satisfying their preferences.

However, there are two important problems with Regan's proposal. In the first place, the idea of "preference autonomy" is not a useful understanding of autonomy. Regan has stripped autonomy down to simple volition—removing key ideas central to the concept. After all, autonomy is usually considered to be a "second-order" capacity—referring to our ability not simply to have desires, but to reason about, reflect on, and willingly alter those desires.[37] Moreover, even if we accept Regan's alternative understanding of autonomy, it still does not justify recognizing that animals possess an intrinsic interest in freedom. After all, and unlike human persons, animals are perfectly able to exercise their particular autonomous capacities even when they are unfree.[38] Consider, for example, an animal in a well-run wildlife park, who has all of his desires met: he has no desire to leave the park and has his desires for food, company, stimulation, sex, and the like all satisfied.[39] Clearly this animal is unfree, and yet he is also able to exercise his preference autonomy. However, the case is quite different for human persons. A human slave may well be happy and have his desires met, but because he is a slave he cannot frame, revise, and pursue his own conception of the good. The capacity for autonomy has an intrinsic link to freedom in the case of persons, but when reconceived in terms of preferences, it has no such link to freedom in the case of animals.

It should be made explicit that none of these arguments implies that impinging on the freedom of nonhuman animals is always harmless. As pointed out above, activities that capture, interfere with, and utilize animals often cause great suffering and distress. And this is certainly true of the practices carried out currently in animal experimentation. But it is absolutely crucial to bear in mind that this harm is caused by the pain inflicted, not by the lack of freedom itself. Most animals are not autonomous beings with interests in leading freely chosen lives; they are creatures whose lives can better or worse based on their capacity for sentience. This means that we have a prima facie obligation not to kill or cause suffering to any animals that we keep or use. It does not mean that each and every animal kept or used by humans is harmed. Animals have no intrinsic interest in freedom. They thus have no interest that is sufficient, all things considered, to impose a duty on us never to use them in experimentation.

HUMAN NONPERSONS, FREEDOM, AND EXPERIMENTATION

If animals do not have an intrinsic interest in freedom because they are not autonomous entities, then the same must also be true of human beings who lack autonomy. In other words, young babies and individuals who are severely mentally disabled must have no intrinsic interest in liberty. So can we then conclude that human nonpersons have no right not to be used in forms of experimentation that are painless and do not result in death?

While such a conclusion might at first sight seem odd, I believe that it is valid. For remember that we are only talking about extremely limited forms of experimentation: if an experiment causes or threatens either immediate or long-term suffering, then it is impermissible, as of course is experimentation that results in death. We must also remember that these individuals have friends and family members who have important interests and rights over the fate of their loved ones. Obviously the wishes of these concerned parties must be taken into account before any such experimentation could be permissible. So really all we are talking about here is painless tests that will have no adverse harmful effect on the individual whatsoever, and that also have the approval of their guardians.

To those who remain unconvinced by this and still feel that nonautonomous humans have an intrinsic interest in freedom and so in not being used in such ways, I would point out that we do regularly impinge on the freedom of nonautonomous humans without controversy. For example, we make children go to school, provide medical care for those who are incapacitated, and deny individuals who are severely demented freedom of movement. Of course, it can be legitimately objected that all these examples are for the individuals' own good; experimenting on babies and those who are severely mentally disabled, on the other hand, will not necessarily benefit the individuals themselves.[40] However, not all our uncontroversial interferences in the lives of nonautonomous humans confer benefits on them. After all, most contemporary societies *already* perform harmless experiments on human nonpersons of the sort outlined above, with little controversy. Think, for example, of those experiments that are carried out in countless hospitals and universities to test babies' learning, cognitive, and language abilities.

Given that we already treat human nonpersons as if they have no intrinsic interest in freedom, and given that we already use them in experiments that cause them absolutely no harm, perhaps the proposals of this chapter are not quite so unappealing and counterintuitive.

In sum, this section has refuted the suggestion that simply by using animals in experimentation we harm them. While it is obviously true that using animals and keeping them in captivity can be wrong, this wrongdoing can be assessed solely on the basis of whether the animals are made to suffer or are killed. As nonautonomous creatures without the ability to reflect on, choose, and pursue their own ends, most animals have no fundamental interest in governing their own lives and in being free from interference. For this reason, from an interest-based approach, animals cannot be said to possess a general right never to be used in any form of experimentation.

This chapter has argued that on the basis of their interests, sentient animals have prima facie rights not to be made to suffer and not to be killed. Moreover, it has argued that all things considered, these rights can be established as concrete rights in the context of animal experimentation. Animals possess the moral right not to be subjected to experiments that cause them pain or that end in death. In other words, painful experiments on nonhuman animals and those that end in death are morally impermissible. Since the vast majority of animal experiments cause pain, end in death, or both, we must conclude that most animal experimentation that takes place is morally unacceptable. Animal experimentation as it currently stands is an affront to the clear moral obligations we have to sentient animals. However, this does not necessarily entail that political communities must take an absolutist stance in relation to animal experimentation. Because most sentient animals are not autonomous agents, they possess no intrinsic interest in liberty. As such, animals have no moral right not to be used for certain purposes if their well-being is respected, and that includes their use in experimentation. If scientists experiment on animals in ways that cause no pain and that do not end in death, then such experiments are permissible.

Having established that animals possess prima facie rights not to be made to suffer and not to be killed but possess no general right not to be used for certain purposes, we need to consider what implications this has for other contexts in which our actions affect animals. The next chapter considers these implications for the ways in which we use animals in agriculture.

Four

Animal Agriculture

Of all of our uses of animals in modern societies, experimentation generates the fiercest debate. However, it does not involve the greatest numbers. While 2.9 million animals were used in scientific experiments in the UK in 2005,[1] around 913.6 million farm animals were slaughtered there in the same year.[2] Moreover, on a global scale, the numbers of animals being slaughtered and consumed is rising at a remarkable rate. Between 1961 and 2007 the global per capita consumption of meat more than doubled, and it is expected to double again by 2050.[3] While the volume of farm animals slaughtered every year is staggering, it really should be of little surprise. After all, the most regular and direct contact many of us have with animals comes through eating their flesh, their milk, and their eggs. In fact, for most people in affluent societies nearly every meal involves the consumption of some kind of animal product. To meet this level of consumption, intensive farming techniques have been developed and promoted since the end of the Second World War to raise productivity; that is, to extract as much protein out of the animals at as little cost as possible. The lives of intensively farmed poultry illustrate this method extremely well. For example, in order to rear more birds per square meter, battery chickens are often held in cages so small that they cannot even stretch their wings. To get more meat from birds, broiler chickens are fed huge amounts to grow quickly and to unnaturally large sizes. Once again, to exploit the space, the birds are usually kept in darkened sheds together with hundreds if not thousands of other birds—both dead and alive. The lives of intensively farmed dairy cows tell a similar story. To get as much milk as possible from the cows, they are artificially inseminated, have their calves removed, and are milked several times a day. They are then inseminated again, milked until before they give birth, have their calves removed, and milked again. This cycle continues until the animals are spent and slaughtered.

While the development of such intensive farming practices has undoubtedly reduced farming costs and resulted in the cheap meat, milk, and eggs that so many of us now enjoy, it has undoubtedly come at the cost of animal welfare. For example, the cramped conditions to which poultry are subjected not only lead to the breaking of limbs, but also "necessitate" the painful process of debeaking. For if the beaks of confined poultry were not trimmed, the cramped conditions would lead them to peck each other to death. Additionally, not only does the dairy cow suffer from both her confinement (often she is kept indoors all her life) and the removal of her offspring, but she is also particularly vulnerable to mastitis, an infection of the udder.

For such reasons, many proponents of animal welfare have been campaigning for better conditions for farm animals and the abolition of so-called factory farming. They favor a return to more traditional farming techniques where animals are given the freedom to move and exercise their natural capacities. At the same time, however, more radical animal rights advocates see animal agriculture as not something that can be fixed by improved welfare legislation. Instead they see the practice of raising animals for food as in itself morally objectionable. Such groups claim that animal agriculture is necessarily exploitative and will always violate the rights of animals, whether free-range or not.

This chapter explores the permissibility of animal agriculture. In particular it asks whether animals have a right not to be raised for food. The first section returns to some of the claims made regarding animal rights that were outlined in the previous chapter and applies them to the case of animal agriculture. Chapter 3 argued that most animals have prima facie rights not to be killed and not to be made to suffer, but they have no such right to liberty. Can these prima facie rights be translated into concrete rights in the context of animal agriculture? This chapter argues that they can: animals have concrete rights not to be killed or made to suffer when being raised for food. This, of course, has radical implications for agricultural policy: it implies that raising animals for food can only ever be permissible when it does not cause animals suffering and does not result in killing them. In other words, political communities need to adopt radically restructured agricultural policies dominated by the cultivation of crops, and with some reduced free-range egg and dairy production. The subsequent sections examine and rebut three possible objections to such a claim. First, how can farm

animals have a right not to be made to suffer or be killed in agricultural practices when, had they not been raised for use in agriculture,
they would never have existed? Second, since nonhuman animals in
the wild kill and eat one another, why can we not do the same? And finally, given that we have to kill some animals in order to survive—even
cultivating crops kills field animals—is a rights-respecting agricultural
policy a utopian fantasy?

Animals in Agriculture and Interest-Based Rights

This book has claimed that for an individual to have a moral right, he
or she must have an interest that is sufficient to impose a duty on another. In the previous chapter it was claimed that the animal interests
in avoiding pain and in continued life were indeed sufficient to ground
prima facie animal rights not to be killed and made to suffer. At the
same time, however, it was argued that animals have no intrinsic interest in liberty and thus have no general right not to be used or interfered
with by humans. Now it is necessary to consider how this theory plays
out in the case of animal agriculture. Given the interests and other considerations at stake in the case of agriculture, do animals have concrete
rights not to be made to suffer and killed on the farm? If so, is it ever
permissible to use them on the farm? This section answers these questions by looking at three areas where the interests of animals in not
suffering, in not being killed, and in freedom are most clearly at stake:
in intensive farming, in the killing of animals for their flesh, and in the
raising of animals for their milk and eggs.

THE SUFFERING OF INTENSIVE FARMING

Chapter 3 claimed that sentient animals have a prima facie moral right
not to be made to suffer. Without doubt, much of what we do to animals
in intensive farming practices causes animals to suffer. The introduction to this chapter gave examples of the ways in which poultry and
dairy cows are intensively farmed. However, these are by no means
the only ways in which these animals suffer, nor indeed are they the
only types of animal that suffer. To illustrate the suffering caused by
intensive farming, we can also consider the life of an intensively reared
pig. Pigs are useful to consider not just because so many people enjoy

eating them in their sausages and bacon, but also because pigs are widely acknowledged to be highly intelligent and social animals. Indeed, in terms of their intelligence and sociability, pigs compare favorably with domestic dogs. Consider, then, the lives of sows, who produce the pigs that are fattened for slaughter. In most countries, upon successful artificial insemination, gestating sows are held in stalls for the whole of their sixteen-week gestation period.[4] These stalls are so narrow that the pig cannot turn around in them and finds it difficult to adopt a normal resting position. Sows in stalls regularly suffer from lameness due to weaker muscles and bones, as well as abrasions caused by the crate itself. It is difficult to measure the consequences of the lack of stimulation and exercise afforded to these sows. However, abnormal behaviors such as bar-biting surely indicate considerable levels of psychological distress. Once the sow gives birth, her plight is not over with. She is then moved to a farrowing crate, which is slightly bigger than the sow crate, to allow room for her piglets to feed. These farrowing crates also severely restrict the movement of the sows, and the lack of bedding prevents the pigs from nest building. Once the piglets are weaned after three to four weeks, the sow is inseminated again, with the process repeated until she is spent and sent for slaughter. As for the piglets, males are usually castrated, tails are docked, and needle teeth are clipped, all normally without analgesia or anesthetic. These pigs are then moved to the finishing or fattening sheds, where they will be held for twenty to twenty-six weeks before being ready for slaughter. These sheds are often crowded and barren, and the pigs have no access to the outdoors and no opportunity to root. As such, fighting and tail biting are common and are both an exhibition of and a further cause of the suffering of these animals.[5]

Now that we have a fuller—if incomplete—picture of the lives of animals that are intensively farmed to provide us with cheap food, what can we say of their rights? Can we say that the interest of these animals in not suffering is sufficient to impose a duty on us to stop treating them in this way? Do animals possess a concrete right not suffer from intensive farming, all things considered?

One relevant factor to consider is the costs that banning such practices would incur. For without doubt, banning the use of intensive methods would reduce the levels of profit available to farmers and businesses and of course would lead to more expensive meat, milk, and eggs. As anyone thoughtful enough to have sought out the free-range products from the supermarket or local shop will tell you, animal welfare comes at a price. Perhaps, then, this price outweighs animals' interest in not suffering and counts against establishing a concrete animal right not to suffer in intensive farming.

I find this argument unconvincing. To claim that an interest is insufficient to ground a duty on another simply because respecting that duty incurs costs is entirely unsatisfactory. All duties incur *some* costs. The relevant question is whether those costs are so burdensome, all things considered, that they count against the establishment of that particular duty. To answer that question, we need to balance the costs that will be incurred against the strength of the interest that the putative right is designed to protect. And when we do that balancing reasonably and fairly in the case of intensive farming, animals' interests in not suffering simply have to win out. After all, the animal interest in avoiding suffering is strong and compelling. Moreover, the levels of suffering inflicted on animals in intensive farming are incredibly severe. In fact many of the practices of factory farms—confinement in cramped spaces, breaking of limbs, debeaking, force-feeding, and so on—would be described as torture if they or their equivalent were done to human beings.

On the other side, the costs incurred by living up to the duty not to intensively farm animals, while real, cannot plausibly be considered to be more pressing than an animal's interest in avoiding suffering. This is because businesspeople, farmers, and consumers can all lead lives of extremely high quality without intensive farming. For instance, it is perfectly possible for farmers and businesspeople to achieve high levels of well-being through the production of fruit, vegetables, grain, and the like. And it is just as possible for consumers to achieve high levels of well-being through the consumption of fruit, vegetables, grain, and the like. The kinds of suffering that poultry, dairy cows, and pigs endure on the factory farm, however, are completely incompatible with a life of well-being. No quality of life is available to animals who suffer the horrors of intensive farming practices. As such, it can only be concluded that animals have an interest in not suffering that is sufficient to impose a duty on us not to intensively farm them.

KILLING ANIMALS FOR THEIR FLESH

Under the theory offered so far in the book, animals not only have the right not to be made to suffer, they also have the prima facie right to life. If this right to life is established in the context of agriculture, then it will have implications that are even more profound than the end of factory farming. For if animals possess a concrete right not to be killed in agriculture, then killing an animal in order to eat that individual's flesh is a rights violation and is thus ordinarily morally impermissible. In other words, if animals possess such a right, then raising animals to produce meat is necessarily impermissible—including when those animals lead good lives under free-range conditions. So do animals have an interest that is sufficient to establish an animal right not to be killed for their flesh, all things considered? Three arguments can be put forward to claim that they do not.

First, it might be argued that granting such a right would be a gross violation of our fundamental human freedoms. It is often claimed that while some people might want to be vegetarian for whatever reasons, that is up to them. However, to force it on people would be to impose a way of life that not everyone accepts. To stop people eating meat, it could be argued, is akin to making people follow the same religion: both are unwarranted infringements on our liberty. Put in the language employed in this book, it might be argued that the human interest in freedom trumps the animal interest in continued life. However, this argument grants too much weight to the human interest in freedom in this case. We must remember that the human interest in freedom is not absolute. Political communities legitimately encroach on human freedom for all sorts of justifiable reasons, whether it be forcing individuals to pay taxes for the maintenance and well-being of that community, or preventing humans from killing and eating their fellow citizens. The question at hand is whether political communities would be justified in preventing individuals from raising and killing animals for food. When the relevant interests are considered fairly and balanced reasonably, there are compelling reasons to believe that communities would be justified in so doing.

Crucially the human interest in being free to eat animals is only trivial. In contrast, the animal interest in continued life is fundamental. Human beings can ordinarily lead exceptionally good lives with high levels of well-being without eating meat. Contrary to some popular opinion, vegetarians can even enjoy immense pleasures of the palate! The welfare costs of following a diet without meat are thus extremely low for human beings. Animals, however, have a much more fundamental interest in staying alive. It is true that their interest in continued life is weaker than that of human persons—recall that the previous chapter argued that this is because animals cannot take immediate satisfaction from the thought of future goods, nor do they have future goals and projects to fulfill. Nevertheless, continued life is obviously the only means by which animals can actually lead good lives. The value of life to animals is thus high indeed. So while the flesh of animals might well taste nice, that does not justify our raising and killing of them for food.

However, there is a second objection to the establishment of a right to life for livestock animals. For it is sometimes claimed that if we cease killing animals for food, it will not just incur costs to farmers and business, but will entail thousands of people losing their livelihoods. Farm laborers, slaughterers, animal feed suppliers, animal transporters, butchers, restaurateurs, pet food suppliers, and the leather industry all face losing their means of making a living. For some the idea of a complete cessation to the killing of animals for their flesh comes at too great an economic price. In response to this, I think it is only reasonable to concede that there is a price to be paid for shutting down the meat industry. However, there is often an economic cost to be paid for respecting the core interests of individuals, but that cost is rarely decisive in deciding the moral issue. For example, there were economic costs in the abolition of slavery—particularly in the southern United States—but that did not render abolition the wrong course of action. In any case, as when any industry shuts down, care must be taken to ensure that the process is gradual and that adverse impact to communities and their families is kept to a minimum. Most crucially, sufficient resources must be provided for the retraining of individuals and the restructuring of local economies.

Finally, it might be objected that we simply must eat meat in order to survive. This objection seems somewhat old-fashioned these days, for as so many lifelong vegetarians have shown, a diet without animal flesh is perfectly healthy. It might be countered, however, that this does not answer every situation. For example, some ice-bound peoples and those living on the edge of starvation may be unable to live off a plant-based diet: to survive they need to kill and eat animals.[6] Here, then, is a case in which the animal interest in continued life clashes directly with the human interest in continued life. Since humans generally have a stronger interest in continued life than nonhuman animals have, in extreme cases of survival, the killing and eating of animals must be considered permissible. In other words, this is a situation where the interests of animals are insufficient to impose duties on us not to kill them, when all the relevant factors are taken into account. In this particular type of context, an animal right not to be killed to be eaten cannot be established. After all, it is completely unreasonable to expect people to sacrifice themselves in order to respect another's interests. That is why we allow people to harm others in cases of self-defense, for example. But none of this should hide the simple truth that the vast majority of us do not need to eat meat in order to survive. On this simple basis, in the overwhelming majority of situations in the overwhelming majority of political communities, animals possess a concrete right not to be killed for their flesh.

RAISING ANIMALS FOR THEIR MILK AND EGGS

As well as discussing their interests in not being made to suffer and in not being killed, this book has also addressed the question of animals' interest in liberty. So far it has claimed that because most animals are not autonomous persons, they have no intrinsic interest in liberty and have no prima facie right to freedom. In light of this, chapter 3 claimed that animals have no general right not to be used by human beings in experimentation. Can the same type of argument be made in respect of those animals used in agriculture? That is, do animals lack a right not to be used in agriculture—used, for example, so that we can enjoy their milk and eggs? I believe that animals do lack such a right and that raising animals for their milk and eggs can be permissible under certain conditions. However, it is necessary to be cautious here. The majority of milk and eggs consumed at present come from animals who suffer terribly. Indeed, the chapter has already outlined some of the pains that are inflicted on intensively raised chickens and dairy cows. So if we are to raise animals for their milk and eggs permissibly, it is necessary that we raise them in accordance with their well-being. This will require an end to intensive farming practices and will result in more expensive dairy products.

At this point, three possible objections can be made against raising animals for their milk and eggs under free-range conditions. First, farming animals for their milk and eggs, even under free-range conditions, still involves the killing of many animals. For example, male chicks and spent dairy cows are routinely slaughtered under present free-range techniques. If these animals have an interest in continued life that trumps our interest in enjoying eggs, milk, and other dairy products, then perhaps all such animal farming should cease. However, such a conclusion is too hasty. The harms of animal agriculture derive from the suffering and killing inflicted upon animals, rather than their use. Their use is not problematic in and of itself because, as non-persons, animals have no interest in framing and pursuing their own freely chosen ends. Given this, surely it is the suffering and killing of animals that should stop, rather than their use in farming per se. In other words, raising animals for their milk and eggs can be permissible when it avoids the routine infliction of suffering on and killing of animals. Clearly such a change to current practices would be burdensome to farmers and business and hence come at considerable expense to consumers. But once again, it should be noted that living up to our obligations always comes at some cost, and that there is neither an obligation nor a need for humans to eat eggs and dairy products.

The second objection to the permissibility of raising animals for their milk and eggs relates to its implications for eating meat. For if we can permissibly raise animals for their milk and eggs provided that we do not cause them to suffer or kill them, surely we can also permissibly raise them for their *corpses*, provided that we do not kill them or cause them to suffer. In other words, according to the theory presented so far in this chapter, it seems that we do no wrong in eating animals who die of natural causes. Some might argue that this implication is incompatible with other aspects of the theory presented in the chapter. Can animals coherently be said to have a right not to be killed to be eaten but have no right not to be raised to be eaten? I believe that this is perfectly coherent, and that there is nothing wrong in itself with eating animals who have died naturally. Our obligations to animals relate to the interests of animals, and interests concern how life goes for the individual whose life it is. If the animal has no life to go well or badly, then she has no interests. So while a living animal has a clear and discernible interest in not being killed, a dead animal has no interest in not being eaten (or in anything else). Our obligation is not to kill animals, rather than not to eat them once they are dead.[7]

But this type of reasoning might have an even more counterintuitive implication. For if it is permissible to eat animal corpses because they have no interests, do we do no wrong in eating human corpses since they have no interests? One answer to this question might be to claim that the interests of human beings can survive death. This is because most human beings are persons with plans, projects, aims, and ambitions in their lives, which do not immediately cease upon death.[8] If this is the case, then we might reasonably claim that dead persons have an interest in not being eaten. However, there remains a fundamental problem with this line of argument—and in attempting to ascribe post-humous interests generally. For in order for there to be interests, there obviously needs to be an interest-bearer, a subject of conscious experience, to have a stake in a particular good.[9] In the case of the dead—including dead persons—no such subject exists. As such, it is surely more plausible to see our aims and projects as ceasing upon our death than to regard them as floating free into eternity attached to no subject.

In any case, whatever our views about posthumous interests, it seems to me that the interests of the living are sufficient to explain why human cannibalism is wrong: I for one do not want to be eaten after my death, and I do not want my friends and relatives to be eaten. In other words, I am happier now for the knowledge that I live in a society in which I will not be eaten once dead, and neither will those close to me. In the case of most nonhuman animals, it is clear that they have no such interest in not being eaten once dead, given their reduced cognitive capacities. Furthermore, unlike human infants and those who are seriously mentally disabled, animals currently lack a significant set of individuals who are happier in the knowledge that animals will not be dined upon after their death from natural causes.

The third objection to raising animals for their milk and eggs is that by using them for our own ends in this way, we will necessarily come to view them as mere things, increasing the likelihood of further animal rights violations. For it is all very well to declare that animals have no interest in not being used for certain purposes, but this neglects the possibility that once these systems of use are institutionalized, humans will instrumentalize these animals, leading to the manifestation of other real and significant harms.

In order for slippery-slope objections like this to stand up, it is very important that evidence be provided to show that real and significant harms would necessarily be caused by the establishment or continuance of otherwise harmless acts. So what evidence is there that real and significant harms would be caused by the type of animal farming system being proposed? If there is any, I cannot think of it. For it has to be remembered that moving to the type of farming model proposed in this chapter would be a dramatic leap forward in terms of animal welfare, and it would have far-reaching consequences for society as a whole, affecting almost everybody. Moreover, the leap could be made only when human beings have a shift in attitude of such significant proportions that they come to recognize that animals are not mere things that we can treat however we please. Thus it is extremely unlikely that moving to an agricultural system of the type proposed here will instill in humans an instrumentalized attitude toward animals that will result in significant animal rights violations.

This section has applied the interest-based rights approach to the issue of animals in agriculture. It has argued that animals have the right not to be made to suffer on the farm and the right not be killed in order that we may eat their flesh. As such, the rights of animals demand that agriculture must change radically. While it is impossible to be absolutely certain how this new rights-respecting industry will look, a few things can be said. Obviously it will not be permissible to raise animals in ways that cause them to suffer, and it will not be permissible to raise animals in order to kill them for their meat. However, animals may permissibly be raised for their milk and eggs (and potentially for their corpses) provided that they have a good quality of life. What this essentially means is that in order to respect animal rights, agriculture will have to focus its attention on the cultivation of crops, with some limited free-range egg and dairy production. While some initial objections to these proposals have already been examined, three more substantial criticisms are explored in the following sections.

Raising Animals Who Would Not Have Existed

So far this chapter has argued that animals used in agriculture have certain rights: the right not to be made to suffer and the right not to be killed. Political communities thus have a duty to restructure their agricultural policies around the production of crops and the production of free-range milk and eggs. Farm animals should not be killed or made to suffer from their use in agriculture. However, there remains a problem with this overall line of argument that has not yet been addressed. How can farm animals have a right not to be made to suffer or be killed in farm practices when without such practices they would not have existed in the first place? Perhaps, when all relevant considerations are truly taken into account—including the fact that farm animals depend on certain agricultural practices for their very existence—animals' interests are not sufficient to establish rights not to be killed and made to suffer on the farm. This brief section outlines and refutes this puzzling argument.

The objection under consideration is that because farm animals owe their existence to farming, they cannot have rights not to suffer and not to be killed by farm practices. So while a farm animal may well have interests in not suffering and in not being killed, given that he owes his existence to farming, those interests are not sufficient to establish rights that he not be killed or made to suffer. Essentially the argument states that because we cause something that is good for an animal (existence), we can also cause something that is bad for him (suffering and death).

There are two significant problems with this line of argument. First, it is not clear that when we cause farm animals to exist we always create something that is good for them. It seems reasonable to suppose that many farm animals, particularly those that are raised intensively, suffer so terribly from agricultural practices that their lives are not worth living. These animals may well owe their existence to farming, but it is an existence that is no good for them. Of course, just as it is probable that some farm animals lead lives that are not worth living, it is also probable that many others lead lives that are of value to them. Animals kept in free-range conditions are one such obvious example. Clearly these animals have lives that are full of valuable experiences. It makes sense, then, to say that causing these animals to exist is good for them. Given this, is it permissible to kill these free-range animals? After all, farming has created something good for these animals, so maybe their interests are insufficient to impose duties on us not to kill them.

This leads us to the second problem with this line of argument. Just because we cause something that is good for an individual, that does not mean that we can permissibly cause something bad for them. This point is dramatically illustrated by recasting the example of free-range farm animals with human beings.[10] So imagine a program in which we produce groups of humans (to remove family ties, we might do this in vitro from anonymous volunteer donors), raising them and letting them lead independent lives of good quality. However, at some point throughout their lives we kill them—if you find the idea of slaughtering them for their meat too implausible, perhaps we might slaughter them for their organs, which will be used in transplants.[11] Should we claim that these individual humans have no right not to be killed? For had we not raised them for their organs, these individuals would never have existed and would never have led valuable lives.

Clearly these humans would still possess the right not to be killed. Just because we do something good for these humans, that does not mean that we can then go on and do something bad for them, such as killing them for their organs. As Jeff McMahan argues, "That justification would allow parents to kill their children."[12] Humans may well be created for some particular purpose, but once those people exist, they have interests that are worthy of ethical consideration in their own right. The reasons behind those humans being created are beside the point; those individuals have rights just like other humans. And just as this is true with humans, so it is true for animals. Yes, free-range animals may well have been created to be killed, and such creation may well be good for them. However, the interests in continued life of farm animals are—as this chapter has argued—of sufficient importance to impose duties on us not to kill them, all things considered.

The Predation Argument

At this point, it might be argued that there is a much more straight-forward objection to the idea that animals have a right not to be killed to be eaten by us. After all, some animals kill other animals in order to eat, so why shouldn't we do the same? Put in the language of the interest-based rights approach, it might be argued that if farm animals have an interest in continued life that is sufficient to establish a right not to be killed to be eaten, then so too must prey animals. If correct, however, this would lead to us having an absurd duty to prevent wild predation through policing nature. Perhaps, then, we should deny prey animals the right to life—and to be consistent, perhaps we should also deny it to farm animals. In other words, perhaps the predation argument informs us that we have no need to restructure our agricultural systems so that they do not raise and kill animals for their flesh.

    This section evaluates this predation argument by looking at three objections to it that can be found in the literature. First is the argument from moral agency. This argument claims that while we—as humans and moral agents—have an obligation not to kill other animals, we are under no duty to prevent animals—who are not moral agents—from so doing. Second is the utilitarian argument. This position claims that if we were to interfere with predator-prey relations we would actually end up causing more overall harm to sentient animals. And finally is the argument from survival. This claim points out that predator animals need to kill in order to survive while we do not, making their killings permissible and ours impermissible. While the first two of these replies fail, the final rebuttal effectively defeats the predation argument and explains why farm animals have a right not to be killed to be eaten, whereas prey animals in the wild do not.

ANIMALS ARE NOT MORAL AGENTS

It is sometimes claimed that there is an important difference between the killing of animals by humans and the killings perpetrated by predator animals. As moral agents, humans are able to reflect up and decide on the appropriate moral action. Animals, on the other hand, lack such capacities. Thus while most humans can be held morally accountable for the killing they inflict, animals cannot.[13] So the claim is that when we as humans kill animals for food, we are blameworthy and such killing should be prevented, but when animals kill other animals for food, they are not blameworthy and this should not be prevented.

However, this argument suffers from a significant problem. As several thinkers have pointed out, while it seems clear that moral agents cannot be held accountable for their actions, that does not mean to say that we should not prevent them from causing harm to others.[14] To illustrate this point, Peter Alward gives the following example: "Consider, by way of analogy, a child too young to know the difference between right and wrong, attempting to slit the throat of his sleeping father. If the child succeeded in his attempt, he would have performed a morally wrong act albeit one for which he ought not to be blamed. However, despite the lack of blameworthiness for his act, we would be morally required to prevent the child from slitting his father's throat if we could."[15]

The simple fact that children and animals are not moral agents does not mean that we should allow them to cause harm. And predator animals do cause harm when they kill their prey: prey animals have an interest that their lives continue. Moreover, if this interest is sufficient to ground a right to life for animals in agriculture and in experimentation, why should it not be sufficient to ground a right for prey animals in the wild? This putative right to life of prey animals would not be held against their predators: predators are not moral agents so cannot have moral duties. Rather it would be held against us: we are moral agents and can act to prevent their deaths.

All this seems to suggest that if it is true that we should not kill animals to eat their flesh, then maybe we should also act to prevent

predator animals from killing their prey. However, perhaps this conclusion can be resisted for another reason.

OVERALL HARM

Some philosophers have pointed out that to interfere with the predator-prey relationship would undoubtedly cause more overall harm in
the long-term than would noninterference. Consider that to avoid the
harms inflicted on prey animals, we would either have to segregate
the prey animals or segregate the predators. Both options seem impossible in practical terms. Nevertheless, even if we could do either, the
impact on the ecosystems in which they reside would be catastrophic.
For example, if we were to remove predator animals from their habitats to avoid the unnecessary harms they inflict, there would be many
so-called cascade effects. First, many scavenger animals who once fed
on the corpses of the prey would suffer and die. Second, the prey animals would become abundant and out-compete other species for the
best habitat, again leading to the suffering and death of animals from
rival species. Moreover, the prey animals might begin to decimate particular plant species. This might deny an important food source to other
animals, who again would suffer and die.

Such harms would also be inevitable if the prey species were seg-
regated: predator animals and scavengers would start to roam miles
in the vain search for food; rival species would grow in number and
decimate other populations; and the vegetation they once fed on might
become abundant, adversely altering the habitat of other species.

Given all this, there is very good reason to believe that in terms of
aggregate well-being, it would be better if we did not interfere with
predator-prey relations. This may well be the case. However, recall that
our obligations to sentient nonhuman animals are not driven solely by
concern for the net amount of well-being in the universe. Instead this
book has argued that individual well-being is what matters, and that
individual rights that protect well-being ought to limit the pursuit of
aggregate welfare. In this case, why should we allow these individual
prey animals to suffer simply for the sake of aggregate well-being? The
interest of prey animals in continued life is clear enough, so it is at least
plausible to suggest that these prey animals possess a concrete right
not to be killed *even if* respecting those rights would diminish aggregate
well-being.

KILLING FOR SURVIVAL

It is possible to deny prey animals a right not to be killed by preda-tors, when it is noted that predator animals need to kill for survival. This makes the situation of prey animals relevantly different from the interests of farm animals, whose deaths are not required for the sur-vival of others. In other words, when we are faced with a predator-prey situation, we are faced with a situation quite different from that in agriculture. For in predator-prey relations, we face a clash of basic sur-vival interests. In effect we have two choices in respect of predation: we can do nothing, meaning that the interests of the prey animals will be sacrificed, or we can protect the prey animal, sacrificing the interests of the predator animals. In both cases the very survival of an animal is at stake. Given that interfering in predator-prey relations is ordinarily far more burdensome on us than doing nothing, it makes sense to say that the right course of action is to adopt a general policy of noninterfer-ence. In other words, when all relevant factors are taken into account, the prey animals' interest in continued life is not sufficient to establish a right that they not be killed to be eaten. This conclusion does not un-dermine the claim that farm animals have a right not to be killed to be eaten because in that situation, the survival of others is not at stake.

However, there is a difficulty with this argument. Dale Jamieson has correctly observed that not all the kills and not all the pain enacted by predators on prey animals are strictly necessary for survival.[16] He points out that sometimes predators will kill more animals than they need to survive. Moreover, and as owners of pet cats will testify, in the process of killing, predatory animals will often inflict more pain on an animal than can be deemed necessary for survival.

But while correct, Jamieson's objection still does not defeat the over-all claim that prey animals have no right not to be killed by preda-tors. For given the struggle for survival of most animals, we have to recognize that the vast majority of kills are absolutely crucial to the well-being of predator animals. Yes, it is true that there will be kills that are beyond what is necessary to keep the predator animal and any dependents alive. And it is also undoubtedly true that sometimes more pain will be inflicted on the prey animal during the kill than is strictly necessary. However, these occasions will be extremely difficult, if not impossible, to determine, and the vast majority of them will also be extremely difficult, if not impossible, to do anything about. For imagine attempting to prevent these unnecessary kills. We would have to somehow locate all those predator animals in the world that are above the survival threshold; follow their movements in anticipation of any unnecessary kills; and then, if such an attempt at a kill were to take place, step in using some nonlethal means to prevent it. Clearly, taking these steps is beyond the realm of possibility—or at least they impose burdens on us that are far too onerous. As such, when absolutely all considerations are taken into account, it is still plausible to recognize that prey animals have no concrete right not to be killed by predator animals.

As a final point, however, I should stress that where it is clear that killings by predator animals are unnecessary for survival, and where it is straightforward for us to do something about them, we *do* have an obligation to interfere. One clear example of such a scenario involves pet cats. Because the survival interests of cats are not at stake when they kill mice, birds, and the like, and because we can take certain meaningful steps to prevent such kills, we ought to try to prevent our cats from killing and inflicting pain on other sentient animals.[17] Perhaps an even more obvious example of predatory hunting where survival is not at stake is that hunting conducted by human beings. Humans are obvious predators and regularly hunt wild prey animals in order to eat them. In the vast majority of cases, such kills are not necessary for survival—and this makes them relevantly different from the kills of other predator animals.

Animals Killed in the Field

Part of the claim of this chapter has been that animals have a right not to be killed in agriculture. However, there remains a final and extremely powerful objection to the establishment of such a right. After all, crop production also involves the killing of some animals. This is because many animals—particularly rabbits, birds, mice, and other small rodents—are killed through working the fields. Since these field animals also have an interest in not being killed, just like livestock animals, surely they must also have a concrete right not to be killed by agricultural practices. But if such a right is established for field animals as well as livestock, humans will be left with nothing to eat. In other words, establishing and upholding the rights of animals not to be killed by agricultural practices seems to entail that we have a duty to sacrifice ourselves. Since this duty is far too burdensome, perhaps the right to life cannot be established for *any* animals in the context of agriculture.

KILLING FIELD ANIMALS FOR SURVIVAL

Perhaps the most obvious way out of this conundrum is to employ an argument similar to that which has been outlined before. After all, it has been pointed out already in this chapter that animals have no right not to be killed when human survival is at stake. If, for example, individuals living in remote areas or in extreme survival situations need to kill animals for basic subsistence, then such killing is permissible. We are not required to sacrifice ourselves to protect the interests of animals. Using a similar line of argument, then, perhaps it can be claimed that since our very survival is at stake, we also have no duty not to kill field animals. After all, given the size of the human population, it is unrealistic to meet the survival needs of humans without using harmful mechanical techniques to cultivate crops.

While initially plausible, there is an important problem with this line of argument. For crucially, why should it be only field animals and not livestock who are sacrificed to meet our survival needs? By allowing all livestock the right to life while denying it to all field animals, we are also effectively privileging the former at the expense of the latter. If some animals will inevitably be killed when we farm, and if such killings are permissible in the name of our own survival, then there seems no good reason to kill only field animals. Given the enjoyment so many take from the flesh of pigs, cows, chickens, and the like, it might seem sensible to kill some of these animals too, in the name of human survival.

UNINTENTIONAL KILLINGS

At this point, some will argue that there is a morally relevant difference between the killing of livestock and the killing of field animals— and that difference is based on intentionality. Many thinkers, since at least the time of Thomas Aquinas, have invoked something called the "doctrine of double effect" to explain the moral difference between intentional and foreseen harms. This doctrine states that an act can be permissible even if it causes serious harm, if that harm is a side effect of promoting some good end.[18] Using such a principle, it could thus be argued that killing animals in the field is permissible because it is a mere side effect of our crop cultivation—cultivation which we need to do to survive. In effect, then, such an argument would claim that there is a relevant difference between the killing of livestock and the killing of field animals: the killing of livestock is *intentional,* while the killing of field animals is merely *foreseen.*[19] On this basis, perhaps we have grounds to argue that the killing of livestock is a rights violation, whereas the killing of field animals is not.

While this argument does have at least some initial intuitive plausibility, there is an important problem with it. After all, it is usually extremely difficult to be absolutely clear about what is and what is not intentional. For if we foresee that our action will have some harmful consequence and decide to go ahead with it anyway, in what sense can the consequence of our action really be described as "unintended"? If a consequence is inevitable and preventable, then it seems perfectly possible to redescribe that consequence as intended.[20] For example, when we cultivate crops, we *do* know that in so doing we will kill animals and cause them serious harm. So much is obvious by the body parts and corpses left behind in the fields and machinery. It is true that we do not cultivate crops *in order* to cause these deaths, but still, we certainly choose a course of action that will inevitably bring them about. As such, some might argue that a morally relevant distinction between the intentional killing of livestock and the foreseen killing of field animals is difficult to identify.

Furthermore, even if intentionality could be identified with clarity, it is unlikely to be decisive in determining the moral permissibility of acts. To explain, it is worth noting that proponents of the doctrine of double effect always include an assessment of proportionality in their analysis. This is simply because a proportionality test is necessary if the principle is to have any plausibility. After all, not just *any* intended good end can justify *any* foreseen side effect. If the analysis is to produce reasonable outcomes, then the intended good aim must outweigh the foreseen bad side effect. Hence, as Peter Singer has argued, proponents of the doctrine might argue that the doctrine can permit the termination of a pregnancy to save a woman's life, but they would not argue that it can permit one for the maintenance of a slim figure.[21] But given that proportionality is so crucial for the principle to have any plausibility, we are left wondering what work intentionality is doing in the analysis. When an action has two foreseen consequences, why not judge its permissibility simply by a judgment about the moral weight of those consequences? Returning to the question of killing animals in agriculture, then, we might more straightforwardly ask whether their deaths serve an end that is of *sufficient* moral importance to justify those deaths. Seeing as the killings serve the end of human survival, we can plausibly state that it is. But since killing field animals and killing livestock can both serve this end, we still have no good reason to view their deaths as morally different. It remains unclear why it would be permissible to kill field animals but not livestock animals in the name of human survival. As such, perhaps it is pointless to grant a right not be killed by our agricultural practices to *any* animal.

OVERALL HARM

In effect, then, we find ourselves in a situation where we need to eat in order to survive, and in order to eat, we need to engage in practices that kill animals. Furthermore, we have yet to find any morally relevant difference between killing a field animal and killing a livestock animal in order to meet our survival needs. Given all this, should we just accept that it is impossible to establish a right to life for animals on the farm? Should we just accept that our survival needs inevitably cause harm, shrug our shoulders, and stop fretting about the animals we kill in agriculture?

Just because we cannot avoid doing harm, that does not provide us with an excuse to do anything we like. After all, while we cannot prevent *any* harm to animals being caused by our agricultural practices, we do have the power to *reduce* the harm to animals caused by our agricultural practices. And since field and livestock animals have compelling interests in continued life, it is evident that we should do as much as is reasonable to respect those interests. What we need to determine, it thus seems, is the agricultural policy that will cause the least harm— the policy that will result in the fewest deaths of animals.

Now it might be thought that adopting agricultural policies that concentrate solely on crop cultivation would cause least overall harm to animals. After all, such policies—while resulting in the deaths of field animals—would cut out all the deaths of livestock.[22] However, Steven L. Davis has argued that it is not clear that a focus on crops would lead to the least overall harm. In fact, Davis argues that a system that involves the raising and slaughter of large herbivores as well as plants would lead to the fewest animal deaths.[23] To reach this conclusion, Davis compares two agricultural systems: one that involves only the cultivation of crops, and one that involves half crops and half ruminant pasture (e.g., grass-fed cows). Using statistics available on field animal deaths, Davis estimates the killing that would be caused by each system. He argues that when crops alone are cultivated, we can reasonably estimate that 15 animals are killed per hectare. However, given that in a system of ruminant pasture the land does not need to be cultivated by the harvester or tractor so much, Davis estimates a much lower rate of deaths of field animals: 7.5 deaths per hectare.[24] In effect, then, Davis claims that if we switched to an agricultural system whereby both large herbivores and crops were produced and consumed, fewer animals would die than if we switched to a system that produced and consumed plants only.

What can we make of Davis's argument? First, it should be pointed out that even fewer animals would die under Davis's proposal if we did not slaughter those ruminant cattle used for grazing but used them only, say, for their milk. This rather obvious point seems to lend further weight to the agricultural system proposed above that is dominated by crops but does allow for some scaled down free-range dairy farming.

However, other thinkers have made even more devastating objections to Davis's argument. Quite simply, Davis's calculations have been doubted. For example, Andy Lamey has questioned Davis's interpretation of the studies used to arrive at his figure of 15 animal deaths per hectare of land.[25] In fact, Lamey goes so far as to doubt whether the science of estimating field animal deaths is anywhere near sophisticated enough to produce a reliable average figure. However, even if we assume for the sake of argument that Davis's figures regarding animal deaths per hectare are correct, that still does not support the conclusion that a crop-only system results in more animal deaths. Gaverick Matheny argues that Davis's comparison of animal deaths rests on a mathematical error: "Davis mistakenly assumes the two systems—crops only and crops with ruminant-pasture—using the same total amount of land, would feed identical numbers of people. In fact, crop and ruminant systems produce different amounts of food per hectare—the two systems would feed different numbers of people."[26] Matheny's essential point is that the appropriate question to ask is not which system produces the fewest animal deaths in total, but which produces the fewest animal deaths *per consumer*. Given that Davis estimates that crop cultivation kills double the amount of animals as ruminant pasture, then so long as crop production uses less than half the amount of land to deliver the same amount of food, crop-only production will result in the fewest deaths. Matheny's concluding calculations are striking: "In fact, crop production uses less than half as many hectares as grass-fed dairy and one-tenth as many hectares as grass-fed beef to deliver the same amount of protein."[27] In sum, assuming that Davis's calculations of animal deaths are correct, an agricultural policy that focuses solely on crop production will result in the least harm being caused to animals, followed very closely by one that also allows for some grass-fed dairy. However, a system that also incorporates livestock—such as grass-fed beef cattle—causes the most harm by an overwhelming margin.

So where does this analysis leave us? It is true, as Lamey points out, that the science of calculating animals killed in the field is imprecise. The kind of calculations discussed above can of course only be estimates. Nevertheless, that imprecision does not mask the striking inefficiency of livestock production in comparison to systems dominated by crops. We would cause far fewer deaths to animals by shifting to policies based on crops only, or crops with some scaled sown free-range dairy farming. On the basis of the interests of animals in continued life, political communities ought to make such policy shifts.

But what does all this mean for the *rights* of field animals? With all this talk of overall harm and numbers of animal deaths, are the rights of field animals being neglected and sacrificed for the sake of aggregate utility? After all, the previous section argued that prey animals should not have to be sacrificed simply for the sake of overall utility. So why are field animals now being sacrificed in this way? The answer, of course, is that these field animals are being sacrificed primarily for the sake of our *survival*. Overall harm is invoked to explain why these animals—and not livestock—are the animals to be sacrificed for human survival needs. As a reminder, then, the question we have been asking throughout this section is whether the interest of field animals in continued life is sufficient to impose a duty on us, all things considered, not to kill them through our agricultural practices. It was initially argued that the interests of field animals cannot be sufficient, given that human survival is at stake. It was then asked why field animals and not livestock animals ought to be sacrificed for the sake of our survival.

Why is the interest of livestock animals sufficient to establish a right to life, but the interest of field animals insufficient? The idea that our killing of livestock is intentional while our killing of field animals is merely foreseen was proposed as a morally relevant difference. However, intentionality was dismissed for being difficult to determine and of dubious moral relevance. The final section thus introduced the idea of overall harm. The morally relevant difference between our killing of livestock and our killing of field animals comes down to the numbers of deaths our agricultural policies will cause. To answer the original question, then, we can justifiably say that the interest of field animals is not sufficient to establish a duty on our part not to kill them in agricultural practices because of two important considerations: first, we need to kill some animals simply in order to survive; and second, choosing policies that kill field animals results in the fewest animal deaths overall. On this basis, it is consistent to say that livestock animals have a right not to be killed by us in agriculture, but that field animals do not.

As a final note, however, this does not mean that we can do what we like to field animals. The harms we cause to field animals cannot simply be forgotten about. Field animals can legitimately be said to have an interest in continued life that is sufficient to impose a duty on us to try to reduce the levels of suffering and death they endure as we cultivate crops. As such, we need to develop much more sophisticated methods of measuring animal deaths in the field. This will allow us to continually reflect on the damage we cause by our practices, and to have a much better idea as to which agricultural policies actually cause the least overall harm. Political communities also have an obligation to take greater steps to reduce the numbers of animals killed in the field. While it would be unrealistic to expect farms to produce sufficient crops to feed current human populations without the employment of harmful machinery, greater efforts to reduce animal deaths can be made. More efficient land use, more efficient crop strains, more sophisticated fencing, more sophisticated scare tactics, and better management of overproduction would all serve to reduce the number of animal deaths caused by our agricultural practices. Finally, there is also the issue concerning the size of the human population. As the human population continues to grow, greater demands are made on agriculture to meet our survival needs. Greater demand means greater amounts of land given over to crop cultivation—which ultimately results in more animal deaths. As such, reflection over the best agricultural policy in terms of animal deaths cannot be detached from questions about the ever-expanding numbers of humans on the planet.

Given the numbers of farm animals that we raise and slaughter in modern societies, the issue of animals in agriculture is indeed pressing. This chapter has applied the interest-based rights approach to the question of farm animals. It has argued that animals have a right not to be killed and not to be made to suffer by agricultural practices, but have no right not to be used in farming at all. This has two radical implications: an end to intensive farming methods, and an end to raising animals for their meat. A number of objections to this proposal have been addressed. The objection that farm animals would not exist at all had they not been raised to be killed fails: being created may be good for farm animals, but that does not mean that we can do what want to them once they are created. The objection that animals kill one another so we should be able to do the same also fails: predator animals need to kill to survive, whereas we do not need to kill livestock animals to survive. It is true that not all predator kills are strictly necessary for survival, but we have to accept the simple facts that the vast majority are necessary, and filtering out those that are not is an unrealistic task. Finally, the objection that field animals are also killed in crop production, while true, fails to undermine the establishment of a right to life for livestock. For not only is killing field animals necessary to our survival, but a policy focused on the production of crops kills far fewer animals than one that includes the killing of livestock.

One increasingly common agricultural practice that has not been addressed in this chapter is that of genetic engineering. Because that topic raises its own difficult and complex ethical problems, chapter 5 is devoted to a full discussion of that issue.

Five

Animals and Genetic Engineering

Genetic engineering refers to the range of technologies in which living organisms are created via genetic manipulation. The process involves inserting foreign DNA molecules into an embryo in order to alter the genetic makeup of that embryo, and thus the resulting animal. Such genetic manipulation takes places so that engineers can create individuals with, or without, specific genetic traits. While human beings have been using selective breeding to produce animals with desirable traits ever since animals were first domesticated, recent scientific advances in genetic engineering have permitted much more rapid and radical results. For example, just some of the animals that have been produced through genetic engineering include goats that produce hormones in their milk to cure human disease; pigs that grow faster and leaner than any of their predecessors; turkeys that do not get broody and thus lay more; and even sheep that produce their own insecticide in their skin to prevent the need for dipping.[1]

From such examples, we can see that genetic engineering is a technique primarily employed in medical experimentation and in agriculture: to model particular genetic diseases, and to select certain traits that are desirable for farmers. Given that the previous two chapters were devoted to experimentation and agriculture, it might be asked why a whole new chapter is being devoted to this topic. For example, surely the routine killing of pregnant mice in order to harvest embryos and the routine killing of those "failure" engineered animals who test negative for the desired trait should be condemned on the same basis that the killing of animals in ordinary experimentation was condemned.[2] Indeed they should. As such, this book does call for the radical transformation of genetic engineering as currently undertaken in laboratories across the globe. But such routine killings are not inherent in the act of engineering itself: genetic engineering can take place without such deaths.

Moreover, and more importantly, the act of engineering itself raises quite specific and complex ethical issues that demand careful consideration in their own right.

For example, it might be thought useful to begin this chapter by asking whether animals possess a moral right not to be genetically engineered. But such a question makes little sense. For engineering is not something that we do to existing animals; rather it is something that we do to prenatal animal embryos. Moreover, by manipulating these embryos and selecting certain traits, we create quite specific individuals who would not have existed without our interference.

Perhaps, then, we should ask whether embryos have a moral right not to be engineered. This question certainly makes more sense. However, it does not get us very far in working out the permissibility of genetic engineering. After all, nonsentient beings have no interest in not being engineered, simply because they have no interests whatsoever. Lacking interests, nonsentient embryos cannot have a right not to be engineered, or indeed any rights whatsoever. Clearly animal embryos have the *potential* to become sentient beings with an interest in continued life. However, establishing rights on the basis of an individual's potential is notoriously problematic. For example, the six-year-old Barack Obama obviously had the potential to become the president of the United States. And yet such potentiality did not ground in that little boy the right to command the armed forces of the United States. Similarly, medical students clearly have the potential to become doctors. However, they do not have the right to practice medicine like doctors until they actually graduate from medical school.[3] Rights are properly established by an assessment of the current and existing interests of individuals—not on the basis of their potentiality. As such, we cannot say that embryos have a right not to be engineered. As nonsentient beings without interests, embryos have no rights whatsoever.

But if embryos have no interest in whether they are engineered or not, does this mean that we can do what we like to them, making all genetic engineering permissible? Not necessarily. For if these engineered embryos are brought to term, they will become sentient animals who can properly be said to possess interests and rights. And it is the interests and rights of these sentient engineered animals—rather than those of any nonsentient embryo—that need to be considered in order to assess the permissibility of genetically engineering animals. As such, the relevant question under consideration in this chapter is whether animals have a moral right not to *have been* engineered.[4]

To answer this question, the first section asks whether animals always have the right not to have been engineered, no matter the type of engineering under consideration. The chapter claims that animals have no such general right not to have been engineered. In particular, animals possess no right not to have been engineered when that engineering results in the animal possessing opportunities for well-being that are similar to or higher than ordinary members of the species. The section examines and refutes some objections to this proposal that claim it is too permissive. The second section considers whether animals *ever* possess the right not to have been engineered. It argues that animals possess such a right in two circumstances: first, when they are engineered with lives so full of suffering that their lives are not worth living; and second, when they are engineered with insufficient opportunities for well-being, where insufficient is defined as fewer than those possessed by ordinary members of their species. The section ends by considering and refuting two objections to this proposal.

Do Animals Always Have the Right Not to Have Been Engineered?

Some activists and philosophers are opposed to genetic engineering in all its forms. Some regard the practice to be simply monstrous; others, to be an affront to nature; and still others, as setting in motion all sorts of unforeseen and disastrous consequences. Perhaps, then, it is appropriate to assign to animals an absolute moral right not to have been engineered that applies in all circumstances. However, given the interest-based rights approach advocated in this book, this would be far too hasty. To consider whether animals always have a right not to have been engineered, we need to consider whether animals have any interest that is sufficient to impose a duty on us *never* to engineer them. This section claims that they do not. First, it argues that animals have no interest in not having been engineered with opportunities for well-being equivalent to or higher than ordinary members of their species. As such, engineering that affords engineered animals these types of opportunities is ordinarily permissible. The section examines and refutes four objections to this proposal, each of which claims that it is too permissive, and that the genetic engineering of animals should be restricted more tightly.

ANIMAL INTERESTS AND THE PERMISSIBILITY
OF GENETIC ENGINEERING

It must be noted at the outset that genetic engineering can have radically different results for the well-being of the created animals. With present technology, predicting just what those results will be is very difficult. The genetic modification of animals usually involves the technique of pronuclear microinjection. This is the injection of the prospective gene into the single-cell embryo of the relevant animal. The procedure breaks up the chromosomes in the cell, and in the process of self-repair the gene is incorporated. At present it is hard to tell exactly how these genes will be incorporated, and often the process is lethal, with those that do survive regularly suffering from serious but unintended pathologies.[5] As will be discussed later in this chapter, these types of consequences—whether intended or not—provide good reason to place tight restrictions on genetic engineering. However, we should of course be aware that these deaths and pathologies are not *inherent* in the process of engineering: sometimes engineered animals lead perfectly healthy lives, just like ordinary members of their species. Moreover, it is reasonable to assume that as the technology keeps improving, so will its ability to avoid such consequences.

Bearing this in mind, let us consider those animals who do not suffer from such pathologies. Without doubt some engineered animals possess opportunities for well-being that are extremely similar to those of animals of the same species created through ordinary sexual reproduction. For example, in the creation of sheep with insecticide in their skin, or goats with hormones in their milk, it appears that the animals have much the same opportunity for a good life as animals created through ordinary sexual reproduction. Furthermore, some engineered animals can actually be said to possess even greater opportunities for well-being compared to the species norm. For example, engineering animals who are resistant to diseases, like creating cows who are resistant to mastitis, surely improves the opportunities for well-being of those animals.

In these cases it would be bizarre to claim that these animals have either an interest or a right in not having been engineered. After all, the engineered animals possess a life with the same or greater opportunities for well-being than animals created through ordinary sexual reproduction. The well-being of these engineered animals is just like that of any other animal. It does not matter to them that they were engineered, for they have lives that can go well for themselves just like any other member of their species. Since we do not regard the creation of animals through ordinary sexual reproduction as a rights violation, I find it hard to see why we should view it as such in these forms of engineering. In sum, sentient animals cannot be said to have a general right not to have been engineered in all circumstances. If genetic engineering gives the animals lives with opportunities for well-being that are similar to or better than ordinary members of their species, then it is ordinarily permissible.

At this point it might be objected that this proposal is far too permissive and allows for too much engineering. The remainder of the section considers four such objections.

GENETIC ENGINEERING INSTRUMENTALIZES ANIMALS

First, it might be argued that animals do have an interest in not being engineered, even if they end up with opportunities for well-being comparable to ordinary members of their species. After all, in all the cases listed above—the sheep, the goat, and the cow—the animal is being engineered with particular traits for the benefit of others. As such, some might wish to claim that these animals are being treated as mere instruments, and that animals have an interest in not being treated in this way.

We encountered a slippery slope version of this argument in the previous chapter. There it was considered whether raising animals for their milk and eggs would lead society to regard them simply as things, which in turn might result in harm being done to animals. Chapter 4 argued that such a consequence is highly unlikely. After all, the kind of agricultural policy proposed in this book would be so different, and require such a transformation in the values and priorities of political communities, it is extremely doubtful that it would inevitably lead to those communities regarding animals as mere things that can be used in any way they please.

The crucial point of the argument made in chapter 4 was that using animals for a particular purpose does not necessarily collapse into regarding animals as objects that we can treat however we like. For example, we use animals for all sorts of purposes, not all of which result in serious animal rights violations: we use dogs to guide blind people and to fetch and carry for people who are disabled; we use horses as modes of transport and for recreation; we use birds to carry messages;

and so on. Obviously just because these animals are used in this way does not mean that they are thereby instrumentalized. It is possible to use animals for purposes without then going on to treat them merely as things without any interests of their own. And the same is true for engineered animals. It is quite possible to engineer them for some purpose without then going on to treat them as mere things with no interests or rights of their own.

However, perhaps the problem with using animals for certain purposes is not that it *leads to* instrumentalizing them, but that it *does* instrumentalize them. In other words, perhaps animals simply have an interest in not being used for our own purposes. Such an argument would presumably be based on the oft-cited Kantian injunction that individuals should always be treated as ends-in-themselves, and never solely as means. However, as was pointed out in chapter 1, it is crucial to bear in mind that the original formulation of this Kantian injunction relates to individuals who *are* ends-in-themselves. That is, the principle relates to *persons*: beings with the capacities for moral and autonomous agency. Given that most animals are not ends-in-themselves, as Kant defines the term, it is unclear why this Kantian principle has any applicability to animals.

Nevertheless, for the sake of argument, let us accept that the principle is valid and can meaningfully be applied to animals. Even if we do this, the principle still does not show that genetically engineering animals is impermissible. For, importantly, the principle does not forbid the use of individuals as means outright. After all, we clearly use individuals as means all the time quite permissibly and uncontroversially: I use the doctor as a means to getting better; I use the shopkeeper as a means of getting food; I use the plumber as a means to fix my leaking radiator; and so on. What the principle does forbid is using individuals *solely* as means to our ends. Thus I cannot keep the plumber locked up in my shed, ready to tend to every plumbing need I have as it occurs. Instead the principle mandates that I must respect that the plumber has his own ends and does not exist solely to benefit me.

Clearly the same argument applies mutatis mutandis to animals. Using animals for certain purposes would be fine under this principle, so long as we respect that animals have their own interests and do not exist solely for our benefit. Importantly, some types of genetic engineering seem perfectly able to live up to this. For example, engineering a goat to produce hormones in her milk would be permissible if the goat ends up with plenty of opportunities for well-being, and if we respect the interests deriving from her well-being. Certainly it would be wrong to keep the engineered goat shackled, barely able to move, and without sufficient food and water; nor could we simply kill the goat once she is spent. But none of these practices is intrinsic to the practice of genetic engineering. It is possible to use a goat—or any other engineered animal—as a means and also to respect her interests. Genetic engineering does not always instrumentalize animals in harmful ways.

GENETIC ENGINEERING IS REPUGNANT

For some philosophers, however, the permissibility of genetically engineering animals cannot be decided solely by an evaluation of their interests and rights. Engineering can be impermissible, they claim, even when no harm is done to the animal. For example, imagine an animal who is engineered with similar opportunities for well-being compared to other members of her species, but with some bizarre alteration in her appearance. Indeed, let us imagine that the rabbit Alba—who was engineered by the French artist Eduardo Kac to glow in the dark—had opportunities for well-being equivalent to other rabbits.[6] Some individuals have claimed that such engineering is wrong in spite of the fact that the well-being of the animal is perfectly normal. Some philosophers have claimed that we can tell that such engineering is wrong by the feeling of repugnance we get when we consider it.

One of the most famous uses of the repugnance argument comes from an article by Leon R. Kass, "The Wisdom of Repugnance." While the article's main focus is human cloning, it was prompted by the arrival of perhaps the most famous engineered animal, Dolly the cloned sheep, and can be applied to other forms of genetic engineering. Kass writes:

Revulsion is not an argument; and some of yesterday's repugnances are calmly accepted—though, one must add, not always for the better. In crucial cases, however, repugnance is the emotional expression of deep wisdom, beyond reason's power fully to articulate it. Can anyone really give an argument fully adequate to the horror which is father-daughter incest (even with consent), or having sex with animals, or mutilating a corpse, or eating human flesh, or even just (just!) raping or murdering another human being?[7]

Kass's point is clear enough. Some acts set back no interests and violate no rights, but our revulsion and horror in response to them indicate that they are morally wrong. Utilizing this argument, then, we might say that the revulsion some of us have toward the creation of animals that glow in the dark or have other unusual and bizarre traits illustrates their moral wrongness.

In response, it seems evident that the argument from repugnance suffers from at least two damning problems.[8] First, repugnance is an indeterminate method of ethical reasoning. For instance, how many people have to be appalled for a particular act to be morally wrong? Must there be a *consensus* on repugnance in order to determine an act wrong? Surely, given our different feelings and intuitions about so many things, requiring a consensus would be far too demanding. Perhaps, then, a majority would do. But would just any type of majority be decisive? What if the individuals making up that majority were completely ignorant about the details of what they were deciding on? It is hard to see why we should rely on the gut feelings of such an ill-informed group in order to make important ethical decisions.

Perhaps only the repugnance of an *informed* majority would count. But how are we to decide when the threshold for being sufficiently informed is passed? Moreover, if being informed and rational is what counts, we have to question just what work, if any, the feeling of repugnance is left doing in the argument.

As well as the problem of *who* is appalled, we also face the problem of deciding just *how* appalled the relevant set of people has to be. For instance, many are greatly appalled by the body odor of other individuals. Does that make being smelly morally wrong? It might be replied that the feelings of revulsion people have toward body odor are qualitatively less than those attached to other issues, such as cloning, genetic engineering, and the like. But even if we accept this dubious assertion, just how are we to measure when any such feeling of revulsion passes the threshold to become sufficient?

All these questions highlight the grave problem of indeterminacy in using repugnance as a means of locating moral wrongdoing. Some are greatly appalled by very insignificant things, while others are hardly moved in the face of utter tragedy. Repugnance is an emotional feeling that can never on its own form the basis of a good reason to say that something is morally wrong.

The second damning problem with the argument from repugnance is that it has a clear potential to be discriminatory. For example, many people have been and remain revolted by all sorts of harmless acts, particularly around the issues of sex and sexual reproduction. These include revulsion at same-sex couplings and mixed-race relationships. However, is it really plausible to consider such relationships morally wrong simply because some people feel disgusted by them? In the absence of any good reasons whatsoever to believe that such acts are harmful, condemning such relationships is clearly absurd.

What about Kass's examples concerning incest, bestiality, cannibalism, rape, murder, and the like? Does a focus on interests force us to accept such acts, even when so many of us feel horror and revulsion toward them? No, it does not. The proper moral assessment of all these acts can be done very well by focusing on the rights and interests of individuals. So much is obvious in cases like rape and murder. But it is also true for issues such as cannibalism and bestiality. Chapter 4 explained how the interests of those who are alive make dining on the dead ordinarily impermissible. Bestiality too is easily explained using a framework of rights and interests. For the moral wrongness of bestiality does not depend on the feelings of revulsion that many people have toward it. Nor, given their lack of personhood, does it depend on the lack of consent to sex granted by the animals themselves. Rather it depends on the suffering the animals will endure from the sexual acts: from being forced into various positions and penetrated.

It may be objected that in some small number of cases, bestiality will involve no animal suffering. Perhaps even in certain situations the animals can plausibly be said to enjoy the sexual acts.[9] However, how can one be sure of this, either before or during the act itself? Animals are not the types of being that one can simply ask. And while it is certainly possible to use behavioral evidence and the like to determine whether an animal is suffering, gathering such evidence while already performing a sexual act will often be rather difficult, and almost always too late! As such, there is good reason to prohibit bestiality on the basis of the probable suffering that will be caused to the animal.

However, that still leaves us with Kass's example of consensual father-daughter incest. Must an interest-based account permit such a repugnant relationship? Once again, I believe that interests and rights are a perfectly good guide to evaluating the permissibility of such relationships. For we have good reason to be extremely skeptical with respect to the consensual nature of any such relationship. It is highly unlikely, if not impossible, that any such relationship could have been embarked on without serious and harmful mental and physical coercion on the part of the father. As such, we have excellent reason to prohibit such relationships on the simple basis that the vast majority of them, and in the real world most likely *all* of them, violate the rights of the daughter.

It is true that relying on interests and rights to determine the permissibility of certain practices may prove counterintuitive to some in a very small number of extreme and bizarre cases. But that is still preferable to relying on an indeterminate and often discriminatory feeling of repugnance simply to confirm some people's hunches. As such, the permissibility of genetic engineering is best assessed primarily by an evaluation of the interests at stake. This section maintains that engineering animals that glow in the dark, or with other bizarre traits, is permissible so long as those animals have opportunities for well-being similar to other animals of their species.

GENETIC ENGINEERING IS VICIOUS

But perhaps engineering animals is not wrong because it instrumentalizes them or because it feels repugnant; perhaps engineering animals is wrong because it exhibits a flaw in our character. In other words, perhaps engineering animals is *vicious*. This type of reasoning has its basis in virtue ethics and is sometimes used to discuss the permissibility of genetic engineering. Indeed, we sometimes hear that genetic engineering is objectionable because it involves "playing God" or "offends nature"—not because it causes harm to individual animals. And yet many philosophers have argued that objections of these kinds—whether against genetic engineering or anything else—are deeply problematic. After all, playing God seems perfectly acceptable and morally praiseworthy in many situations: performing life-saving operations, administering disease-curing drugs, allowing infertile couples to procreate, and so on. Why other acts of playing God should be unacceptable thus remains something of a mystery.

And as for offending nature, just what is natural? Is it even logically possible for human beings to act against nature? If we decide that it is, surely acting against nature can often be positively good. For instance, preventing murderous acts, relieving pain, and overcoming drought and famine all seem like worthwhile endeavors, despite the fact that they could be claimed to offend nature.[10]

Because of these kinds of problems, contemporary philosophers who use virtue-based arguments to attack genetic engineering rarely fall back on claims of playing God or offending nature. Instead, they more commonly claim that genetic engineering lacks humility. Elaborating on this idea, David Cooper argues that humility is a virtue for human beings because it turns us away from mere selfish concerns. Furthermore, we abandon our "proper humility" when we "programme animals with ends to suit ourselves and otherwise bend them to our will."[11]

However, determining the rightness and wrongness of an action by the humility of the actor is far too prohibitive. For example, consider a brilliantly talented yet supremely arrogant surgeon who performs many life-saving operations over the course of any week. Let us assume that his success stems from the self-satisfaction he receives from honing his ability to conquer nature and cheat death, rather than from any concern for the well-being of his patients. It is probably safe to assume that this surgeon fails to show "proper humility." Despite this, it would be extremely odd to judge his actions as morally wrong or impermissible, given the lives he saves. This is simply because his actions result in great benefits at little or no cost.

At this stage it might be argued that I am misrepresenting proponents of this humility argument. For perhaps what is found objectionable is not the arrogance of the individual scientists undertaking the acts of genetic engineering, but the arrogance of humanity as a whole for relentlessly attempting to harness and alter nature for its own ends. Mary Midgley certainly writes in this spirit. When talking of the overconfidence that she feels is inherent in genetically engineering animals, she writes: "To feel this kind of confidence, we would need to stop thinking of the natural world as a colossally complex system with its own laws, a system that we, as a tiny part of it, must somehow try to fit into, and begin instead to see it simply as a consignment of inert raw material laid out for our use."[12] According to Midgley and others, the attitude of overconfidence leads to an attitude on the part of human beings that is not just bad for the environment and animals, but ultimately bad for humans themselves.

In response to this argument, two claims can be made. First, it is unclear from this reworked understanding of humility whether the problem with genetic engineering derives from the arrogance of humanity or the harms to humanity that are alleged to follow from this arrogance. Indeed, there is reason to think that these arguments concerning humility are, at bottom, arguments about the *harm* that can result from a lack of humility. In other words, it seems that we are back assessing the permissibility of genetic engineering in terms of its impact on the interests and rights of affected individuals.

Second, leaving that issue aside, we can question whether genetic engineering necessarily leads to an inappropriate attitude toward the natural world. Midgley is surely correct to point out that viewing the nonhuman world simply as a giant pool of resources that we can use however suits us best can lead to disastrous results. One need only refer to the environmental problems faced by the world today to understand this point. However, it is unclear why all instances of genetic engineering involving animals *necessarily* entail or encourage this general attitude. For example, I see no reason why an act of genetic modification that produces a cow that is resistant to mastitis needs to also involve a rapacious and arrogant attitude toward all nature. In fact, if political communities adopt systems of genetic engineering that are thoughtful, considered, and focused on the interests and rights of the animals involved, they could well foster a more appropriate attitude toward the natural world than we have at present.

In sum, the concept of viciousness should not be used to prohibit the genetic engineering of animals. Prohibiting acts that appear to play God, offend nature, or lack humility would rule out not only all acts of genetic engineering but many other practices that provide great benefits at little or no cost.

GENETIC ENGINEERING VIOLATES ANIMAL DIGNITY

There is another basis on which to judge the proposal of this chapter as too permissive. For if it is permissible to engineer animals with similar opportunities for well-being compared to other members of their species, then it must be permissible to remove and alter traits, capacities, and functions of animals if they do not affect the well-being of the animal. Let us imagine that it were possible to engineer a dog with no capacity (or desire) to wag his tail. For domestic pet dogs, the capacity to tail-wag does not ordinarily contribute to their well-being. While it is an *expression* of their happiness, it certainly does not contribute to it. Given this, the proposal defended in this chapter would regard such engineering as permissible. However, some philosophers might object to such engineering on the basis that it undermines the dog's dignity.

To assess this objection we need to establish a workable understanding of dignity. For animal dignity cannot be exactly the same as the Kantian dignity already referred to in this book. Recall that Kantian dignity is possessed solely by those entities with sufficient cognitive complexity to be described as moral and autonomous agents. Clearly most sentient animals do not have this type of dignity. Balzer, Rippe, and Schaber argue that animal dignity is rather different. For them, animal dignity relates to a being's ability to pursue those functions that a member of his or her species can normally perform.[13] Sara Elizabeth Gavrell Ortiz reaches a similar conclusion, arguing that "the goods necessary for the good life of an animal are those functions, whatever they may be, that a member of its species can normally perform; and respecting the uninhibited development of those functions is respecting the dignity of the animal."[14] Martha C. Nussbaum has also claimed that animals are entitled to a "dignified existence," which involves the ability of an animal to flourish as the kind of being that he or she is.[15] All these authors, then, see dignity as referring to an animal's ability to perform natural species functions.

The problem with this is that it is unclear why it is necessarily good that animals perform their natural functions or flourish as the kinds of beings that they are. From the Ortiz quotation above, the answer seems to be that being able to perform such functions is necessary "for the good life of an animal." In other words, the claim is that normal species functions necessarily make life go well for individual animals. But that is simply not the case: tail wagging does not contribute to the well-being of dogs. And as chapter 3 argued, it is simply a mistake to think that individuals' lives *necessarily* go better when individuals fulfill their natural biological functions: some natural biological functions can cause sentient animals considerable harm. It is certainly true that some of us prefer to see animals performing normal species behavior, such as dogs wagging their tails. Indeed we might say that dogs with wagging tails are better examples of their kind in a perfectionist sense. But these judgments should not be confused with an assessment of what contributes to the quality of life for the animals themselves. Since it contributes nothing to their well-being, dogs have no interest in having been created with a wagging tail.

Some readers might accept all this and still argue that engineering animals without certain of their natural species functions should be prohibited. They might accept that such engineering does not harm the animal but still maintain that it violates their dignity and is wrong and impermissible as such. But we are left wondering just *why* it is wrong. An explanation that appeals to "playing God," "unnaturalness," or "lack of humility" could of course be made. But as seen in the previous section, these types of argument have implications that are far too prohibitive.

Maybe, then, we ought to simply rule out such engineering on aesthetic and perfectionist grounds: such engineering should be prevented simply because we have an interest in living in a world where dogs look and behave like dogs. Perhaps. But even if this were true, we should be clear that such action would not be based on any obligation to the animals themselves—the primary focus of this book. Rather, it would be out of concern of *taste*. And it is hard to believe that such a prohibition could be justified on the basis of taste alone. For if people do have an interest in living among dogs who look and behave like "natural" dogs, it must be an immensely trivial interest. In fact such an interest would be so trivial that it is hard to see why we should go to the effort of introducing coercive legislation to protect it. After all, we could all lead lives of extremely high quality in a world where some dogs do not wag their tails. We would surely adjust to such a world with considerable ease. Communities have adjusted easily to the establishment of new dog pedigrees—with all the bizarre and outlandish traits that many of them possess—so it is likely that they could adjust successfully to the establishment of dogs who do not possess all the functions that we are used to them having.

This section has argued that animals do not always have a moral right not to have been engineered. When engineering results in animals with opportunities for well-being similar to other members of their species, such engineering is ordinarily permissible. Thus it is ordinarily permissible to engineer sheep with insecticides in their skin, goats with hormones in their milk, cows who are resistant to mastitis, rabbits who glow in the dark, and dogs who cannot wag their tails, so long as these engineered animals have opportunities for well-being comparable to other members of their species.

It is now necessary to ask whether animals *ever* have a right not to have been engineered.

Do Animals Ever Have a Right Not to Have Been Engineered?

So far this chapter has argued that it is ordinarily permissible to engineer animals when those animals have opportunities for well-being that are similar to other members of their species. But genetic engineering does not always have such effects. Very often animals are engineered in ways that cause them serious pain or reduce their capacity to perform tasks that make their lives go well. Is such engineering permissible? This section argues that it is not, on the basis that it violates two important animal rights. First, animals possess the right not to have been engineered with lives that are so full of suffering that their lives are not worth living. This right imposes strict limitations on engineering, particularly given the somewhat random nature of the technology as it currently stands. Second, animals possess the right to have been engineered with "sufficient" opportunities for well-being, where sufficient is defined as similar to those possessed by ordinary members of their species.

ENGINEERING ANIMALS WITH LIVES NOT WORTH LIVING

Just as some cases of genetic engineering can lead to unchanged or improved lives for the engineered animals, others can lead to them having lives of intolerable misery. In these latter cases, I want to claim that an animal right has indeed been violated. This section argues that animals have a right not to have been engineered with what philosophers have called a "wrongful life."[16] A wrongful life is one in which the individual suffers so much and so terribly that her life is not worth living. In other words, a wrongful life is one in which nonexistence would be preferable. The basis for recognizing the animal right not to have been created with a wrongful life comes down to their fundamental interest in avoiding suffering. Sometimes animals can suffer so much in their lives, with no prospect of it ever coming to an end, that it is reasonable to say that it would be better for them not to be alive. This kind of argument forms the basis of justifications for euthanasia, whether it be with respect to humans or animals. Given that it is meaningful to say that sometimes sentient individuals can have lives that are not worth living, it must be the case that sentient individuals have an *interest* in not having a life that is not worth living. Indeed, this must be one of the most basic and fundamental interests that sentient creatures possess. And given that sentient animals have a basic interest in not *having* a life not worth living, it must also be the case that they have an interest in not having been *engineered* with a life not worth living.

But is that interest sufficient, all things considered, to establish an animal *right* not to have been engineered with a life not worth living?

Quite simply, it must be. For one, the interest that sentient animals possess in not having a life full of absolute misery and pain is incredibly strong. As mentioned above, it must be one of the most fundamental interests of all sentient creatures. Second, while the creation of such lives might well serve human interests either in terms of agricultural productivity or in terms of medical progress, as we have already seen, these human interests are not all-conquering. In the previous chapters we saw that these human interests do not even trump the standard animal interest in avoiding pain in the contexts of experimentation and agriculture. They therefore cannot coherently be claimed to trump the animal interest in not leading a life of intolerable misery! Given this, it is only sensible and consistent to conclude that animals have a concrete right not to have been engineered with lives not worth living.

Unfortunately many animals that are currently genetically engineered do have such lives. The classic example is that of the Beltsville pigs, named after the U.S. Department of Agriculture research station where they were born. The embryonic pigs had a human growth hormone gene inserted into them so that they would grow faster and leaner than any of their predecessors. In some respects they were a success: the pigs' rate of gain increased by 15 percent, their feed efficiency increased by 18 percent, and their carcass fat was reduced by 80 percent.[17] However, these changes came at considerable costs to the pigs' own well-being. For one, the pigs suffered from liver and kidney problems that shortened their lives. Bernard Rollin goes on to describe the additional problems these pigs endured: "The animals also exhibited a wide variety of disease and symptoms, including lethargy, lameness, uncoordinated gait, bulging eyes, thickened skin, gastric ulcers, severe synovitis, degenerative joint disease, heart disease of various kinds, nephritis and pneumonia."[18]

We have an obligation not to produce animals who suffer so terribly in this way. And while it might be objected that side-effects such as those described above are unintended, that provides no excuse, given that those effects are foreseen and avoidable. Adopting a "precautionary principle" seems apt when we are embarking on such radical alterations of sentient beings. That is, when we have little idea concerning the effects of an alteration, we should refrain from making it. Given the somewhat random nature of the current practice of genetic engineering, as explained above, this precautionary principle would indeed be prohibitive. The onus must be on engineers to prove that their actions will not cause lives of intolerable suffering for the engineered animals.

ENGINEERING ANIMALS WITH DISEASES AND DISABILITIES

So far this chapter has argued that animals possess a right not to have been engineered with so-called wrongful lives but have no right not to have been engineered with opportunities for well-being comparable to those of ordinary members of their species. However, what about engineering that results in animals possessing opportunities for well-being somewhere in between absolute misery and normality? For example, do animals have a right not to have been engineered with disabilities or genetic diseases?

If animals are engineered with diseases but with lives that are minimally worth living, then it might be hard to see how any of their rights have been violated. This is because of what has been referred to as the "nonidentity problem."[19] Nonidentity problems arise when actions *seem* to harm future individuals but, because they lead to the *creation* of those individuals, actually harm no one. Consider once again animals who are engineered with worthwhile lives but debilitating conditions. If these animals had not been engineered in this way, they would never have existed at all. After all, genetic engineering leads to the creation of specific individuals: take away the genetic manipulation of the embryo and either no individual would have been created or a completely different individual would have been created. Given this, we cannot say that these engineered animals are worse off for having been engineered with diseases or disabilities. It thus also seems that we cannot say that these engineered animals have either an *interest* or a *right* in not having been engineered with diseases or disabilities. To reiterate, without such engineering these animals would not exist at all. If this is correct, then it would appear to be permissible to engineer, for example, laboratory rats with terminal cancers, poultry with no capacity to fly or nest, and dogs with no sense of smell.

While some might be happy to accept such an implication with respect to animals, they would be unhappy to accept it with respect to human beings. For if it is permissible to engineer animals with diseases or disabilities so long as they have a life that is minimally worth living, then the same must also be true for human beings. That is, it must also be permissible to engineer humans with cancers, reduced intelligence, blindness, deafness, and so on.

Some philosophers have claimed that this kind of human engineering is wrong despite the fact that it harms no one. They claim that engineering individuals with diseases or disabilities is wrong because it leads to a reduction in aggregate well-being. The general point of arguments of this type is that an impersonal (or non-person-affecting) wrong is done when the creation of one set of individuals results in a world with less well-being than would have resulted from the creation of a different set of individuals.[20] Jeff McMahan calls these types of argument "impersonal comparative principles": "If in either of two possible outcomes the same number of people would ever live, it would be worse if those who live are worse off, or have a lower quality of life, than those who would have lived."[21] While impersonal comparative principles have been invoked to explain the wrong done when engineering disabilities in human beings, similar principles have been invoked with respect to animals. For example, Robin Attfield calls his the "reduced capacity principle": "It is wrong to generate creatures which lead lives more truncated than ones which *could* have been brought into existence instead."[22]

Unfortunately there are two very important problems with these impersonal comparative principles. First, they are far too demanding. This is because they condemn the creation of normal individuals when an individual of superior capacities could have been created instead. Consider two examples. In the first, imagine a woman choosing whether to breed her dog. According to impersonal comparative principles, this woman should not breed her dog but should have a human baby instead. After all, because of the greater capacities of human beings, having a human baby is very likely to lead to there being more aggregate well-being in the world.

In the second scenario, imagine that the woman has heeded the advice of aggregate welfarists, has put her dreams of a puppy on hold, and is now considering whether to have a child with her husband. Her husband, let us say, has average genes, contributing to him being of average appearance, intelligence, athletic ability, emotional sensitivity, propensity to hard work, and so on. According to impersonal comparative principles, this woman should not have a child with her husband but should procreate with a man with greater genetic quality. After all, by breeding with a man with superior genes, she gives herself a greater chance of producing a child with greater capacities and thus a greater chance of contributing to more overall well-being in the world. Clearly these examples serve to show that if each of our procreative choices is to serve aggregate well-being, our options are impossibly restricted.

But there is a second problem with these impersonal comparative arguments: they work only in same-number situations—that is, when we compare the actual world with an alternative world in which there is the same number of individuals. For example, it demands that we compare a world in which we engineer an animal with a debilitating disease with a world in which we engineer an animal without a debilitating disease. The problem with this is that most instances where animals are engineered to have diseases and disabilities are not same-number situations. That is, in most such situations the relevant choice is not whether to engineer an animal with a debilitating disease or to engineer an animal without a debilitating disease, but whether to engineer one with a debilitating disease or *not create one at all*. For as we have seen, these animals are created for quite specific purposes: to model specific diseases, to produce hormones in their milk, and so on. Thus it is not the case that if individuals were prevented from engineering these animals, they would automatically go on to create animals with normal species functions. Instead, the likelihood is that they would not create any other animal at all. Furthermore, when the relevant choice is between engineering an animal or not engineering one, aggregate well-being will always support the former if it leads to the creation of a worthwhile life.

In many cases, then, arguments from aggregate well-being do not explain the wrong in creating animals with diseases and disabilities. Instead they sometimes actually support such creation. This is because of the simple fact that such engineering sometimes increases the amount of aggregate well-being in the world.

THE INTEREST IN HAVING BEEN ENGINEERED WITH
SUFFICIENT OPPORTUNITIES FOR WELL-BEING

So if impersonal comparative principles are flawed, should we simply accept that engineering individuals with diseases or disabilities is permissible? In short, the answer is "no." This section argues that animals (and humans) possess an interest in having been engineered with sufficient opportunities for well-being. Diseases and disabilities provide these engineered animals with fewer opportunities for well-being compared to ordinary members of their species, and this, I argue, sets back their interests.

Such an assertion has an important difficulty to overcome before it can be accepted: namely, the nonidentity problem. For how can animals have an interest in not having been engineered with diseases and disabilities when, had they not been created in that way, they would never have existed at all? These animals are no worse off for having been so engineered, so how can they plausibly be said to have been harmed?

Simply put, the answer comes down to the adoption of a more subtle understanding of harm: an understanding that recognizes that an individual can be harmed by an action, even if that action leaves him or her no worse off. To illustrate, consider an example put forward by James Woodward: "Suppose that Smith, who is black, attempts to buy a ticket on a certain airline flight and that the airline refuses to sell it to him because it discriminates racially. Shortly after, that very flight crashes killing all aboard."[23] Here is a clear case in which an individual is left no worse off by an action. In fact, in overall terms, Smith benefits from suffering from racial discrimination, for he avoids being killed! Nevertheless it would be odd to think that Smith is not harmed by the racial discrimination of the airline. After all, Smith has a clear interest in not suffering from such discrimination, and that interest is explicitly set back. This example illustrates that it is possible for an action to harm someone even if that action benefits the individual overall. This more subtle understanding of harm is the appropriate one to help us evaluate the permissibility of engineering individuals with diseases or disabilities.

Although animals are not made worse off for having been engineered with diseases or disabilities, they have nevertheless been harmed. This is because sentient animals have an interest in having been engineered with *sufficient opportunities* for well-being. Recall that this does not mean that individuals actually have to be *interested in* having been created with such opportunities. Rather it simply means that having such opportunities makes their life go well for them. So in effect I am arguing that it is good for sentient animals to have been created with a sufficient range of opportunities to allow them to achieve a life that goes well for themselves.

But what counts as sufficient? The claim of this chapter is that sufficiency equates to the normal range of opportunities for well-being for that species. Consider a mouse who is engineered with terminal cancer, but with a life worth living. The mouse cannot be said to be worse off overall for having been so engineered. Still, the mouse has been harmed. He has been harmed not because he has *reduced* well-being, but because he has fewer opportunities for well-being compared to what is the norm for mice.

But why is species norm the relevant threshold criterion? The species norm is the appropriate comparative standard because it plays an important role in our ordinary determinations of harm done to individuals. For instance, when an individual loses a normal species capacity that provides an opportunity for well-being, this is commonly and uncontroversially considered to be harmful. Moreover, such a loss is usually considered to be harmful irrespective of its effect on the individual's *overall* well-being.

For example, imagine an individual who is blinded by an industrial accident that is the fault of a negligent employer. Suppose that as a result of this accident that individual leaves his factory job where the accident took place and sets up a campaign group to improve health and safety legislation. Suppose further that the individual proves a great success in his new career, takes huge satisfaction from it, and ends up with higher levels of well-being overall when compared to his previous life. Even though the accident ends up increasing this individual's well-being, it still makes sense to consider that accident harmful. We consider it harmful precisely because the man has lost one of the normal and significant opportunities for well-being that human beings ordinarily possess.

Furthermore, it is not just the *loss* of an opportunity for well-being that is considered harmful for individuals, but also the *absence* of such opportunities. For example, some individuals who were born with malformations due to their mothers taking thalidomide clearly lack certain opportunities for well-being that are available to most ordinary humans. Moreover, they have *always* lacked such opportunities. Nevertheless it still makes sense to say that such individuals have been harmed. And it makes sense precisely because their range of opportunities for well-being falls below the species norm. For human beings it is simply better to have been created with the normal range of opportunities for well-being. Indeed, all sentient animals have an interest in possessing a range of opportunities for well-being that is consistent with their species norm. If correct, this means that engineered animals also possess an interest in having been created with a range of opportunities for well-being similar to ordinary members of their species.

PERFECTIONISM

At this stage it might well be objected that this whole argument is sliding into perfectionism. After all, throughout the book so far it has been claimed that well-being is a prudential value and concerns how life goes for the individual whose life it is. Hence previous chapters have been critical of theorists who argue that it is necessarily good for sentient animals to pursue their biological ends, or to exercise their natural functions. Such arguments, it has been pointed out, mistakenly conflate what makes an animal a good example of its kind with what makes an animal's life go well. However, by claiming that sentient animals have an interest in possessing a similar range of opportunities for well-being compared to their species norm, is the same error not being made?

I do not believe that it is. The argument here is not that engineered animals possess an interest in having the same *capacities* as other members of their species; rather it is that they possess an interest in having a similar range of *opportunities for well-being* compared to other members of their species. As such, the argument is still very much focused on how life goes for the animals themselves, rather than on how they rate as an example of their kind. Moreover, the theory permits quite radical alterations in animals' capacities. If a species capacity or trait does not provide an opportunity for well-being—as was the case with dogs and tail wagging—then it is not ordinarily harmful to engineer an animal without that capacity or trait. Also the removal of a capacity that does provide an opportunity for well-being can be compensated by the addition of another. The proposal here, then, is difficult to see as perfectionist: it does allow for quite radical alterations in the capacities and functions of engineered animals. What matters is not that engineered animals conform to the normal appearance or functions of ordinary members of their species; what matters is that they are provided with a similar level of opportunities for well-being.

NONCONSCIOUS CHICKENS

Before finishing this section, it is necessary to consider a final objection to the claims made so far about engineering animals with reduced opportunities for well-being.[24] Suppose we were to engineer a nonconscious chicken—a nonsentient "lump of flesh."[25] Perhaps we might do this in order to crowd such chickens into tiny spaces to maximize protein production without having to worry about any suffering caused. Would the theory here see anything objectionable about such forms of engineering? Do chickens have a right not to have been engineered as nonsentient lumps of flesh? Given what was said in the previous section, it might seem that they do. After all, these chickens clearly have far fewer opportunities for well-being compared to ordinary members of their species. In fact these chickens do not just have fewer opportunities for well-being, they have none!

However, and as proponents of this objection point out, this response is not available to the theory outlined in this chapter. These chickens do not have a right not to have been engineered in this way for they can have no rights at all. Remember that since these chickens lack consciousness, they cannot possess any interests. As such, and perhaps counterintuitively, the proposal of this chapter would see no harm in engineering nonconscious chickens and no harm in engineering any other nonconscious entities, including human beings.

I accept this implication of the argument presented here: ordinarily there is nothing harmful or wrong with engineering nonconscious entities. The reason this implication can be accepted comes down to a more rational analysis of what this type of engineering actually involves. For the objection seems to trade on ideas that are pretty implausible in terms of the science of genetic engineering. When we picture engineered nonconscious chickens, we imagine otherwise normal, fully grown chickens crammed into tiny cages, able to breathe, move, eat, and lay eggs. In our imaginations the only difference between these and normal chickens is that the former can feel nothing. Similarly, in the case of engineered nonconscious humans, the first things that come to mind are zombielike creatures: humans with consciousness switched off. But the idea that a genetic engineer could simply switch off a capacity as complex and little understood as consciousness, while permitting that individual's growth to maturity and the retention of its other normal functions, is fantastical. For given the complexity of consciousness and brain function more generally, it would surely be the case that switching off consciousness in an engineered animal would involve switching off many important neural functions. As such, any nonconscious engineered individuals that could be created would be very unlike zombies and more like embryonic vegetables.

But all this might be accepted. Is there anything wrong with engineering such vegetable-like entities? It is hard to see what. After all, the creation of such vegetative individuals would be just like the creation of plants themselves. It would be the creation of entities without the capacity to experience the world, without the capacity to have a life that can go well or badly for themselves, without interests, and without the ability to be benefited or harmed. Unlike plants, such entities might look like entities who ordinarily possess sentience. Some people would no doubt find this repugnant, lacking in humility, or a violation of dignity. However, we have already seen in this chapter that these reasons are not persuasive bases on which to enact prohibitions. Well-being provides a more determinate basis with which to make such decisions. And while it can lead to results that some people find counterintuitive—like the permissibility of engineering nonconscious chickens—that conclusion is preferable to invoking mysterious and indeterminate concepts simply to confirm some people's hunches.

THE ANIMAL RIGHT TO HAVE BEEN ENGINEERED WITH
SUFFICIENT OPPORTUNITIES FOR WELL-BEING

So far this section has argued that sentient animals have an interest in having been engineered with sufficient opportunities for well-being. What needs to be considered finally is whether that interest can be translated into a right. Is the interest of sentient animals in having been engineered with sufficient opportunities for well-being sufficient to ground in us a duty not to engineer them with opportunities below the species norm?

To establish this, let us consider the competing interests at stake. Why would anyone want to engineer an animal with reduced opportunities for well-being? The two most likely reasons are for agricultural purposes and to undertake medical experiments. With respect to the first, individuals might want to make animals more amenable to conditions on the farm: for example, they might want to create poultry without the desire to nest, spread their wings, scratch, and so on. However, the previous chapter argued that the human interest in eating the flesh of dead animals and in eating the cheapest possible animal by-products is only very weak. Plenty of healthy alternatives to meat and cheap animal by-products are available, and humans are able to lead lives of extremely high quality without cheap meat, eggs, and dairy in their diet. Given that these competing interest are so weak, there is a very good case for establishing the animal right in this context. In other words, in agriculture, animal interests are sufficient to establish a concrete animal right to have been engineered with sufficient opportunities for well-being.

The second likely reason for engineering such animals is to model particular diseases in order to develop drugs and therapies for human disease and disability. Here the case is more difficult than that of agriculture because it is clear that human beings have a very strong interest in being free from disease and disability. However, as we saw in chapter 3, while this interest is strong, it is not all-conquering. There are limits to what can permissibly be done in the name of medical research. For instance, engineering *human beings* with severe disabilities and crippling diseases could well make a substantial contribution to medical progress. However, the interest of human beings in not having been engineered with such diseases or disabilities is surely strong enough to impose a duty on us not to conduct such engineering. And it is still strong enough in spite of the fact that those individuals would be no worse off for having been so engineered, no matter what benefits that engineering might confer. If this is the case for human beings, then to be consistent it must also be the case for animals, who share that same interest. In sum, engineered animals possess a concrete right to have been engineered with sufficient opportunities for well-being, even in the context of medical experimentation.

This chapter has claimed that animals do not always have a right not to have been engineered. Animals have no right not to have been engineered when they are afforded opportunities for well-being similar to other members of their species. This makes such engineering, all else being equal, ordinarily permissible. However, some philosophers have objected to all engineering of animals on the basis that it instrumentalizes them, is repugnant, is vicious, or undermines their dignity. Upon scrutiny, however, all such objections have been found to be implausible. But this is not to say that animals never have a right not to have been engineered. Animals have a right not to have been engineered when they end up with lives that are so full of pain and suffering that they are not worth living. Given the rather random nature of the technology as it currently stands, acknowledgment of this right and our corresponding duty is indeed prohibitive in practical terms. Furthermore, the chapter has also argued that animals have the right to have been engineered with sufficient opportunities for well-being. This means that engineering animals with fewer opportunities for well-being than other members of their species is ordinarily impermissible, even when those animals are able to lead worthwhile lives.

Interestingly, this right to have been created with sufficient opportunities for well-being has important implications for the breeding pedigree animals. This issue is considered fully in the next chapter, which examines our use of animals in entertainment.

Six

Animal Entertainment

The previous three chapters claimed that sentient animals possess prima facie moral rights not to be killed and not to be subjected to pain. Given that the infliction of pain and death are routine elements of animal experimentation, modern industrial farming techniques, and much genetic engineering, the implications of the theory for these practices were reasonably clear. This chapter, however, examines a more complex use of animals: their use in our entertainment. This use includes such practices as pet keeping, displaying animals in zoos, keeping them in safari parks, making them perform in circuses, and using animals in sport. I say that this use is more complex than that of experimentation, farming, and engineering because these entertainment activities affect animal well-being in such different ways. For example, the well-being of a dancing bear who is chained and beaten every day is markedly different from that of a cosseted pedigree cat. However, the bear and the cat are alike in that they are both being kept and used for the entertainment of human beings. This chapter examines whether such uses of animals are permissible by asking whether animals have a right not to be used for the entertainment of human beings.

The first section outlines the rights theory that has been developed so far in the book and applies it to three contexts in which animals are used for our entertainment: pet keeping, circuses and zoos, and sport. Throughout it is argued that animals have no right not to be used for our entertainment but do have the rights not to be killed or made to suffer when being so used. As such, this section argues that political communities are under no obligation to abolish all the ways in which they use animals for entertainment but do have to radically overhaul those practices in order to make them permissible. The second section addresses three possible objections to this proposal, all of which claim that it is too permissive. The first claims that it is wrong to use animals to entertain us because it undermines their dignity. The second claims that it is wrong to use them for our entertainment on the basis that it involves showing them disrespect. The final objection claims that we have an obligation not to use animals in entertainment on the grounds that such use necessitates owning animals as property, and that animal ownership is necessarily morally wrong. The chapter claims that all these potential objections fail—and that the proposal of reforming animal entertainment rather than abolishing it remains valid.

Animals in Entertainment and Interest-Based Rights

The book has claimed that animals have prima facie moral rights not to be made to suffer and not to be killed. However, it has also argued that because animals have no fundamental interest in liberty, ordinarily they have no right not to be used by human beings. Perhaps the most obvious implication of this is that the use of animals for entertainment should not be ruled out per se. Such a claim stands in opposition to many other proponents of animal rights. For although only some of these proponents condemn the practice of pet keeping,[1] the vast majority of philosophical and political advocates of animal rights regard keeping animals in zoos and making them perform in circuses as necessarily harmful and thus morally illegitimate.[2] This book does not share this view, and it claims that none of these practices is intrinsically harmful to animals. This does not mean that using animals in entertainment is *never* harmful. Often these practices result in the infliction of suffering and the loss of life; and in these cases, political communities have a moral obligation to change their ways. Indeed, the remainder of the section—by looking at the rights of animals in the contexts of pet keeping, circuses and zoos, and sport—examines in more detail the precise nature of those required changes.

PET KEEPING

A basic application of the interest-based rights theory set out in this book suggests that keeping pets is permissible so long as it does not lead to the infliction of suffering and the loss of life. While this does not sound very demanding to most of us, given the love and affection so many of us heap on our nonhuman family members, it is evident that the practice of pet keeping involves a significant amount of animal pain and death. Starting with pain, it is evident that some people abuse their pet animals. Worryingly, in the UK reported cases of cruelty to pet animals are actually going up. The Royal Society for the Prevention of Cruelty to Animals (RSPCA) reported a 77 percent rise in the number of animals it dealt with in 2005. Of the 94,130 abused animals that the RSPCA saw in 2005, 24,000 were dogs and 11,400 were smaller domestic animals.[3]

However, pet animals do not suffer just from such obviously cruel actions, they also suffer in more indirect ways. Sentient animals obviously need sufficient room to move around, sufficient stimuli to prevent them becoming frustrated, and sufficient company to prevent them being bored. They also need the right type and amount of food and the opportunity to exercise. The amount of bored, frustrated, or morbidly obese pet animals is not a statistic that the RSPCA produces. However, the number of animals suffering in this way is surely vast. For example, it has been estimated that one-third of Britain's pet dogs are obese, even though obesity is causally linked to health problems such as diabetes and heart, kidney, and liver damage.[4] In terms of boredom, some argue that confining birds such as parrots in cages for all their lives frustrates them as they are unable to carry out significant aspects of their behavior, such as flocking, social interaction, and foraging for food.[5] Others have pointed out that domestic dogs who are maltreated or who are bored suffer from similar behavioral disturbances to humans: compulsive eating, sympathy lameness, sibling rivalry, extreme jealousy, aggression, depression, and refusal to eat.[6]

Our pet animals have an interest in not suffering in such ways. Clearly it takes time and resources to provide our pets with the appropriate conditions and care. But these costs are minimal. More important, none of us is under any obligation to keep an animal as a pet, so these costs can easily be avoided. As such, it is perfectly reasonable to conclude that pet animals' interests in not suffering are sufficient, all things considered, to impose on us a duty not to cause them to suffer. Our pet animals have a concrete right not to be made to suffer by us. Importantly, this requires more on our part than simply housing, feeding, and refraining from beating them.

The practice of pet keeping also results in huge numbers of animals being killed. Ignorance about what keeping a pet involves often means that humans take on pet animals with little thought. However, once the costs of owning a pet are realized, or a family is started, or a move of house is undertaken, many pets are abandoned. This abandonment might take the extreme form of dumping them with the rubbish or in the canal, but more often it involves leaving them in the street to become strays, or handing them to a rescue home. Many strays, including those in rescue homes, are killed. For example, according to a report by the Dogs Trust, 100,000 stray dogs were found in the UK in 2005, and 7,800 were killed.[7] Once again, when the relevant interests are weighed, it is straightforward to establish that animals have a moral right not to be killed simply because we have gone off them or are moving home. While it is true that humans have an interest in keeping pets, it is not true that that interest must be satisfied at any cost. Pet animals have an interest in continued life that is real and important and must not be sacrificed simply to make life more convenient for humans. It is worth reiterating that none of us has any obligation to keep a pet animal, and we can lead lives of high quality without so doing.

If it is correct that animals have a concrete moral right not to be killed or made to suffer through their use as pets, then pet keeping must be regulated much more rigorously than it is in contemporary political communities. One obvious way to do this would be to make all potential keepers of pets have to apply for a license. The granting of that license would depend on the keeper registering the animal and proving that she will uphold the animal's well-being.[8] That does not just mean that the owners must commit to refraining from beating their animal or to taking the steps to prevent him from starving. Instead potential pet owners should be made to prove that they have the appropriate accommodation, time, and knowledge to care for the particular animal in question. For if animals have a right not to be made to suffer or to be killed from their use as pets, then it is only proper that we—and they—have some assurance that those rights be respected. After all, when we entrust human children to foster guardians or adoptive parents, great care is taken to ensure that those individuals will act in the best interests of the child. It is appropriate that equivalent steps should be taken for those wishing to keep pet animals.

The practice of pet keeping raises three further and more complex issues that have rarely been discussed in the literature: euthanasia, neutering, and breeding. These are common practices among pet owners, and it is necessary to assess them in the context of the interest-based rights approach. The issue of euthanasia can be handled quite straightforwardly by the theory defended in the book. Animal nonpersons have an interest in continued life on the sole basis that they may have future valuable experiences. If an animal is so sick that she has no opportunity for future valuable experiences and instead will suffer for the remainder of her life, then her interest in continued life fades, her right to life is not grounded, and killing that animal, other things being equal, is permissible.[9] However, huge numbers of sick animals are killed every single day even though they still have the opportunity for future valuable experiences. Presumably this is because the owners cannot or do not wish to pay for the necessary operation or care of the animal. This is wrong. If an animal has the opportunity for valuable experiences, then she has an interest in staying alive that cannot simply be ignored on the grounds of cost alone. As mentioned above, no one is under any obligation to keep a pet, and as such, these costs can easily be avoided by those who do not want to bear them. Returning to the practical proposal of licenses, then, it seems feasible that states could make the taking out of insurance a necessary condition for the award of a pet license.

The issue of neutering is much more difficult and needs to be considered carefully. First, we need to consider whether neutering animals harms them. Five possible reasons can be given in support of the harmfulness of neutering. First, it might be claimed to be harmful simply because of the pain that animals suffer from the process itself. The problem with this argument, however, is that it seems to be negated by the fact that anesthetic can be used to make the process painless. Second, it could be argued that animals have an interest in not being interfered with by being made to undergo such surgery without their consent. And yet chapter 3 argued that, lacking autonomous agency, animals do not have an interest in this kind of negative liberty. Perhaps, then, it might be argued that neutering animals is a constraint on their ability to control their own lives. Once again, however, as nonautonomous beings, animals do not have an interest in being "self-governors" of this sort. Fourth, it might be claimed that it is wrong to alter animals so that they are prevented from having and acting on their natural sexual desires. But this argument once again assumes that what is natural for an individual is equivalent to what makes life go well for an individual. And as has been argued throughout the book, this simply is not the case. Finally, and perhaps most persuasively, it might be claimed that neutering diminishes an animal's opportunities for well-being. This claim is significant given one of the arguments of the previous chapter. There it was claimed that genetically engineering an animal with fewer opportunities for well-being compared to the species norm is ordinarily wrong, even if that animal ends up with a life worth living. If this is true, surely it must also be true that operating on a pet animal to reduce his opportunities for well-being is wrong, even if that animal subsequently has a life worth living. Animals, we might argue, have an interest that they not be neutered in order that they may have sufficient opportunities for well-being. What are we to make of such an argument?

If this argument is valid, it needs to be shown that sexual intercourse and rearing young necessarily contribute to the well-being of pet animals. This is an extremely difficult topic—and given the differences across species, it is impossible to generalize. Nevertheless a few remarks can be made. There is evidence that some animals take pleasure from sexual intercourse in much the same way as human beings. Dolphins and bonobos, for example, are both well known for engaging in sexual relations simply for the pleasure of it, rather than solely for the purpose of reproduction.[10] Furthermore, Jonathan Balcombe has argued that a much wider range of animal species can and do enjoy sex.[11] And if animals suffer from similar things to what we suffer from, it is reasonable to suppose that they also take pleasure from similar things to what we take pleasure from.

However, in spite of such claims, we should be hesitant to conclude that the possession of sexual desire and sexual capacities necessarily makes life better for most domestic pet animals. Take the case of pet cats, for example. It is doubtful that female cats take much pleasure from sexual relations, since the penis of the male cat is barbed and scratches the walls of the vagina in order to induce ovulation. And while male cats may enjoy the act itself, it is questionable whether this outweighs the suffering their sexual urges bring about. For example, the bites and scratches that tomcats suffer from fighting with rival males often cause pain and infections. These animals can also be driven to travel many miles to satisfy their urges, often leading to attacks from other cats defending their territory, as well as the possibility of traffic injury and malnutrition. In terms of rearing young, we should again be cautious to assume that female cats necessarily take great value from the act itself. For one thing, cats can easily become pregnant, often producing two or three litters a year. Producing such volumes of offspring is a great strain on the cat's body and leads to unspayed female cats living much shorter lives than their spayed counterparts.

Turning to dogs, it is certainly possible that dogs take more pleasure than cats from sexual intercourse itself. However, once again, the value that dogs take from the sexual act must surely be outweighed by both the frustration and suffering that such sexual desires induce, and the greater likelihood of disease and injury. For example, like cats, rates of cancer in both male and female dogs are greatly reduced by spaying, although there is evidence that the process should not be enacted too early in the animal's life.[12]

For all these reasons, there is good reason to be skeptical of the claim that pet animals have an interest in not being neutered on the basis that it removes a significant source of well-being for them. Yes, we must acknowledge that some animals enjoy sexual intercourse. However, many domestic animals suffer from the desires their sexual capacities produce, from the act of intercourse itself, and from the increased risk of disease that results from producing and rearing young. Given this, and pending further evidence to the contrary, it is possible to argue that most pet animals have no moral right not to be neutered.

If we combine the idea that most pet animals have no moral right not to be neutered with the fact that thousands of unwanted domestic animals are being killed each year, might we not conclude that we all have a moral obligation to neuter our pet animals? This is certainly the claim of those animal charities that have to deal with the grave problems of strays and overpopulation generally. However, we must bear in mind that the problem that these charities face comes down to the fact that these animals are unwanted, rather than from the breeding itself. In other words, if the animals were wanted and were well looked after, then there would be no problem. Given this, perhaps we might claim that we do not have an obligation to neuter our animals, but we do have an obligation to guarantee the welfare of any offspring if we allow our pets to reproduce.[13] Once again, on the practical level, this could easily be woven into the conditions for granting licenses to potential pet owners.

Finally, we come to the issue of breeding. Domestic animals are far removed from their wild predecessors. They have been bred for particular purposes, and many of these breeds have become popular as pets. For example, different breeds of dog have been established for fighting, hunting, sheep herding, looking pretty, and countless other reasons. Some human beings prefer to keep a particular breed of animal rather than a mongrel for a pet and have continued these lines of breed through deliberate mating. For example, pedigree animals actually make up 75 percent of the seven million dogs in the UK.[14] The previous chapter argued that there is nothing wrong in itself with creating animals through genetic engineering. Similraly, so long as the parent animals are not made to suffer in the process, there can be nothing wrong in itself with creating animals through more conventional breeding. However, it was also claimed in that chapter that animals can be wronged when engineering them will cause them to have lives of intolerable suffering, or indeed when they have reduced opportunities for well-being compared to ordinary members of their species. To be consistent, it seems that this same argument should apply in the case of breeding. Unfortunately many pet animals do have fewer opportunities for well-being compared to ordinary members of their species, precisely because of their breeding. For example, both Manx cats and dachshunds suffer from spinal defects. Boxers are more vulnerable to cancers than other dogs. Cavalier King Charles spaniels suffer from syringomyelia, and bulldogs suffer from breathing difficulties.[15] In all cases, these sufferings are the result of the deliberate mating of animals to reproduce genetic traits.

It might be claimed that none of these animals lead lives of complete misery and suffering. That is, despite their suffering, these animals are still able to enjoy a reasonable quality of life. Given this, it might be argued that these animals have not been harmed. After all, by bringing them into existence we have given them some positive quality of life. However, as chapter 5 argued, it is possible for an action to harm an individual, violate an individual's rights, and wrong an individual even if that action benefits the individual overall. That chapter claimed that animals have a moral right to have been engineered with sufficient opportunities for well-being—where sufficient means in keeping with ordinary members of their species. It seems that it is only consistent to apply this right in the context of breeding: animals have a moral right to have been bred with sufficient opportunities for well-being. Thus when animals are bred to reproduce genetic traits that leave them vulnerable to levels of suffering greater than those of ordinary members of the species, this right is violated. As such, this breeding is morally impermissible, all else being equal.

Some might object that this right should not be established in the context of breeding. They might object that because respecting this right would result in the permanent loss of several breeds, which bring a great deal of joy to many people, that right cannot be established. I disagree. As previous chapters have argued, the animal interest in avoiding suffering is strong and compelling. The human interest in maintaining a suffering breed, on the other hand, can only be described as trivial. Humans obviously can lead lives of extreme high quality without the hobby of breeding dogs with novel and bizarre genetic makeups. Because of this, it seems only reasonable to conclude that pedigree and other animals have a concrete moral right to have been bred with sufficient opportunities for well-being.

Because of the length of this section, it may be useful to summarize its main points. It has been argued that animals have no right not to be used as pets but do have rights not to be made to suffer or killed when they are so used. Rather than offering a justification of the status quo, this conclusion demands a radical transformation of the practice of pet keeping as it currently stands in contemporary societies. On a practical level, this section has proposed the use of licenses, whereby potential keepers of animals are granted permission to do so only when they satisfy three conditions: they prove that they have sufficient time, resources, and understanding to maintain the well-being of the particular animal in question; they take out pet insurance in case of disease or accident; and they agree to take responsibility for the well-being of any offspring that are produced as a result of accidental mating or deliberate breeding. The section has further argued that pet animals have no moral right not to be bred to be pets but do have a moral right to have been bred with sufficient opportunities for well-being. While not ruling out all forms of animal breeding, this conclusion does require the end of breeding that creates animals who are more vulnerable to suffering than ordinary members of their species. This conclusion thus implies the loss of certain breeds of pet animals.

CIRCUSES AND ZOOS

Having discussed the use of animals as pets, it is now necessary to consider their use in zoos and circuses. Given that the book argues that animals have no general right not to be used by human beings for certain purposes, it might seem obvious that it also claims that animals also have no right not be displayed in zoos and circuses. However, it must be remembered that animals do have prima facie rights not to suffer or be killed from their use by humans. Moreover, some animal welfare activists have argued that the infliction of suffering—if not death—is intrinsic to the practices of zoos and circuses. If they are correct, animals would seem likely to possess a concrete right not to be displayed and used in circuses and zoos. If that right could be established, then all else being equal, political communities would have an obligation to abolish circuses and zoos in all their forms. This section considers and ultimately rejects this proposal.

Circuses and zoos often come under attack for certain of their cruel practices. We are all familiar with reports exposing how certain zoos keep animals confined in cramped and unstimulating environments causing untold misery to the animals held there.[16] Sadly we are also familiar with reports of cruelty in circuses, not only in relation to the conditions in which the animals are held, but also with regard to the violent forms of training that are used.[17] Clearly it does not take much ethical consideration of the relevant issues at stake to conclude that such practices are illegitimate and should cease. Moreover, it does not take much complex balancing of interests to conclude that the animal interest in not suffering is sufficient to impose on us a duty not to treat them in these horrific ways. It serves no important human interest to cause such suffering to these animals. It is plausible to suggest that keeping animals in horribly confined spaces or training them violently may allow there to be more zoos and circuses, say, by keeping their costs down. But the human interest in viewing animals in zoos and circuses is obviously rather trivial, and certainly too trivial to justify us having access to zoos and circuses *at any cost*. Humans can lead lives of high quality without visiting zoos and circuses, whereas the quality of life for many of the animals used in such institutions is miserable indeed. Animals clearly have a concrete moral right not to be made to suffer from their use in zoos and circuses.

It will be pointed out that not all zoos and circuses treat their animals in such obviously cruel ways. Indeed, it should be noted that many zoos and circuses are concerned for the welfare of their animals and take steps to ensure that they are healthy, suitably housed, and well stimulated. Do animals in these conditions have a right not be used in zoos and circuses? As noted above, some animal protection campaigners might argue that even where animals seem to be kept in benign conditions, they are still suffering. They would presumably argue that animals kept in zoos and circuses *necessarily* suffer.

There is clearly something to be said for the idea that *some* animals necessarily suffer from their use in zoos and circuses. For example, if zoo and circus animals are actually taken from the wild—as is still the case in some situations—then suffering cannot be avoided. The levels of distress caused by the capturing of such animals, both to that animal and to those left behind, are sufficient to impose on us a duty to stop such practices of capture. But what about those animals that have been bred in captivity—do they necessarily suffer from being used in zoos and circuses?

Taking the issue of circuses first, it is hard to see how the traditional circus animals—elephants, lions, tigers, bears, monkeys, horses, dogs, and so on—can have much quality of life when in a circus. Even if these animals are trained successfully in a way that does not cause them to suffer (which itself seems far-fetched given the bizarre tasks they are made to do) and perform acts that are not dangerous or onerous, it would be practically impossible to provide them with the type of living conditions they require in order to live well. Circuses travel, meaning that the performing animals must also travel. None of the animals mentioned above can enjoy much quality of life when continuously locked up in a cramped cage on a trailer. They are all large, intelligent, and social animals that need plenty of room to exercise and interact. It is hard to envisage a traveling circus being able to meet such requirements. However, this is not to say that it is absolutely impossible to construct a circus that caused no harm to its animals. If the circus did not travel, or did not travel much, and if the animals were kept in appropriate conditions—including many acres of space—then it might be possible for a circus to violate no rights. However, whether such a circus would be economically viable is quite another matter. It seems fair to say that the animal right not to be made to suffer from their use in circuses calls for the end of the use of animals in circuses, as traditionally understood.

Given that zoos do not travel, it seems much more possible to envisage a zoo that does not harm its animals. But to be truly harmless, not only would such zoos have to ensure that the interests of their animals are met in terms of health, nutrition, exercise, stimulation, social interaction, and all else, they would also have to refrain from displaying certain species of animal. After all, it may be the case that some species of animal *necessarily* suffer from being held in captivity. As mentioned in previous chapters, it is possible that some animals such as the great apes and cetaceans have sufficient mental complexity to be justifiably described as autonomous agents, and thus to have an intrinsic interest in liberty. If this is proven to be the case, then such animals have an interest in leading their own lives free from captivity. This would provide legitimate grounds to prevent the holding of great apes in zoos, as well as the display of dolphins, killer whales, and other cetaceans in ocean parks.

Furthermore, even for some of those animals who can straightfor-wardly be regarded as nonpersons in the sense used in this book, it might be extremely difficult to hold them in captivity without also caus-ing them to suffer. For example, polar bears and elephants are often cited as animals that need specific and unique environments to have their interests satisfied—environments of such complexity and magni-tude that it would be impossible for any current zoo to live up to. How-ever, as the zoologist Brian Bertram quite rightly argues, "there is no reason *in principle* why it is not possible to build a polar bear . . . enclo-sure of such a scale and design that almost everyone would consider it adequate."[18] Once again, it may well be that implementing these condi-tions is not so much impossible as completely impractical given limited resources.

In sum, it would be wrong to say that all animals possess a general right never to be displayed in zoos and circuses. Not all the ways in which animals are and can be displayed in zoos and circuses set back their interests, let alone violate their rights. Nevertheless animals do have concrete rights not to be made to suffer and not to be killed by their use in zoos and circuses. Upholding such rights imposes severe limitations on the types of animal that can be kept, the conditions in which they are kept, and the tasks they are made to perform.

SPORT AND HUNTING

Finally, we must consider the interest-based rights approach and its implication for the use of animals in sport. Are animal interests suffi-cient to impose duties on us not to make them suffer, kill them, or even use them in the context of sport?

It seems obvious that the interests of animals in not being killed and made to suffer are sufficient, all things considered, to impose duties on us to refrain from sports such as hunting, cockfighting, dogfighting, bear baiting and bullfighting. Each of these activities causes extreme pain to the animals involved, often involves killing them, but provides only fleeting and trivial entertainment to certain sections of the human population.[19] Human beings can lead lives of extremely high quality without getting their kicks from harmful activities of these kinds. As such, the interests of these animals is certainly sufficient to establish animal rights not be treated in such ways.

However, what about less obviously cruel sports? One such sport that must be considered simply because of its popularity is fishing. It is reasonable to assume that anglers do not ordinarily regard their activities as cruel, and no doubt many are opposed to such practices as cockfighting and bear baiting. But do anglers violate animal rights when they engage in this pastime? It must be acknowledged, first, that given their comparatively limited cognitive abilities, fish are likely to have a relatively weak interest in continued life compared to many other animals. However, weak as it may be, that interest in continued life is still discernible and cannot be violated without good reason. And in any case, even though recreational fishing need not result in death, it necessarily involves the painful capture of sentient animals, whether that be from their capture via a hook or lure, or simply from the struggle to avoid being dragged out of the water.[20] As such, it is impossible to envisage any kind of fishing that does not involve the painful capture or death of a fish. Fishing thus violates the clear and discernible interests of animals. Moreover, the pleasures gained from fishing are only very trivial and can easily be replicated by other pastimes. Once again, human beings can and do lead lives of extremely high quality without fishing. Given all this, there is good reason to conclude that the interests of fish are sufficient, all things considered, to impose on us a duty not to fish for sport.

Other hugely popular sports involving animals that are not commonly regarded as cruel include greyhound racing, horse racing, and equestrianism more generally. These sports do not seem to necessitate pain and death in animals in the same way that hunting, fighting, baiting, or fishing does. Unfortunately the way that these sports are currently organized and practiced does involve the routine suffering and death of animals and ought to be condemned as such. For one thing, many of the methods used to train animals for use in these sports involve instilling discipline by causing pain. For example, traditional methods of breaking a horse have usually involved the use of violence. Moreover, some of the practices within the sports themselves also inevitably cause pain, whether from the use of the whip to control the horse or from the inevitable breaking of limbs in races such as the celebrated Grand National in the United Kingdom.

Furthermore, it is not only animals' interest in avoiding pain that is set back by these sports, but also their interest in continued life. For example, those horses and dogs who are past their sporting peak, and those who never attain the required level of achievement, are routinely killed. Although retirement homes for horses do exist, as do rehoming centers for greyhounds, the lucky animals that end up in these places are very much in the minority. A concrete figure for the number of animals that are killed once their racing life is over is hard to come by, but the *Sunday Times* claimed that one builder's merchant in County Durham had killed over ten thousand dogs in the past fifteen years.[21] An investigation by the *Observer* newspaper found that around seven thousand racehorses are killed per annum in the UK, with many being sold abroad as meat. In the United States the figure is as high as ninety thousand.[22]

However, it is important to remember that neither of these types of harm is *intrinsic* to greyhound racing, horse racing, or equestrianism. When it comes to training the animals, for example, the infliction of pain is avoidable. For it is possible to train an animal without using violence. For example, in equestrianism the nonviolent methods advocated by Monty Roberts and others are gaining in popularity.[23] It is also possible to race animals in ways that do not involve violence: without whips, and without fences that result in the inevitable breaking of limbs. It is even possible to imagine the sports making proper provisions for the well-being of those animals who are past their peak or who have not lived up to sporting expectations. That is, it is possible for these sports to invest sums to look after those animals who never make it or who have been retired. Slaughtering these animals because they are of no use is done simply to save money. At present the horse-racing industry in the UK spends just £250,000 per annum on retired animals.[24] Given the profits the industry makes on the back of the work of these animals, and given their clear interests in avoiding pain and in continued life, this sum is pathetic.

Crucially, then, it is possible to use dogs and horses in races and agility competitions in ways that do not cause them harm. As such, we must conclude that these animals do not have any general right not to be used for sport in all and any circumstances. Given their interests, however, it is clear that we have a duty not to make them suffer or kill them if we do decide to use them for sport. After all, the interests of these animals are real and compelling. Moreover, as I have argued throughout this chapter, we are under no obligation to use animals for our entertainment and can lead perfectly decent lives without so doing. These animals thus have concrete rights not to be made to suffer and not to be killed if they are used for racing, agility, or other competitions. To respect these rights, political communities do not have to abolish horse and greyhound racing per se; but they do have to abolish these institutions as they currently stand. Greyhound racing, horse racing, and equestrianism must be completely restructured if they are to respect the rights of animals.

So far this chapter has argued that, in general, animals have no right not to be used by humans for their entertainment, so long as they are not made to suffer or are killed from that use. This argument calls for a radical overhaul of the ways in which political communities use animals to entertain us. If these animal rights are to be respected, there must be tight regulations on the way we keep animals as pets. Moreover, several popular breeds of pet animal must eventually be phased out. Using animals in circuses—as traditionally understood— would also have to end. And while rights-respecting zoos are possible to imagine, it is clear that there would be far fewer of them, and they would look radically different from how they do now. To respect animal rights, all uses of animals in fights would have to cease, as would recreational hunting and fishing. Sports that use animals for racing or to test agility in other ways would be permitted, other things being equal, only when the training and use of those animals respected their well-being for the whole of their lives.

Despite the radical nature of the changes outlined here, it nevertheless remains the case that this position is outside of animal rights orthodoxy. Many proponents of animal rights will attack its conclusions for being too permissive. For this reason the next section anticipates some of the possible objections that can be raised against them.

Objections to Using Animals for Our Entertainment

Proponents of animal rights usually object to their use in entertainment on a number of grounds. Some of those arguments center on the alleged interest that animals have in being free. Thus to domesticate animals and keep them as pets, to display them as exhibits in zoos, to train them to perform acts in circuses, and to make them compete against each other for our amusement are all considered to be necessarily harmful and impermissible because they stop animals from leading their own free lives. This book has criticized such arguments for erroneously treating animals as autonomous agents with an intrinsic interest in liberty, or for erroneously conflating an animal's fulfillment of its natural biological functions with what serves her interests. Most sentient animals, the book has claimed, have no intrinsic interest in leading their own freely chosen lives. As such, they have no interest in not being used for certain purposes, including being used for our entertainment. This leads to the conclusion that animals have no concrete moral right not to be used for our entertainment, provided that they are not killed or made to suffer as a result.

But some critics might argue that using animals for our entertainment is still wrong even when it causes no pain or death, and even if we accept the arguments about animals' interests in liberty. For they might claim that the wrongfulness of using animals in entertainment lies somewhere else. This section looks at three possible objections of this sort. The first returns to the notion of dignity that was discussed in the previous chapter. It argues that using animals to entertain us may not violate their interests or rights but may nevertheless be impermissible on the basis that it undermines their dignity. The second objection returns to the insights of virtue ethics, arguing that some uses of animals may not cause them to suffer or die but are nevertheless impermissible because they involve showing a disrespectful attitude toward them. The final objection introduces a novel but very important argument. It claims that the interests and rights of animals can never truly be respected while they are the *property* of human beings. As such, it claims that keeping animals as pets, displaying them in zoos and circuses, and using them for sport will always be impermissible while they remain our property. This section refutes each of these objections, maintaining that using animals for entertainment in ways that do not cause them to suffer or die is ordinarily permissible, given a proper account of their interests and rights.

ANIMALS IN ENTERTAINMENT AND ANIMAL DIGNITY

The previous chapter examined how some philosophers use the concept of dignity to argue against certain forms of genetic engineering, particularly those that create a different or bizarre trait in the engineered animal. The argument from dignity is also used to object to displaying animals in zoos and making them perform in circuses. For example, Suzanne Laba Cataldi provides an account of the use of bears by the Moscow State Circus. She reports some bears being dressed up in clown collars and holding balloons for photographs; she also describes another dressed up as a "momma bear": "a bear with a frilly pastel apron draped over its torso and tied around its waist—standing on its hind legs and pushing a toy baby carriage around the singular ring."[25] Cataldi argues that such performances are an affront to the bears' dignity, irrespective of the physical abuses and cruelty that the bears had undoubtedly suffered.[26] In other words, Cataldi is arguing that even if these bears had not suffered in any way from having been used and trained to perform these acts, such use would still be undignified and thus wrong.

Of course the question still remains, just what is dignity and why is undermining it wrong? Cataldi begins to provide us with an answer in the following passage:

> Wild animals are belittled, rather than dignified, as a result of their circus performances because they are viewed and treated as (or reduced to) something less or something other than what they are. In the carnival atmosphere of the circus, their dynamic charm is obscured. Costumed bears are "cute" and "funny"—"funny" human beings and "funny" bears—which decreases the likelihood that they will be taken seriously as the creatures they (really) are.[27]

Cataldi seems to be saying that to treat another individual with dignity is to treat him or her as the kind of being that he or she is. For example, it is to treat a bear not as a dressed-up human, but as a bear. Moreover, Cataldi also claims that this understanding of dignity applies to humans. For she argues that treating a child with dignity involves treating her as a child as opposed to a fully grown adult. She also argues that treating an individual with mental disabilities with dignity involves treating him as an individual with mental disabilities, as opposed to someone without them.[28]

The problem with all this, however, is that it is not entirely clear what treating something as the kind of being that it is actually requires of us. If it means that we should treat the individual in accordance with his or her own particular interests, then I quite agree. Throughout this book, it has been argued that it is imperative to pay careful attention to the particular interests of individuals and not simply regard the interests of all individuals with moral status as equivalent. For it does not make animals, children, or people with mental disabilities any less valuable or less worthy of consideration to acknowledge that they often have quite different interests from those of adult humans.

However, such an understanding of dignity is not what Cataldi has in mind. For if treating a being as the kind of entity it is simply involves respecting that entity's own particular interests, then clearly Cataldi would have to allow all harmless uses of animals. But she does not. Cataldi claims that there is something wrong with treating animals as beings other than they are, even when it causes no harm. Thus treating bears as human beings is wrong even when it does not lead to their death or cause them suffering. But why?

Presumably such a claim must be based on a judgment that it is simply good that animals perform their own *natural* functions, rather than those of some other entity. And yet such a claim is implausible. For, as has been argued previously in the book, it is a mistake to believe that it is always good that individuals act naturally. Preventing the natural human actions of rape and murder, for example, seems to be an obvious moral good rather than a moral bad. What is natural for an entity is one thing; what is good is quite another.

Importantly, this does not make the use of the bears as described by Cataldi permissible. The use of bears in circuses does, after all, usually involve serious harms: the killing of mothers to secure the capture of their cubs; suffering from the violent training methods that are employed; and suffering caused by the inadequate ways in which the bears are housed and transported. Bears have a moral right not to be subject to such harms for our entertainment. Rights and interests provide more powerful and determinate normative tools in this case than the rather hazy notion of dignity.

However, perhaps it is too hasty to dismiss the concept of dignity in this way. After all, an interesting use of a dignity-based argument comes from Dita Wickins-Dražilová, who draws an analogy between contemporary zoos and the eighteenth- and nineteenth-century practice of opening up mental asylums to the paying public.[29] Wickins-Dražilová argues that although the patients in the asylums did not seem to mind the visitors, and thus did not have their well-being adversely affected, the practice came to an end because "we perceive using the mentally ill for entertainment as bad, because we respect their dignity."[30] Wickins-Dražilová argues that if we regard displaying these humans as impermissible on the basis of their dignity, then we must also regard the display of animals in zoos as impermissible on the basis of theirs. It is claimed that the notion of dignity does the work where interests and rights cannot.

But still, we are left wondering just what this notion of dignity means. What does it actually signify to say that the dignity of patients and animals is violated by displaying them in this way? Again, and in keeping with the understandings of animal dignity discussed previously in this and the previous chapter, Wickins-Dražilová sees dignity as related to the ability to perform natural functions: "a bad zoo makes it impossible for the animals to keep their dignity if it prevents them from their basic natural behaviour, like cleaning themselves, or socializing with their own kind."[31] But as was explained above, it is unclear why allowing individuals to perform natural functions is always a good thing. We still have no reason as to *why* it is morally problematic to sometimes disallow or even prevent individuals from acting in line with their biological functions. Furthermore, it is also possible to imagine zoos—and indeed care homes for individuals with serious mental disabilities—that do allow individuals to perform their natural behavior. As such, it is unclear why displaying these individuals for the entertainment of others is always problematic, even when using the concept of dignity that Wickins-Dražilová provides.

However, the important wider objection remains. Does the logic of the argument presented in this chapter lead to the conclusion that it would be permissible to reinstate the practice of opening up asylums to the paying public? Certainly not! It is crucial to remember that this chapter has not been defending each and every form of zoo. Rather it has argued that radically restructured zoos, which display certain species of captive-bred animal, and which respect every aspect of those animals' well-being, are harmless and violate no rights. The practice of displaying patients can hardly be described as harmless. For example, contrary to what Wickins-Dražilová states, patients who were displayed in asylums in the eighteenth and nineteenth centuries certainly did mind being treated in that way. At Bedlam in London, for instance, visitors poked the inmates with sticks with the deliberate intention of enraging them. Importantly for our purposes, it is very difficult to imagine *any* form of display of people with seriously mental disabilities that would not result in serious harms being caused. For we must remember that mental illness is extremely complex and is experienced differently by different individuals. Most important, it certainly does not mean a simple and permanent loss of self-awareness: even the most serious forms of mental illness do not necessarily obstruct feelings of distress and shame. Given this complexity, and thus the inevitable harm that such human displays would cause, we have an overwhelming reason never to return to the practice of displaying individuals who are mentally ill for the entertainment of the paying public. Moreover, that reason rests not on any notion of dignity, but rather on the concrete interests and well-being of the individuals themselves.

ANIMALS IN ENTERTAINMENT AND RESPECTFUL TREATMENT

David DeGrazia has used the notion of respectful treatment to describe certain acts that wrong animals but do them no harm. It is possible to use such a notion to argue that zoos are wrongful and should be prohibited, irrespective of whether they cause the animals to suffer.[32]

To illuminate his conception of respectful treatment, DeGrazia offers an example of a potential instance of disrespect shown to animals. He asks us to imagine a family dyeing its white-haired poodle in the colors of the American flag for a Fourth of July Parade. Further, he asks us to imagine that the dog shows no sign of distress. DeGrazia claims that although this act may not cause the dog to suffer, perhaps it is a sign of disrespect, and objectionable as such. He explains: "I am inclined to believe that the human conduct described . . . [is] objectionable for evincing disrespect towards the animals. If this and similar judgments are defensible, an adequate account may implicate virtue ethics, which connects the manner in which we act, our attitudes, and our character."[33] Maybe, then, dyeing poodles, keeping them as pets, displaying them in zoos, and using them for our entertainment are all instances of disrespect and thereby wrong in that they illustrate flaws and defects in our character.

However, on further reading, DeGrazia himself does not rule out all uses of animals for entertainment. For he also considers the example of a massive zoo that meets all the needs of its animals and "provides them with lives at least as good (long, healthy and satisfying) as the lives they would probably have in the wild."[34] Such a zoo, DeGrazia claims, is not obviously disrespectful and would probably be permissible.

So not all uses of animals in entertainment are disrespectful according to this account. Some, like dyeing poodles, are impermissible, and others, like keeping them in harmless zoos, are permissible. DeGrazia presumably bases this judgment on the fact that the zookeepers act out of concern for the animals, and thus somewhat virtuously, while the poodle's owners act for their own amusement, and thus viciously.

However, as was argued in the previous chapter, we should be extremely wary of determining the permissibility of actions based on the virtuous attitude or character of those behind them. For example, imagine a film star who decides to devote a considerable amount of time to promoting some worthwhile charity. Suppose further that because of her involvement, the charity raises more money than it would have otherwise been able to raise and uses that money to improve the lives of many individuals. At this point this act seems not only permissible but positively virtuous. However, imagine now that we somehow found out that this star had no concern for the charity's goals whatsoever. Instead she spent her time in this way because she had a new film to promote and was actually using the charity work to boost her profile and that of the film. Clearly this changes our attitude toward the character of the film star: we would no longer find her virtuous, and many would see her as exploitative and vicious. Nevertheless it is extremely difficult to give credence to the view that this individual's actions are *wrongful*. It is even more difficult to believe that such behavior is *impermissible*. The film star's intentions may be dishonorable, her actions vicious even, but they can only sensibly be regarded as permissible: they cause no harm and provide a great deal of benefit.

It is preferable to determine our obligations on the basis of the interests and rights of individuals, and not through the attitudes of agents. That would mean that the kind of harmless zoos DeGrazia describes are permissible, all else being equal. But what, then, of dyeing poodles in the colors of the national flag? I doubt that it is obvious that such a poodle would not be distressed by the events described by DeGrazia. After all, if the dog is being mocked and laughed at, it seems highly probable that a creature as sensitive and sociable as a poodle would suffer as such. However, if there were no mocking, and if it could be shown that there would be no suffering on the part of the dog, then it is difficult to understand why the dyeing of the dog should be prevented.[35] This conclusion may run contrary to the intuitions of some proponents of animal rights. However, it is better to formulate our obligations to animals on the basis of the concrete interests of animals themselves, as opposed to the hunches of campaigners for animal protection.

ANIMALS IN ENTERTAINMENT AND PROPERTY STATUS

Recall that the notion of respect for animals is also used—albeit in a quite different way—by Tom Regan. As a reminder, Regan argues that those beings with what he calls "inherent value" have a fundamental right to respectful treatment. Regan argues that all entities who are subjects-of-a-life—that is, those entities with beliefs and desires, perception and memory, the ability to feel pain and pleasure, the ability to initiate action, an individual welfare, and so on—possess a value in and of themselves, irrespective of their value to anyone or anything else.[36] This inherent value grounds Regan's respect principle: "We are to treat those individuals who have inherent value in ways that respect their inherent value."[37] Essentially this is a Kantian injunction whereby "individuals who have inherent value must never be treated *merely as means* to securing the best aggregate consequences."[38]

Crucially, some scholars have used this notion of respect to argue against all uses of animals in entertainment. For example, Gary Francione claims that the respect principle logically entails that animals have the right not to be the property of others.[39] This is because he claims that once a thing is the property of another, it is necessarily treated in a purely instrumental way:

> The status of animals as property renders meaningless our claim that we reject the status of animals as things. We treat animals as the moral equivalent of inanimate objects with no morally significant interests or rights. We bring billions of animals into existence annually simply for the purpose of killing them. Animals have market prices. Dogs and cats are sold in pet stores like compact discs; financial markets trade in futures for pork bellies and cattle. Any interest that an animal has is nothing more than an economic commodity that may be bought and sold when it is in the economic interest of the property owner. That is what it means to be property.[40]

Francione would argue that since the animals used in entertainment are our property, we necessarily disrespect them. As such, Francione claims that all such forms of animal use should be abolished—irrespective of the suffering that those used animals endure.

There are two problems with this line of reasoning. First, as has been mentioned previously, there is reason to question the applicability to animals of this Kantian principle of respect. Once again, since most animals are not ends-in-themselves, as Kant defines the term, it is unclear why they must always be treated as ends-in-themselves.

However, let us leave aside that wider issue with Regan's respect principle and assume, for the sake of argument, that the principle is valid. Even with this assumption, there is still a problem with the way that Francione uses that principle to condemn all the ways we use and own animals—as pets, in zoos, in circuses, in sport, and so on. While Francione's argument has considerable rhetorical force, when we analyze his claims carefully, there is good reason to doubt it. In particular, we must question whether owning a piece of property necessarily leads to treating it as a mere economic commodity. For once we start to analyze the criteria of ownership, we soon see that things are much more complicated than Francione suggests.

To explain, A. M. Honoré has famously listed twelve standard incidents of ownership.[41] These incidents include such things as the right to the possession of that property, the liberty to use the property at one's discretion, and the power to transfer possession of the property to another. If in every case of ownership all these incidents manifest themselves without qualification, then Francione's claim concerning the necessary connection between ownership and disrespect must be valid. That is, if one can use, transfer, and destroy one's property *however one likes and whenever one likes*, then the property status of animals would seem to obstruct the goal of respecting animals' interests. However, as Jeremy Waldron has pointed out, the incidents Honoré outlines should not be regarded as the necessary or jointly sufficient conditions of ownership. Instead they are the general and qualified features of ownership.[42] Thus just because the power to sell a piece of property or the liberty to use it as one wishes might be very limited in some situations, that does not mean that the entity in question is not owned. For example, I sometimes have to let government officials onto my land, I cannot sell cans of beer to children playing outside my house, and I cannot burn down my listed cottage on a whim. However, none of these facts means that I do not *own* my land, my cans of beer, and my cottage.[43]

What I am getting at here is that people can be said to own property, without being able to do what they like with that property. Accordingly, Francione is wrong to contend that the property status of animals *necessarily* means that animals will not be respected. For example, most people regard pet keepers as the owners of their animals. However, pet keepers do not usually treat their pets "merely as means to securing the best aggregate consequences." For torturing a cat for the pleasure of sadists might lead to increased overall happiness in the world, but not many cat owners would consider performing such an act. The cat may well be property, but that does not necessarily lead to treating "animals as the moral equivalent of inanimate objects with no morally significant interests or rights," as Francione contends.

Francione's more persuasive argument, however, is that even if we recognize that animals possess significant interests, so long as they remain property, their interests will always be subordinated to those of property owners: "As property, animals are *chattels,* just as slaves once were. And just as in the case of human slaves, virtually *any* interest possessed by animals can be 'sacrificed' or traded away as long as the human benefit is sufficient."[44] And yet just as the ownership of animals does not necessarily entail ignoring their interests, nor does it necessarily entail subordinating their interests. As Cass Sunstein has pointed out, it is possible for us to protect animal interests and even grant them rights without necessarily declaring that they cannot be owned.[45] Indeed, some of the suggestions that have been proposed in this chapter with regard to the licensing of pet keeping can be regarded as an example of interest-protection within a system of ownership.

However, perhaps the more important aspect of Francione's claim is his analogy of owned animals and human slaves. For it has been argued that the ultimate harm done to slaves derives from the fact that they are *dominated.*[46] Thus even if one treats a slave well and satisfies his interests, that slave is still harmed from the fact that he is *dependent* on the goodwill of others for such decent treatment. The slave may be treated well, but as property he is dominated by and dependent on his property owner, which is necessarily harmful. Clearly the same argument can be made with respect to animals. For just like slaves, no matter how kindly we act toward them, so long as animals are property, they will always have a second-class status and be *dependent* on our goodwill for the protection of their interests.

The great problem with this argument is that animals always depend on our goodwill for the protection of their interests to some extent. This is clearly the case with domesticated animals living in modern societies who obviously require human provision and care in order to live well. However, even if we were to totally abolish domestication—which is the ultimate goal of Gary Francione—some forms of animal dependence would not cease. For the effects of human actions can be felt in every corner of the natural world. As such, even those animals living in the wild depend on decisions humans make: those decisions might relate to whether to hunt those animals, to develop the land where they live, to burn fossil fuels, and so on. Because of human domination and power, the dependence of animals will not be eroded by abolishing all forms of animal ownership. Given this, the appropriate task must be to work out what obligations we have to animals, given that they are so dependent on us.

In all, then, when we adopt a more subtle understanding of property than the one adopted by Francione, we can see that not all forms of ownership necessarily harm animals. Once it is understood that property is a fragmented concept, we can see that it is perfectly possible to own animals—and own them to use them for our entertainment—but also to respect them. However, this is not to say that the current system of animal ownership adopted in modern societies is legitimate. Animals may well have no basic right not to be owned under any circumstances, but because of their interests, animals should not ordinarily be made to suffer, nor be killed, as a result of their ownership. Given this qualification, it is possible to think of two important constraints on the permissible incidents of animal ownership.

First, it is not ordinarily permissible to take possession of an animal existing in the wild. After all, taking possession of a wild animal—say, by going into the countryside and trapping him—runs contrary to the animal's interests in not suffering. Such capture would cause the animal to suffer in at least four ways: he would be removed from his familiar habitat; he would be removed from his social network; he would feel threatened and fear for his life; and he would grow frustrated at not being able to escape. Domesticated animals, on the other hand, are born into human society and are thus not only used to but sometimes dependent on human care for their well-being. Moreover, domesticated animals have been bred for generations specifically for domestication and are thus far removed from their ancestors in terms of their ability to live a decent life in the wild. As such, while it seems reasonable to allow for the possession of domesticated animals, that permission should not be extended to the possession of animals living in the wild.

Second, the transfer of possession of animals should be much more restricted than is currently permitted. After all, often the transfer of possession can cause significant harm to animals. This is especially true for those infant animals who are taken from their mothers too young; but it is also true for mature social animals who can suffer greatly when uprooted from familiar environments and social networks. Clearly this does not render all animal transfers impermissible. Nevertheless it does demand much greater regulation than is in place in most states.

It requires breeders and vendors of animals to be closely monitored to ensure that all the interests of animals are protected when such exchanges take place. Once again, this could plausibly be woven into some kind of licensing system.

The fundamental argument should be clear. There is nothing inherent in the idea of owning animals that means that they will be disrespected: it is possible to have certain ownership rights in relation to animals and to respect their interests.

To sum up, this section has examined three arguments that claim that animals should not be used to entertain us irrespective of whether they are made to suffer or are killed. It has examined the possibility that such uses of animals are wrong because they violate their dignity, show them disrespect, and involve owning them as property. All these types of claim have been found to be flawed. As such, we do not have an obligation *never* to use animals for our entertainment, but we do have an obligation not to make them suffer and not to kill them if we do so use them.

This chapter has argued that animals have no moral right not to be used for the entertainment of humans but do have concrete rights not to be made to suffer and killed if they are so used. This claim is not a justification of the status quo, but calls for a radical transformation of many of the practices of contemporary societies. Pet keeping needs to be completely overhauled so that the well-being of pet animals is ensured. The chapter has tentatively suggested a system of licensing to facilitate this goal. Circuses, as traditionally understood, must be abolished. Zoos must be radically transformed so that they display only those animals whose well-being they can be certain to uphold. The baiting, hunting, and fishing of animals must end, as must sports that make animals fight. Sports that race animals or test their agility must be completely transformed so that they satisfy the interests of all their animals for all their lives.

Many proponents of animal rights will object that in spite of the radical nature of these proposals, they are still too permissive. This chapter has examined three potential objections of this sort that use the notions of dignity, respect, and property. But each of these arguments has been found wanting. Preventing the use of animals on the grounds of their dignity either remains too vague or collapses into perfectionism.

Rejecting such animal use on the basis that it would exhibit disrespect on our part ends up being implausibly prohibitive. And abolishing all uses of animal in entertainment on the grounds that we cannot properly protect an owned entity's interests has been shown to be false. As such, there are good reasons to maintain that animals have no general right never to be used in entertainment, and on that basis, to regulate rather than abolish all such uses of animals.

Seven

Animals and the Environment

The previous four chapters have outlined our obligations to animals in four different contexts: experimentation, agriculture, genetic engineering, and entertainment. Without doubt, then, the main focus of the book so far has been what we owe to domestic animals, rather than animals existing in the wild. But that is not to say that the consideration of wild animals has been excluded altogether. For example, chapter 4 argued that establishing an animal right not to be raised and killed for human consumption does not imply that prey animals in the wild have a right not be killed by predator animals. The same chapter also claimed that field animals have no right not to be killed when we harvest crops. In chapter 6 it was argued that animals have a right not to be hunted for sport. And in that chapter it was claimed that removing animals from the wild to be owned by humans is ordinarily wrong. This chapter builds on these brief excursions from the subject of domestic animals. This not only involves a deeper analysis of our obligations to animals living in the wild but also includes an evaluation of our moral obligations with respect to the environment itself.

Indeed, it is crucial for any theory of animal rights to address our environmental obligations for at least three different reasons. First, given that a theory of animal rights seeks to extend moral status and rights beyond the human species, it is necessary to ask just how far that extension should go. For example, do all living entities have moral status and rights, as some environmental ethicists have claimed? Second, a full account of our obligations to animals cannot just focus on issues such as farming and animal experimentation. The actions and behavior of political communities also affect sentient animals living in the wild, and it is necessary to ask what obligations we have with respect to such animals. Finally, and crucially, some philosophers have suggested that theories of animal rights are inimical to the goals of environmentalism.[1] It is thus important to evaluate such claims and to ask how the rights of animals affect our obligations with respect to endangered species, deforestation, pollution, climate change, and so on.

The first section of the chapter outlines the implications of the interest-based animal rights theory for our environmental obligations. This section argues that our environmental obligations should not be founded on a "biocentric" ethic that assigns moral status and rights to all living entities. Instead, the chapter proposes a "welfare-centric" ethic that delineates our environmental obligations from the interests and rights of individual sentient beings. This kind of approach, the chapter argues, is not only rationally sound but also offers robust protection to sentient and nonsentient living organisms.

The second and third sections anticipate and consider two specific problems that might stem from this account of our environmental obligations: how to account for our obligations to endangered species, and how to deal with such wildlife management problems as overpopulation and the threat posed by nonnative species. The chapter argues that the interest-based rights approach is well-equipped to offer sensible proposals with respect to both issues.

To begin, it will be useful to outline the implications of the rights-based approach for our environmental obligations.

Environmental Obligations and Interest-Based Rights

Concern about the health of the environment is no longer the exclusive preserve of a few environmentalist groups and fringe political parties. Over the past decade environmentalism has become very much mainstream. In most developed states, for example, political parties try to outdo one another in terms of their green rhetoric. In several states green parties have even achieved success in local and national elections. Recently this rhetoric has focused mainly around anthropogenic climate change and the challenges it poses, but it has also encompassed such issues as air and water pollution, resource depletion, biodiversity loss, and much else besides. In philosophical terms, mainstream environmentalism is clearly "anthropocentric." That is, politicians, activists, and the public have become increasingly concerned about such issues as pollution, climate change, and resource depletion because of the threats and harms they pose to human beings.

However, many philosophers working in environmental ethics are scathing of anthropocentrism. Such philosophers claim that anthropocentrism is narrow and self-interested and fails to capture an appropriate attitude toward the natural world. Importantly, these critics of anthropocentrism claim that our environmental obligations are not exhausted by those we have to human beings. Instead they claim that we also possess certain obligations to the environment itself: to trees, species, ecosystems, and areas of wilderness. Only by extending moral status in this way, it is argued, can an adequate account of our environmental obligations be delineated. As such, these thinkers urge that we move beyond anthropocentrism to a "biocentric" or "ecocentric" position, which will result in a fuller and deeper environmental ethic.[2]

This section explains how the interest-based rights approach lies between the two poles of anthropocentrism and biocentrism. In fact, the approach of this book might be best described as "welfare-centric": recognizing moral status on the basis of the capacity for well-being. This section thus makes three important claims: first, that nonconscious entities such as plants, species, and ecosystems cannot possess interests; second, that these same entities do not possess moral status; and finally, that a full and demanding account of our moral obligations concerning the environment can be arrived at from a theory based on the interests and rights of sentient individual animals.

THE INTERESTS AND RIGHTS OF THE ENVIRONMENT?

Some philosophers have claimed that we have environmental obligations to entities such as plants, species, and ecosystems for their own sake. For example, they claim that we have duties to preserve and not to damage these entities irrespective of whether they benefit humans or other sentient animals. No doubt because of the centrality of interests and well-being to ethics, many of the thinkers who put forward this argument base it on the claim that these natural entities possess interests. However, the idea that such nonconscious entities can possess interests is at odds with the understanding of interests put forward in this book. Chapter 2 defended what was termed a "welfarist" understanding of interests. In other words, it was claimed that interests are components of well-being; so in order to have an interest in something, that thing must make life go better *for the individual whose life it is*. On this basis, vases, books, bicycles, and other nonconscious objects were excluded from the class of interest-holders. For while events can make the conditions of such inanimate objects better or worse, nothing can make life better or worse for those objects themselves. Importantly, plants were also excluded from the class of interest-holders. For although events can make the biological functioning of plants better or worse, nothing can make life better or worse *for the plants themselves*.

To put it plainly, this welfarist understanding requires an individual to have the capacity for conscious experience in order to possess interests. No nonconscious entity such as a plant, species, or ecosystem can possess interests under this account; and thus no such entity can possess moral status or rights.

However, some philosophers have argued that this account of interests is too restrictive and have claimed that nonconscious entities can meaningfully be said to have interests. For example, Paul W. Taylor and Robin Attfield have both argued that all living things have interests based on the full development of their biological powers. However, the problem with this kind of argument, as has been mentioned throughout this book, is that it mistakenly confuses interests with what makes an organism a better example of its kind. A tree can be a better or worse tree in a perfectionist sense, but lacking conscious experience, its life cannot go better or worse *for itself*. And given that interests properly concern what makes an individual's go life better for the individual whose life it is, the possession of interests depends on an entity having the capacity for conscious experience.

But perhaps we should not be so hasty in dismissing the idea that nonconscious entities possess interests. After all, both Gary E. Varner and Lawrence E. Johnson have claimed that limiting interests to beings with the capacity for conscious experience is in fact implausible. They do so by pointing out, quite reasonably it seems, that not all interests are tied to conscious experience.[3] To illustrate, Varner asks us to consider the following statement: "Nineteenth-century mariners needed ten milligrams of ascorbic acid a day to avoid scurvy."[4] Now clearly it makes sense to say that nineteenth-century mariners had an *interest* in that daily dose of ascorbic acid. Moreover, it makes sense to say that they had such an interest in spite of three facts: first, that those mariners had no conscious desire for ascorbic acid; second, that they had no conscious understanding of what ascorbic acid is; and finally, that they lived at a time when they could never attain that kind of understanding.

According to both Varner and Johnson, it makes sense to recognize that these mariners possessed an interest in their daily dose of ascorbic acid because of the simple fact that it met a biological need of theirs. As such, they point out that not all interests are attached to conscious experience—some are attached to simple biological need. Moreover, they argue that if we admit the existence of such nonconscious biological interests in humans, we must also recognize them in plants and other natural entities.

However, such an argument fails to undermine the welfarist understanding of interests defended in this book. It is true that not all interests are tied to conscious desires, or the possibility of having such desires. But that does not undermine the point that the capacity for conscious experience is necessary for the possession of interests. Nineteenth-century mariners certainly did possess an interest in their daily dose of ascorbic acid. And this is not because they had a conscious desire for that acid; for clearly they had no such desire. But nor is it because the mariners had a biological need for it. For as has been repeated in this book, to conflate biological needs with interests is to mistakenly conflate what makes an entity a better example of its kind with its own well-being. Well-being is a prudential value and concerns how life goes for the individual whose life it is. Instead, then, the mariners had an interest in the acid because, as a result of receiving their daily dose, their lives went better *for those individuals themselves.* This is where conscious experience becomes so important for the possession of interests: not to have the capacity to be consciously interested in a good, but to have the capacity to *experience the benefit* of that good.

As such, and in spite of Varner's and Johnson's arguments to the contrary, the welfarist understanding of interests remains valid. Only entities with the capacity for conscious experience possess interests because only those entities have lives that can go well or badly for themselves. As such, plants, species, ecosystems, and tracts of wilderness all lack interests. And since they lack interests, these entities can possess no rights.

THE MORAL STATUS OF THE ENVIRONMENT?

At this point, some might want to claim that even if these nonconscious entities possess no interests, they nevertheless have moral status. So perhaps we have obligations to plants, species, and ecosystems in spite of the fact that they have no interests. Given the centrality of interests and well-being to morality and ethics, such a claim is difficult to sustain. For recall the argument that was made in chapter 2 in defense of the idea that sentient animals possess moral status. It was claimed in that chapter that the reason philosophers usually assign moral status to animals is not their sentience per se, but what their sentience represents: well-being. Sentient animals have lives that can go well or badly for themselves, can be benefited and harmed, and possess interests that can be set back or promoted. Well-being is the fundamental concern of ethics, and as such, the capacity for well-being is necessary in order to possess moral status.

However, some philosophers have claimed that this is an impoverished understanding of ethics. They call for a fuller, more inclusive ethic that moves beyond the welfare of individuals. Perhaps the classic statement of such a view in environmental ethics is Aldo Leopold's "land ethic." Leopold makes the claim that the land itself has moral status, irrespective of its possession of welfare, interests, or conscious experience. For Leopold the land is much more than just soil. Rather he regards the land as a fountain of energy flowing through a circuit of soils, plants, and animals. Food chains conduct the flow of energy upward, while death and decay return that energy back to the soil. Under this account, then, the flow of energy within the land depends on the complex interrelations between living organisms. Clearly these relations are not static, with evolution gradually making changes to them. However, Leopold claims that human interventions in these relations have a much more violent and destructive impact than the changes brought about by evolutionary processes. Thus to maintain the *proper* relations within the land, Leopold argues for a land ethic, whereby we grant moral status to the land community itself. Such an outlook is embodied in his famous ethical injunction: "A thing is right when it tends to preserve the integrity, stability and beauty of the biotic community. It is wrong when it tends otherwise."[5]

The question remains, *why* should we follow Leopold's land ethic and grant moral status to the land community? After all, even if we agree with Leopold's account of how the land is, there remains the question of why we should preserve it. What is it about these relations in the community that make them the *proper* relations? What is it about the biotic community that merits awarding it moral status? At this stage, J. Baird Callicott would argue that I am asking the wrong question.

According to Callicott, Leopold is not claiming that we should grant the land moral status on the basis of its possession of some particular characteristic. Rather, Leopold is asking us to grant it on the basis of our own moral sentiment and affection.[6] So the appropriate question to ask is not, what quality does the land possess that makes it worthy of moral status? Instead the question should be, how do we *feel* about the land? Under Callicott's interpretation, the land ethic is an injunction to humanity to move away from self-interest and broaden its ethical commitments to include the biotic community.

But if this is a correct interpretation of Leopold's land ethic, then the land ethic remains entirely unsatisfactory as a means of determining who and what possesses moral status. It is unsatisfactory because it is indeterminate. Callicott's interpretation of the land ethic urges us to widen our affections beyond humanity and to assign moral status to the biotic community as a whole. But *why* should we do this? Not because of some quality that the nonhuman world possesses, it is claimed. Instead, the answer comes down to our positive moral sentiments and feelings about the biotic community. However, while Leopold, Callicott, and others might have such feelings about the biotic community, many others do not share them. For example, some human beings regard the natural world as something alien and to be feared, while others regard it as something to be controlled, dominated, and exploited. And even among those who consider the natural world to be a wondrous thing, such affection usually falls far short of recognizing that it has moral status. Given this diversity of sentiment, how can we be sure that Leopold and Callicott possess the correct moral sentiments, and others possess the wrong ones? Without making an argument through pointing to some characteristic of the biotic community, it is hard to see how such a question can be answered.

Ultimately, then, it would seem that the granting of moral status to the biotic community in the land ethic is based solely on a feeling that Aldo Leopold possessed and J. Baird Callicott shares. Without doubt this foundation is far too flimsy. Instead we need a determinate account of moral status: one that can explain why we have obligations to some entities but not to others. The most plausible necessary characteristic for the possession of moral status is well-being: our moral obligations are fundamentally concerned with making the lives of individuals go better for themselves and avoiding making them go worse. As such, plants, species, and ecosystems lack interests, rights, and moral status. We have no moral obligations to such entities.

A WELFARE-CENTRIC ENVIRONMENTAL ETHIC

If, as has been argued, our moral obligations are owed exclusively to entities with the capacity for well-being, where does that leave the content of our environmental obligations? Does it make for a rather impoverished and weak environmental ethic? This section argues that it does not. After all, just because only sentient individuals have interests, moral status, and rights, that does not mean that we can permissibly pollute the air and rivers, tear down forests, drill for oil in tracts of wilderness, build human settlements wherever we see fit, and so on. For the well-being of sentient individuals is absolutely dependent on the health of nonconscious nature. Humans, for example, require a healthy environment simply in order to lead a tolerable life: to have clean air to breathe, sufficient food to eat, unpolluted water to drink, and an environment in which to shelter. For this reason some theorists have argued that there is a human right to a healthy environment.[7] Even an anthropocentric environmental ethic can impose strict environmental obligations upon us.

However, the interest-based rights approach proposed in this book moves beyond anthropocentrism. When formulating our obligations with respect to the environment, not only must the interests of human beings be accounted for, but so must the interests of all sentient creatures.[8] Indeed, the animal interests in not being killed and not being made to suffer place important limits on the activities of humans. As an example, even if it were shown that the development of some piece of land would violate no human interests or rights, it might still be impermissible. For if that development were to have a deleterious impact on the habitat of sentient animals such that it resulted in their suffering or death, then that development would be impermissible, all else being equal. Thus the rights-based theory defended here offers protection to nonconscious natural entities such as plants, species, and ecosystems because of their contribution to the well-being of all sentient individuals.

Of course, it is quite clear that a theory founded on the interests and rights of sentient individuals takes us only so far in terms of our environmental obligations. For example, it will ordinarily find it difficult to prevent certain actions—including the destruction of nonsentient plants, species, and ecosystems—if they could be proven not to have any harmful effects on sentient individuals. For many environmental ethicists, this makes a welfare-centric environmental ethic far too permissive.

Indeed, Bryan G. Norton has argued that welfare-centric ethics, such as the one proposed in this chapter, can even permit the destruction of the habitats of sentient animals. That is because, in his view, the relationship between habitat destruction and animal suffering is only contingent: "It is possible . . . for humans to accept the obligation to avoid unnecessary suffering resulting from their actions without accepting the obligation to save environmentally important areas. They could, for example, humanely capture and relocate all creatures in an area slated to become a parking lot or a condominium complex, thereby sparing them suffering."[9] In other words, Norton is arguing that a welfare-centric ethic would permit environmental degradation in the form of habitat destruction, provided that the sentient animals who live there are captured and relocated.

But Norton underestimates the harmful effects of capturing and relocating animals. Capturing the animals can be extremely stressful for them, particularly when it involves the separation of individuals from social groups. Transporting wild animals also inevitably causes frustration and anxiety for the animals. And most important, relocating animals to new and unfamiliar territories often causes them to be confused, disoriented, and vulnerable to predators and competitors for food.[10] It is true that there is not a *necessary* link between habitat destruction and animal suffering. Perhaps in some very specific and isolated situations these harms could be avoided. But generally it has to be recognized that habitat destruction causes serious harm to sentient animals, which gives us a compelling reason to prevent it.

Before leaving this topic, however, it is necessary to briefly consider one thinker who has attempted to show that habitat destruction and harm to animals *are* necessarily linked. John Hadley has put forward an argument that is of particular relevance to the theory advanced in this book. For Hadley ingeniously proposes that nonhuman animals have property rights over their habitats.[11] Hadley argues that if human property rights are founded on the human interest in using natural resources to satisfy their basic needs, then the very same interest can be used as a justification for animal property rights.[12] If Hadley is correct, then each and every instance of habitat destruction involves a harm done to animals on the basis that it violates their property rights. As such, it is possible for an interest-based rights approach to have the same implications as a deeper environmental ethic: that is, the destruction of any piece of the environment is prima facie impermissible.

Unfortunately this attempt at a reconciliation between animal rights and deeper environmental ethics is flawed. First, it is not at all clear that property rights really are properly founded on the interest of individuals in satisfying their basic needs. After all, most understandings of property recognize that individuals can possess rights to goods over and above what is necessary to meet their basic needs. As such, there is good reason to question the link between property and basic needs. However, even if we ignore this objection and accept Hadley's understanding of property rights, there is a second and more important problem with this attempt at reconciliation. This proposal is unlikely to appease environmental ethicists simply because it would permit the destruction of environments where no sentient animals exist. After all, if there is no sentient animal with a property right over the land, then destruction of that land would ordinarily be permissible under this kind of account.

So where does all this leave the interest-based rights approach and our environmental obligations? It leaves us with extremely strict environmental obligations based on the interests and rights of sentient individuals. Whenever our actions are to have a significant impact on the environment, whether immediately or in the future, we have a duty to consider how such actions will affect the well-being of sentient individuals. If such actions are to cause suffering or death to sentient individuals, then there is a strong prima facie case against such actions. For example, the implications of this theory for such practices as clearing forests for farming are obvious. Deforestation necessitates the deaths of the sentient animals who reside there. As such, this widespread practice can usually be considered to violate the rights of animals, and to be impermissible as such.

Furthermore, the interest-based rights approach also has implications for actions that involve less direct harms. For example, climate change is having and is predicted to have a devastating impact on the habitats, food sources, and migratory patterns of sentient animals—including humans. The prima facie rights of animals in continued life and in not being made to suffer give us good reason to slow the impact of climate change by cutting the volume of greenhouse gases we release into the atmosphere.[13]

At this point many will argue that all this is too quick. Recall that the animal rights not to suffer and not be killed are only prima facie.

Perhaps, then, when all things are considered, these rights cannot be established in contexts that involve policies of deforestation and the release of greenhouse gases. After all, forests are cleared and fossil fuels are burned not for trivial reasons. In particular, these actions are undertaken by states to facilitate economic development. Moreover, they are undertaken by developing nations to raise the standard of living for their people, and to raise it to levels comparable to something like that which is enjoyed in many developed states. This can hardly be described as a trivial or minor interest. Why should developing states forestall real economic progress and welfare increases for the sake of sentient animals?

There are several responses that can be made to this objection. However, the most devastating one is simply that it rests on a false premise. There is an increasing consensus that economic progress and increased standards of living will *not* be achieved by such environmentally destructive policies as deforestation and the increased burning of fossil fuels. This is simply because such practices contribute to climate change that will not only slow economic development for us all but hit developing states the hardest. The *Stern Review* on the economic impact of climate change is unequivocal on this point:

> While all regions will eventually feel the effects of climate change, it will have a disproportionately harmful effect on developing countries—and in particular poor communities who are already living at or close to the margins of survival. Changes in the climate will amplify the existing challenges posed by tropical geography, a heavy dependence on agriculture, rapid population growth and poverty. . . . Climate change threatens the long-term sustainability of development progress.[14]

As such, it is simply false to claim that economic progress rests on environmentally destructive policies that involve the harming of sentient animals. In fact, the contrary is the case: long-term economic progress requires much more benign environmental policies. Given this, when all things are considered, concrete animal rights not to be made to suffer and not to be killed through such policies as deforestation and the burning of fossil fuels can be established.

This section has outlined the implications of the interest-based rights approach for our environmental obligations. In a nutshell, the claim is that our obligations are properly based on the well-being of sentient individuals, rather than on any putative obligations some have claimed we have to nonconscious entities such as plants, species, or ecosystems. Rather than being a weak or permissive environmental ethic, it has been argued that this theory imposes strict environmental obligations on us—including with respect to such issues as deforestation and the release of greenhouse gases.

Still, however, two objections from environmentalists that have not yet been considered can be anticipated. First, some will claim that the theory does not deal adequately with our obligations with respect to endangered species. Second, some will argue that the theory does not offer sensible conclusions regarding therapeutic hunting. The remainder of the chapter tackles these two concerns head on.

Endangered Species and Interest-Based Rights

If our obligations concerning the environment are based solely on the interests and rights of sentient individuals, where does that leave endangered species? Does the individualistic and welfarist focus of the theory advocated in this chapter mean that it is blind to the plight of endangered species?

First, it is important to emphasize that the theory advocated in this book does not mean that it is permissible to drive endangered species to extinction. Although species have no interests, rights, or moral status, they are often comprised of individuals who do. Thus we have an obligation not to drive gorillas to extinction, quite simply because we have an obligation not to kill gorillas. According to this theory, no interest or right of the gorilla *species* either needs to be or should be invoked to explain this obligation. Endangered species merit protection because sentient individuals merit protection.[15]

However, some environmentalists would undoubtedly find such an account of our obligations concerning endangered species to be unsatisfactory for two reasons. First, they would claim that it is unsatisfactory because it cannot explain the wrong done when nonconscious species, such as plants and insects, are driven to extinction or the brink of it. Second, they would find it unsatisfactory because it cannot explain the *special* and *stronger* obligations we have to individuals from endangered species.

This section examines two possible principles that might be incorporated into the interest-based rights approach in order to meet these sorts of objections. The first invokes the idea of "superkilling" and claims that killing a species is a special kind of wrong, and worse than the killing of an individual member of that species. The second principle invokes the notion of "compensatory justice" to explain the special obligations we have to endangered species. This section claims that not only are these two proposed principles flawed, they are also unnecessary. For the interests and rights of sentient individuals can straightforwardly explain not only the wrong of destroying endangered nonconscious species, but also the nature of our special obligations to endangered species.

SUPERKILLING

Some environmental ethicists not only consider holistic entities such as species and ecosystems to have moral status, they also regard them as having *priority* over the individuals who make them up. For example, Holmes Rolston III writes: "In an evolutionary ecosystem, it is not mere individuality that counts. . . . The individual represents (re-presents) a species in each new generation. It is a token of a type, and the type is more important than the token."[16] He goes on to argue, "The species line is quite fundamental. It is more important to protect this integrity than to protect individuals."[17] Because of the importance of species, Rolston considers their extinction as a form of superkilling.[18] As such, for Rolston, we most certainly do have obligations to species of nonconscious entities; and we most certainly do possess special obligations to members of endangered species. Should then the interest-based rights theory of this book incorporate this notion of superkilling?

No, it should not. And it should not do so because there is no good reason to award such fundamental ethical importance to species. Consider why Rolston places so much value on species. Perhaps surprisingly he does not believe that species are ethically significant in and of themselves. Rather their importance rests on their contribution to the maintenance of "natural processes." After all, Rolston is dismissive of policies that attempt to preserve species in zoos or in botanical gardens. This is because zoos and botanical gardens cannot simulate "the ongoing dynamism of gene flow under the selection pressures in a wild biome." Similarly, *natural* extinctions of species are not a matter of regret for Rolston, and we have no duty to prevent them. This is because "nature takes away life when it has become unfit in habitat, or when the habitat alters, and supplies other life in its place."[19] What is of importance to Rolston, then, is not so much the preservation of species, but the preservation of natural processes. Thus our obligations with respect to endangered species are duties not to cause *artificial* extinctions because such extinctions will upset natural processes.

Unfortunately this invocation of the "natural" is deeply problematic. First, it is unclear why we are under any duty to preserve natural processes. After all, very real harms are caused by natural processes such as disease and famine, and it seems obvious that these should be prevented as far as possible. Second, even if we concede for the sake of argument that these, or some, natural processes should be preserved, that still leaves us with the grave problem of delineating a clear understanding of just what "natural" is. For it has been pointed out that we human beings are just as natural as every other living organism. Moreover, what is more natural than fighting off competitors and expanding our ecological niches, just as we do when we drive other species to extinction?[20] If preserving natural processes is what matters, then there seems to be no good reason to obstruct those extinctions caused by human beings. In spite of his intentions, then, the real implications of Rolston's argument offer a much more permissive set of obligations with respect to endangered species compared to the welfare-centered theory defended in this chapter.

COMPENSATORY JUSTICE

In the first edition of his book *The Case for Animal Rights*, Tom Regan dismissed the idea that we have special obligations to members of endangered species. Regan argued that the rarity or abundance of an animal makes no difference to the weight of its claims against us.[21] However, when returning to these arguments for the revised edition of his book, Regan changed his mind. For in the revised edition he argues that something more is indeed owed to members of endangered species than is owed to members of plentiful ones. Moreover, he believes that his rights-based theory can accommodate this special obligation by using the notion of "compensatory justice." Essentially the idea behind compensatory justice is that something more should be done for individuals who have been disadvantaged by a grave injustice to their ancestors. For example, claims to compensatory justice have been made in the United States by the descendents of both African slaves and Native Americans. Importantly, Regan thinks that such a compensatory principle can be applied to animals: "If it is true, as I believe it is, that today's rhinos have been disadvantaged because of wrongs done to their predecessors, then, other things being equal, more should be done for rhinos, by way of compensatory assistance, than should be done for rabbits."[22]

Should this notion of compensatory justice be incorporated into the interest-based rights theory of this book? No, it should not. There is good reason to question the very idea of compensatory justice. After all, there are two problems facing the idea. First, there is the problem of identifying who should bear the duties of this compensation.[23] For it is one thing to identify a wrong done in the past that disadvantages present individuals, but it is quite another to identify who, if anyone, should compensate those individuals for that wrong. For example, it is not obvious that innocent members of present generations are obliged to compensate for an injustice that they played no part in. As well as locating the duty-bearers, there is also a problem with identifying the relevant beneficiaries of the duty. Compensatory justice tells us that we should compensate those whose ancestors were victims of a serious injustice. But just how far into the past should we delve? It is probable that if we dug far enough back, any one of us could find some ancestor who was seriously wronged. But we cannot all be entitled to compensatory justice if the idea is to have any plausibility. And even if it were possible to resolve this problem by identifying a relevant group worthy of these special obligations, should we then compensate *all* members of that group? It would be odd to devote resources to members of the group who did not want compensation, say, because they found it patronizing. It would also be odd to devote resources to those members of the group who are now extremely well-off, in spite of the disadvantages they have faced. The grave and difficult problems of identifying the relevant duty-bearers as well as the appropriate beneficiaries give us good reason to question the very idea of compensatory justice.

However, let us for the sake of argument assume that these problems can be overcome and that compensatory justice is, at base, a useful ethical principle. Even with this assumption, the principle still does not do the work that Regan thinks it does. That is, it still cannot establish special obligations to all members of endangered species. To explain, the idea of compensatory justice depends on the idea that certain individuals from a group have been disadvantaged by a historic injustice. Regan seems to believe that rare animals have been so disadvantaged. But is that necessarily the case? It could be argued that rarer animals have fewer mates to find and choose from. This may cause them frustration, and it may also cause them to roam farther in search of mate, in turn making them more susceptible to attack and malnourishment. It could also be pointed out that rarer animals live in smaller social groups, possibly resulting in less stimulation and also making them more vulnerable to competitors. But even if these disadvantages are considered to be real, they clearly do not apply to *all species* of endangered animals. For one, not all animals live in social groups, so the problem of decreased stimulation and increased vulnerability to competitors does not apply. Furthermore, it is quite easy to imagine that some endangered animals are actually *advantaged* by their rarity. After all, rarer animals will have fewer cospecies competitors for mates, territory, and food, which could conceivably make their lives easier.

Plainly, then, the link between being rare and being disadvantaged is not a necessary one. As such, if compensatory justice is a valid notion, which we have good reason to doubt, it will ground special obligations only to those endangered animals that can be proven to be disadvantaged by their rarity. In other words, it will not appease the environmentalist objection that a rights-based approach cannot establish special obligations to all members of endangered species.

ENDANGERED SPECIES AND THE
INTERESTS OF SENTIENT BEINGS

As a reminder, this section has been considering two alleged problems with the interest-based rights account of our obligations regarding endangered species. The first claims that it cannot account for the wrong done when nonconscious species are driven to extinction. The second claims that it cannot explain the *special* obligations we have regarding endangered species. It has been argued so far that incorporating notions of superkilling or compensatory justice is not a satisfactory response to these objections. This section claims that these principles are also unnecessary. They are unnecessary because the interest-based rights approach can perfectly adequately explain the wrong of driving species of plants and insects to extinction, as well as the nature of our special obligations to members of endangered species. It can do so on the basis of the interests and rights of sentient beings.

Let us start with the destruction of species whose members are nonconscious, such as plants and insects. There is an excellent case against such destruction based on the prima facie rights of sentient individuals not to be made to suffer and not to be killed. For example, it is obvious that sentient animals—including human beings—depend on plants and insects for their well-being: as sources of food, as sources of medicine, as sources of shelter, as sources of camouflage, and so on.[24] This point is driven home by recent fears over the impact of the decline of pollinators, such as honeybees, on global food supplies.[25] Obviously, then, the extinction of a species of plant or insect can have a deleterious impact on sentient animals. Moreover, many of these impacts are difficult to predict. Because of such effects on sentient animals, there is a good prima facie reason not to drive species of nonconscious entities to extinction.

However, some environmentalists might consider this response to be unsatisfactory. They would regard it as unsatisfactory because it makes our obligation to preserve nonconscious species *contingent*. Thus if it could be shown that a species provided no benefit to sentient individuals, or even that it were inimical to the well-being of sentient individuals, then all else being equal, that species could permissibly be destroyed. For some environmental ethicists, this makes our obligations with respect to species insufficiently stringent. They argue that all species have an *intrinsic value* that cannot be reduced to their value to other beings.[26] As such, they argue that species are very much like great works of art, whose value derives from the intrinsic properties of the work, and not from the appreciation of those who view them.[27]

But we should be extremely cautious about this kind of reasoning. Appeals to the intrinsic value of natural entities—and indeed of works of art—have a tendency to be indeterminate. For if the value of an entity is entirely independent of the appreciation of the valuer, then how can we know that the *Mona Lisa* has value, whereas the tissue I have blown my nose on does not? Or even more pertinently for this investigation, how can we know that yellow orchids are a species worth preserving, whereas the AIDS virus is not? Of course, none of this is to deny that species or works of art have value; it is simply to recognize that this value—in order to be meaningful and determinate—must ultimately derive from an entity who can experience that value. That is why we can and should say that orchids are worth preserving, but that the AIDS virus is not.

What, then, of our supposed *special* obligations to members of endangered species? Can the approach defended in this chapter support the environmentalists' view that our obligations to preserve members of endangered species are stronger than our obligations to preserve abundant entities? When it comes to our obligations with respect to nonconscious entities, we can say, using the type of argument sketched above, that our obligation to preserve such entities depends on their contribution to the well-being of sentient individuals. Thus we may often have a stronger obligation to preserve rare plants than we do to preserve abundant plants, if the loss of the former can be shown to have a much more harmful impact on sentient animals. But this cannot be taken to mean that we *always* have a special and stronger obligation to preserve nonconscious endangered species. If, for example, entities from such a species can be shown to have a limited or even deleterious impact on the well-being of sentient animals, then there is no good reason to see ourselves as having a special obligation to preserve them.

This still leaves the question of endangered species of *sentient* animals. Is it plausible to say that we have special obligations to preserve rarer sentient animals? Such a claim could perhaps be supported if those rare animals could be shown to have a *stronger* right to life compared to animals of abundant species. At first sight, however, it might seem rather strange to argue that rare animals do have a stronger right to life. For one, it is unclear whether the very idea of a stronger right makes much sense. As we have seen throughout this book, once an interest of an individual is shown to be sufficient to impose a duty on another when all other considerations are taken into account, a concrete right is established. Crucially, that concrete right tells us what finally ought to be done: it cannot be outweighed by some set of other considerations, for they have already been accounted for! Saying, then, that one concrete right can be weaker or stronger than another concrete right does not make much sense. All concrete rights seem to be equally strong and compelling.

Perhaps the issue is whether rare animals have a stronger prima facie right to life than abundant animals have. That is, the issue is whether these rare animals can have their concrete right to life established more easily than abundant animals can, when all else is equal. I do believe that this is often the case. Importantly, however, this is not because rarer animals necessarily have any stronger interest in continued life themselves. The interest that animals have in continued life depends on their opportunities for pleasurable experiences in the future, as well as their psychological continuity over time. Whether animals belong to a rare or abundant species does not seem to affect either of these issues in any way that can be generalized. That is, it seems hard to provide reason to conclude that rarer animals necessarily have more (or less) to gain from continued life in comparison to abundant animals. Nevertheless it must be remembered that an animal's right to life is not established solely by the strength of its interest in continued life: all other relevant considerations also have to be taken into account. And two considerations support the claim that it is often easier to establish the concrete right to life of a rarer animal than it is of an abundant one, when all else is equal.

First, it has been pointed out that wiping out endangered species of sentient animals wipes out a source of awe and wonderment to future human beings.[28] After all, it seems sensible to acknowledge that future humans have an interest in living in a world with a rich abundance of biodiversity for aesthetic, spiritual, and recreational reasons. Second, as has been pointed out before, human and nonhuman animals are not isolated entities, but depend on creatures of their own species and other species to live well. Thus when we kill an animal, the harm inflicted will not be isolated to that animal alone: the animal's dependent kin may suffer, and the animal's social group may suffer. Importantly, if the numbers of that animal's species are dwindling, other species in that animal's ecosystem may suffer. For instance, it is widely assumed that the poisoning of prairie dogs in North America has led to the demise of their natural predator, the endangered black-footed ferret. These so-called cascade effects alert us to the fact that destroying one species of sentient animal will often lead to the harming of other species of sentient animal. Because of these two factors, I believe that we can legitimately say that the prima facie right to life of a rare animal is often stronger than that of an abundant one.

In sum, the interest-based rights approach can explain our obligations not to destroy nonconscious species and can account for the nature of our special obligations to members of endangered species. Crucially, it can do so without invoking notions of superkilling or compensatory justice—all it needs to do is to point to the interests and rights of sentient individuals. Sentient individuals have compelling interests in not suffering the harms caused when plants and animals are driven to extinction, and this gives us a powerful reason to preserve such organisms. Clearly, however, those reasons we have are undoubtedly *contingent*: they depend on the interests of those who will be affected by such loss of life. This should not be looked upon as a fault in the theory, however. Rather than making it too weak or too shallow, it simply makes the account plausible, meaningful, and determinate.

Therapeutic Hunting and Interest-Based Rights

The chapter so far has claimed that the interest-based animal rights theory defended in this book imposes strict environmental obligations on us. In the previous section the objection that this theory does not adequately deal with our obligations with respect to endangered species was anticipated, examined, and refuted. In this section a related but different objection is anticipated, examined, and refuted. Environmentalists have criticized other theories of animal rights on the basis that they make so-called therapeutic hunting impermissible. Therapeutic hunting generally refers to that form of killing animals that is done not for entertainment, trophies, subsistence, or cultural reasons, but to manage wildlife. Simply put, therapeutic hunting refers to those policies of killing wild animals that aim to prevent overpopulation and eradicate or minimize nonnative species. This section examines our obligations with respect to overpopulated and nonnative species in turn. In both contexts it is argued that when all things are considered, individual animals possess a concrete right not to be killed by therapeutic hunting.

OVERPOPULATION

Largely because of the decline of natural predators, which in turn is usually the result of hunting by humans, it is claimed that some species of wild animal can become overpopulated. A species is usually said to be overpopulated in two scenarios: first, where so many offspring are produced that the habitat cannot feed them all, the result being that many members of that species die of starvation; and second, where so many offspring are produced that serious environmental degradation takes place. In the UK the classic example of an overpopulated species is the deer of Scotland, 77,399 of whom were killed (culled) in 2006–7.[29] What are the implications of the rights theory of this book for such therapeutic hunting?

First off, it is important to acknowledge that overpopulated sentient animals, like deer, have a prima facie right not to be killed. Like any other sentient animal, these animals have a clear and compelling interest in continued life in order that they may experience future pleasurable experiences—an interest that cannot justifiably be overridden without good reason. The crucial question is whether these animals have a concrete right not to be killed given the particular issues at stake in overpopulation. One reason to think that they might not is on the basis of overall harm. For example, Gary E. Varner has argued that animal rights theorists of all stripes should support some forms of therapeutic hunting. This is on the basis that in many cases it is plausible that fewer animals overall will suffer and die if populations are regulated through therapeutic hunting than if "natural attrition is allowed to take its course."[30]

But even if it is conceded that some forms of therapeutic hunting will result in less animal suffering and fewer animal deaths overall—which is by no means obvious—that certainly does not establish that over-populated animals have no concrete right not to be killed. As we have seen already in this book, rights act as brakes on purely aggregative analysis of this kind. Rights are actually meant to set limits on what can be done to individuals in the name of aggregate welfare. So if this is what rights are meant to do, and if overpopulated sentient animals have prima facie rights to life, we need to ask why it is that these animals ought to be sacrificed for the sake of reducing overall harm. After all, I cannot think of any sensible thinker who would condone the killing of overpopulated *humans* for the greater good. And indeed this question is apt because many humans are overpopulated as defined above: they breed more than their habitat can sustain, and they are causing serious environmental degradation. It makes sense to say that such overpopulated humans should not be killed because they have a right not to be sacrificed in this way. Why, then, not say the same for overpopulated animals?

To his credit, Varner recognizes this objection and tackles it head on. He claims that there is an important difference between killing overpop-ulated animals and killing overpopulated human beings: "There would, I think, be a good reason for not culling overpopulated humans: it is possible for any normal adult human both to understand the gravity of the situation and to alter his or her behaviour accordingly. A human being can recognize and act on the obligation of individuals to avoid contributing to overpopulation; a deer, an elephant, or a water buffalo cannot."[31] However, it is unclear what moral significance this ability to understand and act on an obligation actually has. Furthermore, plenty of human beings do not have the capacity to understand and act on such an obligation: infants and individuals with severe mental disabilities being the obvious examples. The logic of Varner's theory seems to make it permissible to therapeutically hunt these groups of humans.

Another way to claim that killing overpopulated animals is permissible but killing overpopulated humans is not, is to argue that human beings simply have a stronger interest in continuing to live than animals do. Chapter 3 argued that ordinarily this is the case: continued life is of more value to human persons than it is to nonhuman nonpersons. But we also saw in that chapter that not all human beings are persons, and thus not all human beings have this equivalently strong interest in continued life. Some human beings have an interest in continued life simply on the basis of the future pleasurable experiences that it affords—not because of any long-term goals they have, and not because of any immediate satisfaction that the prospect of future life provides them. Given this, we are once again faced with a judgment about the strength of the interest of nonpersons in continued life. Do we judge it as sufficient to impose on us a duty not to kill human nonpersons for the sake of aggregate well-being, or do we judge it as insufficient? If we regard it as sufficient—which is my judgment and no doubt the judgment of most others—then the equivalent interest of nonhumans must also be regarded as sufficient. In other words, the interest that overpopulated animals have in not being killed is sufficient to impose on us a duty not to kill them, all things considered.

Importantly, this claim is bolstered by questioning the supposed dichotomy at the heart of the argument from overall harm. For the argument suggests that we either cull these animals or do absolutely nothing. But while certain animal rights theorists do advocate a hands-off approach with respect to animals in the wild, it is certainly not intrinsic to animal rights theories.[32] And the problem with doing nothing is that it ignores the very real harms that can be inflicted on animals—harms that we might be able to prevent. Importantly, the harms of overpopulation can be prevented with measures that fall short of culling. The existence of such measures undermines the very idea that therapeutic hunting is necessary to reduce overall harm. But what are those measures?

One method to prevent the harms of overpopulation is capture and relocation. That is, part of the population of abundant animals can be caught, removed, and placed in new territories where their numbers are much lower. Unfortunately, even ignoring the stress and suffering this can cause to the captured animals, such relocation programs have not proved to have been very successful. Often relocation programs have resulted in the death of the relocated animals, or the death of members of other species who reside there.[33]

The better option, then, is to adopt the same measures we employ to deal with human overpopulation: contraception. The widespread availability and use of contraception within human societies allows overpopulation to be dealt with effectively and without harm, by lowering birth rates. And just as contraception can do this for humans, so it can do so for animals. Controlling species numbers through contraception violates no animal rights and has the potential to alleviate the very real harms that overpopulation can cause.

Unfortunately, and as proponents of therapeutic hunting are quick to point out, contracepting wild animals is not without its problems. The first problem is finding an effective contraceptive treatment for the specific species. Clearly it is imperative that contraceptives are found that do not cause harmful side-effects or harmful changes in behavior. However, success has been achieved in this regard, with effective contraceptives being developed for a number of species, including horses, deer, captive exotic species, water buffalo, wapiti, and African elephants.[34] The second problem is delivery of the contraceptive. For even if it is known that the contraceptive is effective for that species because of trials on captive animals, that still leaves the problem of administering the drug effectively to animals in the wild. But once again, success has been achieved in this regard with applications to such free-ranging animals as wild horses, white-tailed deer, and elephants.[35]

Without doubt, the greatest problem facing wildlife contraception is cost. Drug companies have little incentive to develop species-specific contraceptives when so few numbers are involved.[36] Furthermore, purchasing those drugs is expensive, as is the employment of large numbers of skilled shooters to deliver the contraceptive darts to sufficient numbers of animals to control the population. Given these costs, and given the scant regard for the interests of animals in most modern societies, it is little wonder that overpopulation is usually dealt with simply by shooting the abundant animals.

But does the cost of wildlife contraception count against recognizing the right to life of overpopulated animals? It certainly does not. Just as we do not kill overpopulated humans when it will save us money, so we should not kill overpopulated animals. The interests of both in continued life are real and compelling and should not be overridden simply because it will save us money.

In any case, and to provide a final argument in favor of the right to life of these overpopulated animals, we have reason to question therapeutic hunting as an effective means of long-term population control. For certain studies have shown that killing overpopulated species simply results in a better environment for the remaining population to breed in, and thus a rapid population recovery. The use of contraception, on the other hand, helps to maintain that population at a lower level for a much longer time.[37] As such, it can be argued to be in the interests of all groups to invest the time and resources in the development and employment of contraceptives to deal with the overpopulation of wild animals.

NONNATIVE SPECIES

There are some species that are regarded as *necessarily* overpopulated, irrespective of their numbers. Many wildlife managers consider nonnative species to be a serious threat to the balance and health of indigenous wildlife, and thus to be justifiable targets of therapeutic hunting. The question for this section is whether nonnative animals, such as the brushtail possums of New Zealand, the European rabbits of Australia, and the gray squirrels of the UK, have a concrete right not to be killed even in the context of the grave harms they pose to indigenous wildlife.

The first thing to consider in addressing the question is whether the premise that these nonnative species cause harm is accurate. It is beyond doubt that the introduction of a new species will change the dynamics of an ecosystem, but ecosystems change through evolutionary processes anyway. What is it that makes these evolutionary changes harmless, but the introductions of nonnative species harmful? As we have seen, claims that invoke the "natural" by way of explanation are dubious in the extreme. Perhaps, then, the harm caused by nonnative species lies in the types of changes they make to the ecosystems they join. Indeed, many claim that nonnative species are the second biggest cause of extinctions after habitat destruction. Moreover, as we saw earlier in the chapter, the extinction of species can have a very harmful impact on sentient individuals, including human beings. Since nonnative species cause extinction, and since extinctions harm sentient individuals, it appears that there is good reason to control or even eradicate nonnative species.

However, the notion that nonnative species are a major cause of extinctions is contested.[38] Some authors have claimed that the impact of nonnative species varies and certainly does not always lead to the extinction of indigenous species. They point out that statistics from the IUCN Red List, which documents the extinct, endangered, and threatened species of the world, show that of those species with data, only 6 percent are listed as being threatened because of alien species.[39] And yet others have claimed that this result is from limited data, and that when other sources are used to examine the causes of extinct species on the IUCN List, of those with data, 54 percent include the effects of alien species.[40]

This is not the place to attempt to resolve such a complex debate. But what seems clear is that the effects of nonnative species are not uniform but will vary from context to context. So let us focus on those situations where it can be established that nonnative sentient individuals are threatening to wipe out the indigenous species of an area, and that such effects will diminish overall well-being. In such circumstances, do those nonnative animals have a concrete right not to be killed, all things considered?

In light of the arguments presented previously in this section, it seems that it is only sensible to recognize that they do. It is not clear why these animals should be denied the right to life simply because they are nonnative. Their interests in continued life are pressing and should be given due consideration, just like those of any other sentient animal. Simply stating that their interests count for less because they are "alien" is extremely prejudicial. We would certainly not countenance similar arguments being used to subordinate the interests of nonnatives in the human context. And while it is true that in the types of situations under consideration, these nonnative animals threaten to reduce overall welfare, we must remember that we have measures to deal with these potential harms that fall short of killing. As we have already seen in this chapter, our options are not "kill" or "do nothing." We can invest in the development of contraceptives and the delivery of these contraceptives to effectively lower the birth rates of these animals. Just like other overpopulated animals, nonnative animals possess the concrete right not to be therapeutically hunted.

This chapter has applied the interest-based rights approach to the question of our environmental obligations. It has been claimed that our environmental obligations are properly owed to sentient individuals, and not to such entities as plants, species, and ecosystems. This is because the latter types of entities lack the capacity for their lives to go well or badly for themselves and thus have no interests. While some environmentalists will argue that this welfare-centric environmental ethic is too weak, it has been claimed that the interests and rights of sentient individuals ground significant obligations on our part, especially in relation to such issues as deforestation, the burning of fossil fuels, and the protection of endangered species. It is quite true that all these obligations are founded on the well-being of sentient individuals. As such, it is also true that when environmentally destructive policies can be shown to cause no harm, they may well be permissible. But rather than being a damning fault of the theory, this is something that makes it plausible. It explains why, for example, there is no wrong in destroying harmful viruses. Some will object that granting animals rights in this way prevents proper wildlife management—where wildlife management includes so-called therapeutic hunting. But wildlife management does not need to include such hunting. It is simply the cheap and easy option. Just as we do not deal with the overpopulation of human beings with mass culls, so we should not deal with the overpopulation of sentient animals with mass culls. Contraception serves as a way of reducing the harm caused by overpopulation—whether human or animal—and ought to be invested in for the sake of the interests and rights of sentient animals.

Eight

Animals and Cultural Practices

This book has argued that animals have prima facie moral rights not to be killed and not to be made to suffer. These rights are prima facie because in some contexts, other considerations—such as competing interests or the burdens imposed by the putative duty—will count against the establishment of either right. Given that circumstances and competing interests are so important to the grounding of these animal rights, it is crucial to look at one last controversial context in which animals are used: cultural practices.

Some cultural groups have claimed that they should be allowed to continue with their traditional practices even when it appears that such practices cause harm to animals, and even when such practices violate the government's existing animal welfare legislation. Several such claims have been made in recent years. Foxhunters in the UK have claimed that a ban on foxhunting is an attack on the rural way of life.[1] Native peoples in North America, Greenland, and Russia have argued that bans on hunting whales threaten their very existence. Jewish and Muslim groups in several states claim that legislation requiring the stunning of farm animals prior to slaughter violates their religious freedom. Representatives of the Santeria religion have gone to the United States Supreme Court arguing that state legislation banning animal sacrifice prevents them from following the traditions of their faith. Advocates of bullfighting in Spain have claimed that attempts to reform the practice to make it more humane involve importing "Anglo-Saxon prejudices."[2]

All such calls have been controversial and have been opposed by campaigners for animals. Moreover, and interestingly, these cultural claims have achieved markedly different levels of success. For example, on the one hand, Jewish and Muslim communities are exempted from UK law that requires animals to be stunned in order that they are rendered unconscious before they are slaughtered. This is because "the Government is committed to respect for the rights of religious groups and accepts that an insistence on a pre-cut or immediate post-cut stun would not be compatible with the requirements of religious slaughter by Jewish and Muslim groups."[3] On the other hand, the UK government has not seen fit to overturn or allow exemptions to recent legislation on banning hunting with dogs, despite hunters' claims that it is a traditional cultural practice. In fact, in a direct response to such claims, the Department for Environment, Food and Rural Affairs (DEFRA) publicly states, "There is no right to be cruel."[4]

Perhaps the UK government's differing reaction to these two issues is based on there being a relevant difference between the two types of claim. After all, cultural groups usually assert one of three quite different types of argument when making their case. The first type is the one often made by foxhunters: the human interest in culture trumps the interests of animals. For it might be argued that what is at stake here is something more than the therapeutic benefits garnered by animal experimentation, the pleasures of the palate offered by animal agriculture, or the trivial amusement we gain from using animals in entertainment. Rather the very integrity and survival of a cultural group are in question. Given this, it might be claimed that animal rights not to be killed and not to be made to suffer are *not* established in the context of culture, because the rival human interests are so strong and pressing.

The second type of claim made by cultural groups invokes religion, and this is clearly the type of argument made by Jewish and Islamic groups regarding animal slaughter. In these claims, groups argue that treating animals in certain ways and using them for certain purposes is integral to their religion. Thus to prevent such treatment or to restrict such uses is effectively to undermine the ability of religious believers to practice their faith. As in the case of culture above, it might well be argued that the human interest in freedom of religion trumps the interests of animals, thus negating the ascription of animal rights in this context.

A final type of claim made by some cultural groups is that it is illegitimate to judge one culture's practices by a different culture's ethical standard. In short, some groups claim that so-called Western standards of animal welfare and rights simply do not apply to them: they have their own ethical standards that relate to animals that cannot legitimately be judged by outsiders. This chapter will not discuss this type of cultural relativist claim, for it rests on two implausible assumptions.

First, accusing animal rights theories of being Western is odd given the strong distinction that Western religions and philosophy have traditionally made between what we owe to humans and what is owed with respect to nonhumans. Indeed, given the previous discussions of animal experimentation, factory farms, genetic engineering, pet keeping, and so on, it is clear that this dichotomy of duties still permeates Western societies, practices, and institutions.

Second, the argument also assumes that ethical standards are entirely relative to the culture in which they are formed. As many philosophers have argued, this ethical relativism can serve to shield all sorts of horrific acts and practices from examination—and the practices of all communities should be the legitimate subjects of reflection and debate.[5] This kind of relativism also mistakenly supposes that cultures are internally uniform, possessing shared standards and norms that all members subscribe to and are happy to follow. In reality, communities comprise a diverse range of views and values that change over time, meaning that we can never establish the ultimate set of norms ascribed to by community X or Y.[6]

In light of these devastating problems, cultural relativist claims will not be addressed further in the chapter. This is not to say, of course, that context is irrelevant to working out what we owe to animals. As this book has repeatedly emphasized, context is crucial to the rights of animals, and the interest-based approach seeks to recognize this by considering all the relevant considerations of an issue when establishing rights. This kind of context-sensitivity, however, is quite different from ethical relativism. It does not prevent us from examining and evaluating any practice by any cultural group.

Given all this, we are left to consider whether the human interests in culture and freedom of religion should take precedence over the interests of animals in continued life and avoiding pain. If they should, then the animal rights not to be killed and not to be made to suffer are not established in the context of cultural practices involving animals. To make this assessment, the interests in culture and freedom of religion are examined in turn. The chapter argues that while the human interests in culture and religious freedom are strong, they do not trump the pressing interests of animals. Indeed, the chapter claims that the animal interests in not being killed and in not being made to suffer are sufficient, all things considered, to impose duties on us not to harm animals in the name of culture. Finally, it is worth noting that the chapter also claims that we should be wary of overestimating the conflict between animal rights and culture. Abiding by the rights theory outlined in this book will not lead to the destruction of vast numbers of cultures, nor will it prevent significant numbers of people from practicing their faith.

The Interest in Culture

The claim of the book is that animals have interests in not being killed and not being made to suffer, but these ground concrete rights only when those interests can be shown to be sufficient, all things considered, to impose duties on others. As noted above, it might be claimed that in the context of culture, these animal interests are insufficient to ground rights. In other words, it could be claimed that the human interest in culture trumps the interests of animals. This section assesses just such a claim. First, the strength of the human interest in culture is considered. Second, the competing interests at stake in cultural practices that cause pain to animals are examined. Third, the competing interests at stake in cultural practices that kill animals are evaluated. And finally, the question of whether prohibiting cultural practices will lead to the annihilation of some cultures is addressed. The section concludes by arguing that although culture is of great value to humans, it does not trump animals' interests in avoiding pain or in continued life. Furthermore, it claims that because it is extremely unlikely that any cultural group's identity is defined solely in terms of its practices relating to animals, the cessation of these practices will not lead to the destruction of cultures.

THE STRENGTH OF THE HUMAN INTEREST IN CULTURE

Virtually every philosopher who has addressed the topic of culture acknowledges that living within a cultural context is of great importance to the well-being of human beings. Humans are clearly social animals, and culture provides a context within which they can flourish: humans can pursue projects, plans, and ideals that would never be available to them in isolation. For example, this very project of outlining the rights of animals depends very much on a culture in which intellectual endeavor and ethical debate are valued and supported. In this way my culture increases my well-being by helping me pursue and realize a project of mine.

However, it is not just the support that culture offers to one's *personal* plans that contributes to well-being; individuals also often take great satisfaction from living by the *communal* norms of their culture. Thus religious believers benefit from being able to worship with individuals who share their faith, ethnic communities benefit from performing customs that celebrate their shared heritage, individuals within nation-states benefit from taking part in the joint support of national sporting teams, and so on. Clearly, then, these communal cultural practices make an important contribution to the well-being of human individuals. And this is no doubt true for those cultural practices that involve the use of animals. But do such practices violate animals' rights?

From the arguments presented so far in the book, its implications regarding cultural groups simply *using* animals should be clear. Animals have no fundamental interest in liberty and thus have no interest in not being used for certain purposes. Thus if a cultural practice involves the use of an animal and that use does not cause the animal pain or death, then that practice is permissible, other things being equal. So if a cultural group claims that racing pigeons, riding horses, using dogs to pull sleighs, and so on are traditional practices of theirs, such uses of animals are permissible so long as they do not cause the animals to suffer and do not result in their death. However, what about those cultural practices that do cause harm to animals?

In the first instance, the interest that an individual has in performing a cultural practice does not serve as an absolute trump that always takes priority over any competing interest. For example, imagine a cultural group claiming that a practice of theirs is "honor killing," where women are murdered for supposedly bringing shame on their family. No sensible person would suggest that the group's interest in performing honor killings should take priority over the interests of the potential victims in continued life. That is, surely we can all agree that in this instance the potential victim's interest in continued life trumps the perpetrators' interest in performing the cultural practice.

However, perhaps this conclusion is more controversial than is being made out. Chandran Kukathas, for example, has argued that freedom of association is of such value to humans that groups who have freely associated should be left to run their affairs and conduct their practices with the minimum restriction.[7] In one paper he argues that these restrictions should be so minimal that "there would in such a society be (the possibility of) communities which bring up children unschooled and illiterate; which enforce arranged marriages; which deny conventional medical care to their members (including children); and which inflict cruel and 'unusual' punishment."[8] Maybe, then, Kukathas's framework provides a means to argue that the human interest in culture is so great that it can justify practices involving "cruel punishments" such as honor killings.

But on closer examination, we can see that even Kukathas—who gives such importance to the value of free association—does not go so far as to sanction all and any cultural practices. For example, he writes that group members are bound and restrained by the norms of the wider communities to which they belong.[9] Thus honor killings would not in fact be permissible if conducted by a cultural group residing in the UK because wider UK values presumably forbid such practices.

Unfortunately, with this type of reasoning, Kukathas seems to be taking us into strange and dangerous territory. In effect he is arguing that honor killing is impermissible only when a community (like the UK) says it is. This means that honor killing would be perfectly permissible in a culture that values its version of moral propriety over the lives of women. But such an argument is bizarre. Honor killing is wrong *everywhere* and should not be permitted *anywhere*. This is simply because a woman has an interest in continuing to live that is stronger, is more compelling, and trumps her family's interest in avoiding shame or ridicule. After all, individuals usually get over feelings of shame or being ostracized, and if they cannot, they can still lead lives of extremely high quality. However, there is no hope of overcoming death, and thus no opportunity to have a decent quality of life.

The human interest in performing a cultural practice cannot sensibly be considered to be all-conquering. Sometimes, when all interests and relevant considerations are taken into account, a cultural practice can be judged to violate rights. What remains, then, is to examine whether there are any cultural practices that violate the rights of sentient animals.

CULTURAL PRACTICES THAT CAUSE ANIMALS TO SUFFER

Some cultural practices involve the gross infliction of pain on animals. For example, take the Indian equivalent of bullfighting, which takes place in the state of Tamil Nadu. *Jallikattu,* as the practice is known, differs from Spanish bullfighting in two crucial respects. First, the primary purpose of jallikattu is not to fight with the bulls, but to grab prizes that have been tied to their horns. Second, no bulls are intentionally killed in the Indian practice, unlike in Spanish bullfighting. Despite these differences, however, it is perfectly clear that just as bulls suffer from bullfighting, so too do they suffer from jallikattu. Individuals will go to great lengths to obtain the prizes that are tied to the bulls, tormenting them, clinging to their horns, and throwing stones at them. The suffering that the hundreds of bulls used in jallikattu endure from anxiety, harassment, and injury is without question. However, it is also clear that many of the people of Tamil Nadu have a strong interest in participating in this practice. Indeed, they even fight with one another for a chance to approach the bull and put their own health and lives at risk for the sake of a prize. In fact, in 2005 five people were killed and over two hundred were injured during the fights.[10] Moreover, organizers of jallikattu claim that it is a sacrosanct tradition that has been carried out for over two thousand years. Given the strong interest that the people of Tamil Nadu have in this cultural tradition, it might be argued that the bulls' interest in not suffering is insufficient to ground a duty on the participants to stop the practice. Do bulls have no right not to be made to suffer from the practice of jallikattu?

Although the interest of the people of Tamil Nadu in jallikattu is undoubtedly strong, it is difficult to see how it can take priority over the interest of the bulls in not suffering. Recall from chapter 3 on animal experimentation that suffering is a serious harm for both humans and animals. That chapter argued that while humans' extra cognitive capacities might sometimes make them capable of more extreme forms of suffering, such capacities can also provide them with the opportunity to rationalize their pain and to take comfort from other goods and projects that are of value to them.

With all this in mind, imagine a cultural group who practiced a "human jallikattu" where prizes are tied to individuals, who are then mauled, beaten, and generally tormented against their will. Every reasonable person would condemn this practice for violating the fundamental rights of the victims in not suffering. And such condemnation would stand even if the practice were ancient and greatly enjoyed by the cultural group. But if we recognize that humans have a right not to suffer from such a cultural practice, can we legitimately deny it to bulls?

One possible way of maintaining the human right not to suffer in such a way while denying it to bulls would be on the basis that the human's interest in not suffering from jallikattu is much greater than the bull's. For it might be argued that the human victim will suffer more from the practice because of added feelings of shame, humiliation, and rejection by the group around him. Personally, however, I'm not convinced that bulls in jallikattu do not also have such feelings. But even assuming that they do not, it can be replied that this additional suffering of the human victim is balanced by the fact that he is likely to understand the value of the cultural practice, that the suffering will soon be over, and that ultimately he will survive. A bull has no such resources to draw on and will be totally consumed by terror, fear, and pain. Therefore, it is only reasonable to regard the bull's and the human's interest in not suffering as being roughly equivalent. Since the interest of humans is sufficient to ground a human right not to be made to suffer by cultural practices, the interest of bulls must also be sufficient to ground an equivalent animal right.

CULTURAL PRACTICES THAT KILL ANIMALS

It will be remembered that in chapter 3, during the discussion of animal experimentation, it was argued that the animal interest in continued life is ordinarily weaker than that of humans. Perhaps, then, we might argue that the interest of individuals in performing cultural practices, strong as it is, trumps animals' interest in continued life. This would make cultural practices that kill animals permissible, all else being equal. Of course, things are not always equal! And one problem comes from the fact that those cultural practices that involve killing animals also invariably involve the infliction of pain. For example, hunting foxes with hounds ends with the fox being ripped apart by the hounds. Even though this means of killing is now banned in the UK, meaning that the fox must be killed "humanely," it would be absurd to claim that the fox does not suffer from being chased for miles by dozens of humans, horses, and dogs. Whaling is another practice in which the primary purpose is death, but the infliction of pain is inevitable. Indeed, a study by Steve Kestin found that some whales live for up to an hour after being harpooned, and Kestin claims that he cannot "currently visualise an acceptably humane way of killing whales."[11] Moreover, while most bullfights culminate in death (including those in Portugal, where the killing is not conducted in the ring), the majority of the spectacle itself involves tormenting and injuring the bull. In a Spanish-style bullfight, for example, lances are speared into the bull, sticks with harpoon points are driven into the bull, and the bull is made to chase and circle his agitators until exhaustion before the matador finally kills him with a sword. Cultural practices that involve killing animals also involve the infliction of extreme pain on animals, violate their rights, and are impermissible as such.

However, let us consider the possibility of a cultural practice that kills animals but does not involve the infliction of pain. For example, imagine a group that wants to kill a pig as part of some kind of public celebration, which ultimately culminates in a hog roast. Imagine further that this practice involves the infliction of no pain on the pig: the pig is not tormented, harassed, or injured before his death, and he is killed in a manner that causes no pain, say, by a shot through his head while he is sleeping. If this group has a strong interest in this cultural practice, might it trump the pig's interest in continued life? It is difficult to believe that it would. While it is true that an animal's interest in continued life is ordinarily weaker than that of most humans, it is still strong and must be considered fairly. Indeed, chapter 3 argued that some humans, such as young infants, have an interest in continued life that is comparable in strength to that of animals. Given this, consider the plausible notion of a cultural group claiming that infanticide is a traditional custom of theirs. They might argue that as part of the ceremony a child must be taken to a special spot and sacrificed painlessly. Without doubt this child's interest in continued life is weaker than that of most adult humans. Furthermore, the group has a strong interest in performing this practice; imagine, for example, that the child's parents have willingly consented to it or will even perform the sacrifice themselves. Do these considerations mean that the child has no right not to be killed in such a ritual?

No, they do not. The interest of infants in continued life is ordinarily weaker than that of adult humans. However, "weaker" does not mean nonexistent. Moreover, the interest of infants in continuing to live is sufficient to ground a moral right to life even when there are very strong competing interests. For example, the therapeutic benefits offered by conducting deadly experimentation on infants might be huge, and certainly more beneficial than relying on results obtained from rats and mice. However, chapter 3 claimed that these potential benefits do not negate infants' rights to life in that context. Accordingly, it seems only reasonable to propose that an infant's right to life is also established even when a group has a strong desire to sacrifice that infant as part of a cultural practice. Furthermore, and to be consistent, if an infant's interest in continued life is sufficiently strong to establish a duty on us not to kill her in cultural practices, an animal's interest in continued life must also usually be considered sufficiently strong. On this basis the pig execution would ordinarily violate the animal's rights, and so the hog roast can be considered impermissible.

THE DESTRUCTION OF CULTURES?

If animals have concrete moral rights not to be killed and not to be made to suffer by cultural practices, what impact does this conclusion have for the future of particular cultural groups? Some communities have claimed that prohibiting such practices is tantamount to destroying their cultures. In light of this, and since the existence of culture is so important to the well-being of humans, we might still have a reason to deny these animal rights in the context of the cultural use of animals.

One way of refuting such an argument would be to claim that while the existence of culture is important to the well-being of individuals, the existence of *any particular* culture is not so important. Thus if one culture dies out, this is not problematic as long as there is another culture to take its place. So, for example, it might be claimed that we need not be concerned if the traditional rural way of life in Britain dies out, since individuals living in the country can adopt a more modern British culture. This argument essentially claims that it is the general context of culture that matters for individuals' well-being, rather than the particular details of any culture.

This type of rebuttal is unconvincing for two reasons. First, it can plausibly be argued that the details of culture *do* matter, that the existence of different cultures is a good thing in itself, and that such diversity is valuable. Second, and more importantly for the purpose of delineating interests, individuals usually have close bonds with and interests in their *own* culture. Having to switch cultures often incurs considerable costs to one's well-being.[12] Thus if ending certain cultural practices leads to the destruction of some cultures, this is a serious cause for concern.

However, we can question whether prohibiting certain uses of animals really will result in cultural destruction. In fact, in the vast majority of cases, claiming that an entire culture will be destroyed by the prevention of certain practices relating to animals is something of an overstatement. As Brian Barry writes: "We can at least reject the idea that the elements in a way of life are so rigidly locked together that no part can change without causing the whole to disintegrate."[13] For example, it would be bizarre to suggest that the Spanish culture is so bound up with the practice of bullfighting that it would simply disintegrate if bullfighting ended.

Having said this, however, several native peoples in Greenland, Canada, the United States, and Russia do claim that whaling is so central to their culture that to prevent it would mean destruction. I believe that we should treat such claims with great caution. After all, in 1999 the Makah tribe in the United States claimed that they had a "cultural right" to kill whales—but they did so having survived as a people without having killed a whale for seventy years.[14] Nevertheless, it is not too far-fetched to imagine that there *might be* a community or communities whose group identity is so bound up with whaling that to prevent it would threaten their very existence. In such a case, should such groups be permitted to harm animals through whaling?

First, we must ascertain just how this group is under threat, and separate the different possible means of destruction: destruction of groups via starvation, destruction from destitution, and destruction of a cultural way of life. Often these three types of threat are conflated when whaling peoples make their claims. Given this, if a group needs to kill whales for *subsistence*, then the rights theory defended here permits such killing. As chapter 4 argued, when the killing of animals for subsistence was discussed, the animal interest in continued life is not sufficient to establish an animal right to life when human survival is at stake. We need not sacrifice ourselves for the sake of animals' interests. However, if a community kills whales because whale meat is their only source of income, then such killing does violate animal rights and is impermissible as such. Once again, chapter 4 argued in the discussion of animal agriculture that economic benefit does not trump animals' interest in continued life. Both meat farmers and whalers are able to change their activity and find new sources of income. Clearly this will be costly and sometimes painful. But it is a price worth paying to meet the compelling interests of these animals in not suffering terribly and in not being killed.

But what if a community kills whales not primarily for subsistence or money but because its members define themselves entirely as whaling people, and because whaling is their only way of life?[15] In other words, to prevent this group from whaling would mean that a discrete cultural community is lost, and that the individuals comprising that community might suffer a crisis of identity and thus a drastic and severe diminishment of well-being. First, the point must be made that although cultural diversity is valuable, it is not valuable at any cost. If some cultures are defined fundamentally in terms of causing serious harm to others—and whaling is a serious infliction of harm—then the loss of such cultures cannot sensibly be considered regrettable in itself. Second, while it can be conceded that preventing the individuals of such a group from hunting whales would impose considerable costs on them, it is hard to believe that it would lead to a complete loss of their identity and the disintegration of their well-being. People change cultural communities all the time; and not only do such people routinely avoid irreversible breakdowns, they often flourish and achieve increased well-being.[16] A particular culture may be a source of well-being for individuals, but it is by no means the only source. Because of these two factors, even if preventing a cultural practice that causes harm to animals results in the loss of that culture, animals still possess rights not to be killed and not to be made to suffer.

To end this section, it will be useful to summarize its main points. The section has evaluated whether the human interest in culture trumps animals' interests in avoiding pain and in being killed. It has concluded that it does not. Although humans have a strong interest in living within a cultural context generally, and their own cultural context specifically, this does not excuse every possible cultural practice. Just as we would not let humans suffer intolerably in the name of culture, nor should we let animals. And just as we would not let human infants be killed in the name of culture, nor should we let animals. Some might argue that such restrictions on cultural practices will lead to the destruction of certain cultural communities. I am extremely skeptical of such arguments: it is difficult to think of any community whose entire identity is based on a particular use of animals. However, even if such a community could be found, it would still not mean that that community could permissibly harm animals. The loss of a culture that is defined entirely by the grave harm it causes to animals is not much of a loss; and humans can lead lives of extremely high quality even when they change cultures.

The Interest in Freedom of Religion

If the human interest in culture does not trump animals' interests, what about the interest humans have in religion? Freedom of religion is widely recognized to be a human right. It is rightly argued that individuals should not be persecuted or discriminated against because of their religion. Moreover, the right to religious freedom also means that individuals should ordinarily be free to practice their religion and live by the customs and values of their faith. However, it is clear that some religious practices violate the prima facie animal rights that have been outlined in this book. In light of this, we must examine whether the interest that humans have in religious freedom trumps the interests of animals.

At this stage one might claim that given the close connection between religion and culture, this interest does not merit separate attention. That is, we might simply argue that because the human interest in culture does not trump the interests of animals, nor can the interest in religious freedom. However, because some people have argued that the human interest in religion is of the highest order, and something stronger and more pressing than mere culture, a specific examination of the interest in religious freedom seems warranted.

In undertaking this examination, this section first briefly spells out the basis for the human interest in religious freedom and evaluates which religions actually *require* harm to be inflicted on animals. It then looks at some possible justifications for the idea that the interest in religion is special and merits priority. Third, the section assesses whether the interest in religious freedom should be considered stronger and worthy of priority on the basis of equal opportunity. Finally, it evaluates the claim that it is hypocritical and unfair to prevent religious groups from conducting their practices that harm animals when other harmful practices are ignored. Ultimately it is argued that none of these arguments justifies giving the human interest in religious freedom a special status and priority over the interests of animals. Thus, pending further evidence to the contrary, it is argued that animals have concrete rights not to be killed and made to suffer by religious practices.

FREEDOM OF RELIGION AND THE REQUIREMENT TO HARM ANIMALS

Previously in the book it has been claimed that most adult humans have a fundamental interest in liberty. As autonomous beings, humans have an interest in not being interfered with and in framing and pursuing their own conception of the good. Given that religion is very much a conception of the good, we can legitimately claim that freedom of religion is fundamental to human well-being. In other words, preventing someone from exercising their chosen religion and living by the terms of their faith is ordinarily a serious harm. Unfortunately, religious freedom sometimes leads to harm being caused to animals.

For example, consider the method of slaughtering animals for kosher and halal meat as advocated by Judaism and Islam, respectively. There has been much controversy around these practices, because stunning animals before slaughter—a requirement under UK and EU law for animal welfare reasons—is forbidden under Jewish and Islamic methods. Currently these religious groups are exempted from the requirement to stun before slaughter in the UK on the basis of freedom of religion.

But even though Jewish and Islamic leaders invoke religious freedom to defend and justify their exemption, such arguments are extremely dubious. This is because neither Judaism nor Islam *demands* that its followers slaughter animals to eat meat; vegetarianism is perfectly permissible under any plausible reading of either religion.[17] All that these faiths require is that *if* an animal is slaughtered to be eaten, then it must be killed in a particular way. Thus preventing Jews and Muslims from killing animals in the first place—as a prima facie application of this animal rights theory mandates—does not prevent free religious practice. Clearly this application would be burdensome to those Jews and Muslims who enjoy eating meat, as it would be burdensome to other individuals who enjoy eating meat, but it would not interfere with religious freedom.

That still leaves us to consider those religious practices that cause harm to animals and are *required* by the mandates of the faith. Interestingly, and also fortunately, these are few and far between. However, perhaps the clearest example is the animal sacrifice conducted by the Santeria religion. Paula Casal provides a useful summation of the religion's history and beliefs:

Santeria, or the Way of the Saints, is a syncretic religion from the nineteenth century. It originated when hundreds of thousands of the Yoruba people were brought as slaves from West Africa to Cuba, and conjoined Catholic iconography and sacraments to their traditional religion in order to escape persecution. Santeria now counts on 50–60,000 practitioners in Dade County, Southern Florida, and has many more in other states and countries. Santeros worship *ori-shas*, living spirits of African origin which, they suppose, can help people fulfil their destinies. Orishas are powerful but not immortal, and their survival depends on animal sacrifices.[18]

The exact numbers of animals slaughtered each year by the religion are unknown. However, one of its churches in Florida has estimated that it alone kills over ten thousand animals each year as part of its services, including goats, sheep, guinea pigs, ducks, and turtles.[19]

Without doubt, preventing these sacrifices would interfere with the religious freedom of Santeros, which is a key human interest. On what grounds, if any, could this interest of free religious practice trump the interests of the animals who are killed?

FREEDOM OF RELIGION AS A SPECIAL INTEREST

It might be claimed that the interest human beings have in freedom of religion merits priority because it is somehow special. Indeed, it is certainly undeniable that for many people in the world their religion is one of their most pressing concerns. To justify the idea that our interest in religion is special and thus merits being given priority, we need to point to something about it that differentiates it from other interests. Several candidates have been put forward in the literature that might make the interest in religion special. They run as follows: religion makes claims on the whole lives of believers; religion is based on immanent beliefs; religious-based desires are intense; religion provides a context for self-understanding; religion transmits ethical values; religious practice permits individual integrity; and finally, religion has been the focus of particularly acute acts of persecution and oppression.[20] Each of these candidates will be considered in turn.

First, it is pointed out that religious believers cannot turn their values on and off, like others can, but must abide by them for life. This, one might claim, makes the interest in living by those beliefs special and worthy of priority. However, this argument is not very persuasive. In the first place, religious beliefs can be changed: individuals can abandon religion, and even swap religion, thus altering their beliefs. Furthermore, those without ties to religion can also have beliefs that last all their lives. For example, a white supremacist might have the sincere belief lasting his entire life that black people are criminally minded and that lynching is permissible as such. However, we would not want to assign any force to this man's desire to perform lynchings, let alone grant it primary importance.

Second, it could be argued that religion is based on beliefs about the divine and the spiritual realm, thus giving the interest in acting upon such beliefs much more importance than our Earthly interests. However, this claim really just begs the question: for *why* are our spiritual interests more important? Perhaps it might be responded that our very salvation depends on religious freedom and practice, thus making it the highest interest of all. Unfortunately, there seems to be no way of proving that there is such a thing as salvation, let alone that certain practices necessarily lead to it. It thus seems difficult to maintain that free religious practice is our highest interest because it leads to salvation.

However, this argument might be recast in terms of the intensity of religious belief: it is not the fact that a particular practice *does* lead to salvation that gives it priority, it is the fact that individuals *believe* it to lead to salvation. And because they believe it to lead to salvation, their desires to perform the practice are incredibly intense and thus deserve priority. There are two obvious responses to this. First, it is extremely dangerous to grant priority to an interest just because it rests on an intense belief. For example, religiously motivated suicide bombers no doubt have an intense belief that their actions will lead to salvation. However, it would be perverse to grant the bombers' interest in carrying out such actions priority over their victims' interest in continued life. Second, one can question the idea that religious beliefs are *always* more intense than nonreligious beliefs. For example, religiously motivated suicide bombers are not the only individuals prepared to bear the highest costs for their beliefs. Indeed, suicide bombings are not only carried out on the basis of religious beliefs, as the use of such tactics by the Tamil Tigers clearly illustrates.

The fourth and fifth candidates for granting the interest in religious freedom special status and thus priority are as follows: that religion provides a context for self-understanding; and that religion transmits ethical values. These two candidates are useful to consider and evaluate together because they both suffer from the same problem: they do not prove that religion is special, because humans can achieve self-understanding and learn ethical values in the absence of religion. While religion is often an important source of identity, so too are nationality, culture, gender, race, family, ambitions, talents, and so on. Moreover, although many individuals learn their ethical values from religion, many also learn them from family, friends, society, school, and books. Clearly, then, religion is not special in either of these regards.

Sixth is the idea that our interest in religious practice merits priority because it allows us to live a life of integrity, where integrity is defined as living in accordance with one's perceived duties.[21] Chandran Kukathas certainly seems to regard this notion of integrity as of the highest importance, although he frames it in terms of adherence to one's conscience: "If there are any basic human interests, that interest is *at a minimum*, an interest in living in accordance with the demands of conscience. For among the worst fates that a person might have to endure is *that he is unable avoid acting against conscience*—that he be unable to do what he thinks is right."[22] So to prevent religious believers such as the Santeros from practicing their religious customs denies them the opportunity to do what they think is required of them, which has the most serious impact on their well-being.

In response, it must be pointed out that leading a life in line with one's perceived duties or conscience is not unique to religious believers. If it is integrity that makes religion special, it also makes other ways of living special. But granting special status and priority to all religious and nonreligious practices because they encompass integrity is problematic. For example, consider someone—and there are surely many such people—who truly believes in the mandate "an eye for an eye, and a tooth for a tooth." If the interest in leading a life of integrity is special and merits priority, then this individual should have the moral right to enact his own form of justice whenever he is transgressed. However, granting such a right would plainly be wrong. This is because the interest of individuals in having a fair and impartial trial trumps the interests of individuals whose conscience demands this form of retributive justice. It seems very unlikely, then, that our interest in integrity always merits priority.

The final justification for the claim that the interest in religious freedom is special and should take priority is based on the fact that religious groups have been persecuted in the past. However, while we can acknowledge that serious crimes and harms have been inflicted on religious groups in the past, it seems odd to atone for that by awarding absolute priority to the interest in religion. For one thing, if persecution in the past means priority now, then priority must also be granted to individuals' interests in culture, nationality, gender, and so on. Moreover, given that animals have been persecuted and seriously harmed in the past, then on the basis of this argument, their interests too must merit special status and priority. Once again, it appears that the argument for special status proves too much.

In sum, there is no justification for the view that humans' interest in religion is special and always merits priority. This, of course, is not to deny that freedom of religion is an important interest of humans. Rather, it is merely to point out that religion cannot be invoked as some kind of absolute trump to defeat any competing interest. Given this, if Santeros wish to argue that their interest in religious freedom trumps the interests of animals in not being killed and not being subject to pain, they will have to find another way.

FREEDOM OF RELIGION AND EQUAL OPPORTUNITY

One course that the Santeros could take is to argue that their interest in religious freedom should be given extra weight on the basis of fairness and equality. This is because without such extra weighting, Santeros will have a diminished opportunity to pursue their conception of the good, something that has been argued to be so crucial for human well-being.[23] So to focus on the example of the Santeria religion in Florida specifically, the argument might run as follows. Established groups and religions in Florida have ample opportunity to pursue their conceptions of the good and live by its mandates: Catholics can take the sacrament at mass; Baptists can gather to sing in worship; Muslims can congregate for prayers; and so on. The animal rights theory of this book does not restrict any of these practices, thus allowing members of such groups to lead what they consider to be a good life. However, the theory does have the clear potential to outlaw a core Santeria practice, thereby denying its adherents the opportunity to pursue their conception of the good. Thus the burden of abiding by this animal rights standard falls much more heavily on members of the Santeros than it does on other groups. This, so the argument might go, is unfair, unequal, and must be rectified by giving greater weight to the interest in religious freedom of the Santeros.

One easy way of rebutting this suggestion would be to suggest that religion is a matter of choice. If religion is chosen, we cannot claim that adherents of Santeria have a diminished opportunity to pursue their conception of the good. Rather, they possess an opportunity equal to that of every other individual; but because they choose to follow the Santeria religion, they cannot avail themselves of that opportunity.

However, this rebuttal is far from convincing. For one thing, given that many individuals are born into a particular religion and brought up and educated in terms of its norms, it is far from clear that all follow-ers of a religion have straightforwardly chosen it. If this is the case with followers of Santeria, as it surely is, we might still justifiably say that an application of animal rights standards will lead to many Sante-ros possessing a diminished opportunity to pursue their conception of the good.[24]

However, at this stage we must ask how far we are prepared go for equal opportunity. Looking back at some of the examples given so far in this chapter, it is extremely doubtful that we would permit *any* type of religious practice in the name of equal opportunity. For example, if a religion claimed that human jallikattu, honor killing, or infant sacrifice were all practices of theirs, no one would seriously suggest that reli-gious groups should be permitted to conduct such practices in the name of equal opportunity. Rather, we would say that opportunity to pursue one's conception of the good is *justifiably* diminished for groups who want to carry out these and practices like them. For example, Jonathan Quong advocates exemptions for minority groups on the basis of equal opportunity but quite rightly mandates that for a practice to even be considered for exemption, "[It] must not violate any basic rights."[25] This raises the question as to what these basic rights are, and when they can legitimately be established, but the point is clear enough. Simi-larly, Paul Bou-Habib, who makes a case for religious exemptions on the grounds of integrity, argues that such exemptions "cannot come at the expense of other people's equal opportunity for well-being," and that "religious practices that harm others severely . . . may not be accommodated."[26]

We can agree, then, that granting all individuals the equal opportu-nity to pursue their own conceptions of the good has justifiable limits. One obvious limit is infanticide. And if we accept this limit, we must also ordinarily accept the limit of animal sacrifice. For the strength of an animal's interest in continued life is extremely similar to the strength of an infant's interest in continued life.

HARMING ANIMALS AND HYPOCRISY

Having said all this, it is possible to think of one final response that fol-lowers of Santeria might make to support their claim that they should be allowed to continue with the animal sacrifices. They might argue that to disallow their religious practice on the basis of animal rights is hypocritical given all the violations of animal rights going on around them.[27] That is, they could point to the factory farms, slaughterhouses, animal laboratories, and so on in and around Florida and argue that if these practices are permitted, so too should theirs be. In other words, they might claim that to outlaw their practices alone is discriminatory and inegalitarian.

One response to such an argument has come from Paula Casal, who argues in effect that two wrongs do not make a right: "Under present circumstances, insisting that nothing be prohibited unless everything comparable is prohibited is tantamount to lifting all existing prohibitions on comparable forms of cruelty. Such reasoning would oppose most gradual reforms and incapacitate incremental political change."[28] Here Casal makes the perfectly sensible point that in the real world, legislation conforming to a certain ethical standard will often have to be piecemeal. Accordingly, some groups will have to suffer the burdens of this legislation sooner than others. Since Santerian animal sacrifice is straightforwardly in violation of the animal welfare standard set out, Santeros have no legitimate complaint when they are targeted sooner than others.

While Casal is certainly correct on this point, the validity of such an argument depends on one crucial premise that she fails to mention: there must be good reason to believe that the standard *will* eventually be applied to *all* groups.[29] For if we do not have good reason to think that all groups will eventually come under legislation enforcing this standard, Santeros can quite justifiably ask why they are being targeted specifically. In such circumstances, singling out Santeria would not be part of overall incremental change but would simply be change for them and them alone. If we return to the present situation in Florida, we can see that there is no significant political will to outlaw other practices that cause significant harms to animals, such as factory farms. Politicians are not drawing up plans to close down such farms, nor are they under huge pressure from the public to do so. To target the Santeros specifically, then, does not appear to be part of a general and piecemeal application of animal welfare standards; rather, it seems inconsistent and inegalitarian. In other words, the claim that it is hypocritical to prevent the Santeros from conducting their religious practices is well founded.

Importantly, however, none of this means that the interest of Santeros in religious freedom should be granted extra weight and take priority over the interests of animals. Just because it would be unfair to
target Santeria specifically, that does not give its followers the moral
permission to conduct animal sacrifices. On the contrary, as has been
argued above, there is no reason to believe that their interest in religious freedom should trump the interests of animals. Animals still have
a concrete right not to be killed by Santerian animal sacrifice. What it
does mean, however, is that the animal rights theory outlined ought
to be applied to *all* groups and individuals without discrimination. It
should not be used as a stick with which to beat cultural and religious
minorities, who quite justifiably often feel persecuted as it is. So while
piecemeal application of the rights theory will inevitably land on some
individuals and groups before others, we must be sure that such application is piecemeal rather than discriminatory.

To sum up this section, it may be useful to outline once again its
key points. The section has evaluated whether the human interest in
freedom of religion trumps animals' interests in avoiding pain and in
being killed. It has been concluded that it does not. First, very few
religions actually require their followers to harm animals. Thus the
animal rights theory of this book has the potential to impinge upon
religious freedom on only a rare number of occasions. When religious
freedom and animal interests do clash, we can concede that humans
have a strong interest in being free to practice their religion. However,
the interest in religion cannot be regarded as special, meriting priority over any other competing interest. Nor can the goal of equalizing
individuals' opportunity to pursue their conception of the good take
priority over all other claims. Just as we would not let humans suffer
intolerably in the name of religion or equal opportunity, nor should we
let animals. And just as we would not let human infants be killed in
the name of religion or equal opportunity, nor should we let animals.
While some groups might justifiably object that it is hypocritical to target their practices specifically while so many other actions that cause
significant harms to animals are allowed to flourish, that does not make
their practices any more permissible.

In conclusion, it is important to reiterate that the human interests in
culture and in freedom of religion are strong and pressing. Indeed, as

far as possible these interests should be accommodated. Unfortunately, however, both of these interests sometimes clash with the interests of animals. Cultural and religious practices sometimes involve inflicting serious harms on animals. This chapter has argued that the human interests in culture and religion cannot simply take priority in these circumstances. While these interests are pressing, they are by no means absolute. Having cultural support and living by a communal way of life are important to individuals, but not all that is important. And while the diversity of cultures in the world is to be celebrated, we should not rigidly preserve this diversity at any cost. In any case, the animal rights theory defended in this book is not much of a threat to such diversity. Similarly, the rights theory defended here is not much of a threat to religious freedom: few religions *demand* harming animals. However, when they do, religion cannot act as a simple trump. There are no grounds for regarding the interest in religious freedom as special, and, like our interest in culture, it must be weighed fairly against other competing interests. When we undertake such weighing, we see that there are limits to religious and cultural practices. If we believe that torture and infanticide are such justified limits, then we must also accept that the interests of animals in avoiding pain and death are justified limits. In other words, animals have a concrete moral right not to be killed or made to suffer by cultural and religious practices.

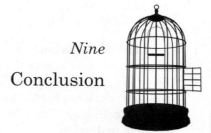

Nine

Conclusion

The aim of this book has been to decouple animal rights from animal liberation. That is, its aim has been to challenge the widely held assumption in animal ethics that a theory of animal rights must necessarily be a theory that demands that all use, ownership, and exploitation of animals be abolished. As was discussed in the introduction, this assumption derives from an unfortunate entrenched dichotomy in animal ethics: a dichotomy that pits a Singer-influenced animal welfarism against a Regan-influenced animal rights position. Recall that theories of animal rights emerged in the main as a response to Peter Singer's hugely influential *Animal Liberation*. Critics attacked Singer's theory for not really being a theory of liberation at all. After all, while utilitarian theories can include sentient animals within their moral analysis with considerable ease, they must also permit the sacrifice of individual animals—whether in laboratories, farms, or other contexts—when such sacrifices can be shown to maximize aggregate utility. In response to Singer's utilitarianism, several scholars claimed that a theory of *animal rights* was required, where rights mark absolute limits on what can be done to an individual, irrespective of considerations of the greater good. Tom Regan's *The Case for Animal Rights* provided the most compelling and celebrated rights theory of this kind, claiming that all subjects-of-a-life possess an inherent value that grounds a basic right to respectful treatment. For contemporary followers of Regan, like Gary Francione, such a rights position is a true theory of animal liberation, requiring that animals must never be used, owned, or exploited by human beings.

The problem with this well-established dichotomy in animal ethics is not that it is false. Clearly there are important differences between the two theories of Peter Singer and Tom Regan. No, the problem is with the way that this dichotomy has become *entrenched* within animal ethics. For there is now an assumption that animal welfarism must be a welfarism of the kind proposed by Singer, and that an animal rights theory must be a rights theory of the kind proposed by Regan. But in fact it is possible to develop theories that can legitimately be considered welfarist or rights-based that deviate significantly from the writings of Singer and Regan. Crucially, as this book has aimed to show, it is quite possible to develop a theory of animal rights that does not demand the abolition of all uses, ownership, and exploitation of animals.

Importantly, not only is an alternative theory of animal rights *possible*, but it is also *preferable*. An alternative theory of animal rights is preferable because Regan fails to offer a plausible foundation for the basic animal right to respectful treatment. As chapter 1 discussed, Regan uses Kantian moral reasoning to argue that animals possess the basic right to respectful treatment: that animals have the right to always be treated as ends-in-themselves and never merely as means. But since most sentient animals are not ends-in-themselves, as Kant defines the term, it is unclear why they must always be treated as such. Kantian reasoning, privileging as it does the moral and autonomous capacities of rational agents, seems an entirely inappropriate means of establishing a theory of animal rights.

A much more plausible means of establishing animal rights is to use an interest-based rights approach—where rights serve to protect certain of the most important aspects of an entity's well-being, or interests. Interest-based theories have at least two important advantages. In the first place, they offer a convincing and inclusive account of who can possess rights. Interest theories ground rights simply in the capacity for well-being: the ability to lead a life that can go well or badly for oneself. This not only explains why sentient animals can possess rights, it also explains why human infants and those who are seriously mentally disabled possess rights. None of these individuals may be able to claim their rights for themselves, or hold moral duties themselves, but as beings with a life that can go well or badly for themselves, they all have some interests that are sufficient to ground duties in others. Furthermore, it is certainly possible to provide reasonable accounts of what their interests are, and we can represent those interests on their behalf.

Interest theories not only have the advantage of offering a plausible account of who has rights, they also provide a compelling means of establishing what rights individuals possess. Joseph Raz has argued that rights are interests that are of sufficient importance to ground duties in others. This provides us with a convincing means by which to establish the rights of individuals—including sentient animals. Under this account, rights are not established by appeal to mysterious metaphysical notions, or simply by falling back on our hunches and intuitions. Instead, rights require justification via an assessment of the interest they protect: is that interest strong enough, when balanced against competing interests, other values, and the burdens it might place, to establish a duty in another?

This book has asked this question in a range of different contexts in which humans use animals. It has argued that when the interests of animals are identified and weighed properly, most animals have no general right to liberation—and hence no general rights not be used, owned, and exploited by human beings. Unlike humans, most sentient animals are not autonomous agents and thus do not share the intrinsic interest in leading a life on their own terms—in framing, revising, and pursuing their own conceptions of the good. This does not mean that all uses of animals are permissible. Obviously animals are seriously harmed by many of the ways in which they are exploited in contemporary societies. However, such uses ought to be condemned on the basis of the fact that they violate the animals' interests in not being made to suffer and in continued life, rather than on any alleged right they have to be free.

The Implications of Animal Rights Without Liberation

This book has thus argued that while animals have certain interests that impose strict duties on us in a range of contexts, we have no duty to refrain from owning, keeping, and using them for particular purposes. The basis of this claim rests on a specific understanding of what is, and what is not, in the interests of sentient animals. Taking what *is* in their interests first, the book has claimed that as sentient beings, animals possess interests in not being made to suffer and in not being killed. These interests, it has been argued, establish prima facie animal rights not to be made to suffer and not to be killed. The chapters have shown that these rights impose extremely strict limits on what we can do to animals in experimentation, agriculture, genetic engineering, and entertainment; in relation to the environment; and in cultural practices. In fact, if these rights were institutionalized and established as legal rights, the results would be incredibly radical. The vast majority of animal experimentation would have to stop, including that which is undertaken in an effort to cure human disease. The meat industry would have to shut down, with farmers limited to raising crops, along with reduced free-range egg and dairy production. The genetic engineering of animals would be prohibited unless it could be shown that the engineered animals would not lead lives of intolerable suffering and would not have fewer opportunities for well-being compared to ordinary members of their species. Pet keeping would be permitted only when the well-being of the animal and any offspring were guaranteed. Zoos would have to expand in size and provide sufficient stimulation in order to permissibly display animals. Circuses would likely have to stop using most species of animal altogether. Routine deforestation and other forms of habitat destruction would have to cease, and our emission of greenhouse gases would have to be curbed for the sake of animals themselves. Therapeutic hunting would have to stop, and investment in the development of effective contraceptive treatments for wild animals would be required. Finally, cultural practices that are harmful to animals, such as bullfighting, jallikattu, whaling, hunting, animal sacrifice, and religious slaughter, would all have to end. Without doubt, the rights theory advanced in this book—while more permissive than those advanced by such thinkers as Regan and Francione—is indeed prohibitive.

However, the interests of animals do not mandate that we refrain from using animals altogether. This is because, as nonautonomous beings, most animals have no interest in leading freely chosen lives. Animals can desire things, can act intentionally toward satisfying their desires, and can pursue their biological functions. But this does not make them autonomous. For autonomy entails the capacity to reflect on and choose one's own life goals. Without such capacities for reflection, animals are locked into their ends and desires in a way that most adult humans are not. Because of this, animals do not ordinarily have an intrinsic interest in not being interfered with or in being prevented from controlling their own lives. In light of this, we do not cause harm or violate any rights simply by owning, keeping, and using animals for certain purposes. As such, and contrary to the claims of many other animal rights philosophers, our obligations to animals fall short of liberating them.

This fact moderates the radical nature of the theory defended in this book. For provided that our use of animals does not cause them to suffer or be killed, we can ordinarily use them for a range of different purposes: to act as experimental models; to provide us with food from their milk, eggs, and even corpses; to exhibit engineered traits that we find useful or interesting; to entertain us as companions, in sporting competition, and in zoos; and to play a role in cultural and religious practices. None of these uses is rendered impermissible simply by recognizing that animals possess rights. This is because rights derive from interests, and most animals have no intrinsic interest in being free.

From Theory to Practice

But what does the theory of animal rights without liberation offered in this book mean in practice? If this is what the rights of animals are—and are not—what does this mean we should do? Recall that this book has offered a theory of *moral* rights: a theory outlining the legal rights that animals *ought* to enjoy. In other words, this book has proposed a set of duties to animals that the state can legitimately make individuals comply with. So, on the one hand, political communities ought to change their legal rules so that they recognize, uphold, and protect the animal rights outlined and defended in this book. And on the other, citizens ought to comply with the duties entailed by these rights, as far as that is possible in present circumstances, and ought to campaign for their political community to enact the legal changes necessary to put these rights into practice.

Note, then, that the call is not that states must enforce these rights in their totality and with immediate effect. Chapter 1 argued that this book strives to be part of the process of "democratic underlaboring."[1] That is, rather than circumventing democratic deliberation and procedures, the theory of this book speaks to them. As such, the theory hopes to *improve* citizens' and politicians' understanding of our obligations to animals. Furthermore, the arguments it offers are also hoped to *persuade* the public that the theory presented here is the best account of our political obligations to animals.[2]

But at this stage an important objection can be anticipated. For it may be pointed out that our powers of persuasion—and particularly in relation to the treatment of animals—are somewhat limited. Without doubt there are a number of entrenched and structural obstacles to successfully persuading contemporary political communities that they ought to transform the ways in which they treat nonhuman sentient animals. Clearly there are cultural obstacles. Most Western societies, for example, simply take it for granted that human beings are of supreme moral value, and that nonhumans count for very little. Part of the explanation for this cultural attitude of course stems from Judeo-

Christian teachings about the special relationship between humans and God—teachings that have been accepted and become embedded over centuries. There are also important material obstacles. Indeed, many of the grossest animal rights violations are committed by agricultural and pharmaceutical businesses with huge resources. Crucially, these are just the kind of resources that governments and political leaders covet and are loathe to shy away from. Our powers of persuasion are also limited by power imbalances between humans and animals. Quite simply, most sentient animals lack the capabilities to speak up and campaign for their own better treatment. This means that animals are necessarily reliant on the motivation and action of human representatives to fight for their cause.

Given all these impediments to our ability to engage with and inform democratic procedures, it can legitimately be asked how far the strategies of representation, discourse, debate, and persuasion can go. Some campaigners might ask themselves why billions of animals have to suffer so horribly while we forlornly attempt to convince the public that such suffering actually matters. Is democratic underlaboring inevitably doomed to propping up the status quo? If so, are more direct and even violent political interventions justified for the sake of animal rights?

It is my firm belief that they are not. It is crucial that we not lose sight of democratic procedures for the establishment and promotion of animal rights, for at least three reasons. First, the process of democratic engagement calls for this theory—and any other—to be opened up to public scrutiny. Such a process is absolutely vital before any steps toward policy implementation are taken. It would, after all, be rather strange if this particular book had hit on the absolutely truthful account of our obligations to animals! Just as there are flaws with theories of animal ethics that have gone before it, there are no doubt flaws with the theory of animal rights proposed here. This is not to go back on the arguments that have been made throughout the book—they are offered with the sincere belief that this account is more compelling and plausible than the alternatives. However, it is to admit to fallibility—and hence the idea that all theories should be open to scrutiny, questioned, amended, improved, or even abandoned, as is deemed necessary.

Democratic underlaboring is also crucial for the sake of legitimacy. The rights proposed in this book are urgent and compelling. The way contemporary societies disregard the interests of nonhuman animals is shocking, and the horrific abuse inflicted upon animals for the most trivial of reasons should be a source of collective shame. However, the appropriate response to these harms and rights violations is not simply to institutionalize and uphold these rights at any cost. Violating basic human rights for the sake of promoting the rights of animals, for example, would obviously be illegitimate, as well as counterproductive. If animal rights are to have political legitimacy, then, it is crucial that they have been arrived at through just democratic procedures. That does not mean, however, that campaigners should just sit around and wait for the political will to emerge. Instead, it means that campaigners should do all they can within those just strategies to establish, foster, and promote that political will. Of course, there are serious and important impediments to realizing that will, as described above. But to think that we have no power or means by which to address and even to overcome those obstacles seems unjustifiably pessimistic. After all, advances in other areas of social justice have taken place across many political communities in spite of similarly powerful obstacles.

Finally, it is crucial that democratic procedures and strategies are followed for the sake of the protection of animals themselves. After all, without any kind of democratic support for these rights, not only will legislation protecting them lack political legitimacy, but it will also lack any realistic chance of achieving lasting results for animals. Citizens will resist and disobey the laws, and governments will lack the will and energy to enforce them. The process of democratic underlaboring—of doing everything in our power to persuade political communities of the validity of these rights—is thus absolutely essential if these animal rights are to be upheld, protected, and enjoyed over the long term.

This book has offered a theory of animal rights without liberation. As such, it stands together with many other proponents of animal rights on certain key and fundamental issues. For example, the book agrees that it is entirely wrong that the interests of animals are subordinated in the politics and morality of contemporary societies simply because they belong to members of different species. The interests of animals should be considered on their own strengths, and equivalent interests should be treated with the same respect, irrespective of the kinds of entities to whom they belong. The fairest and best means of respecting the interests of individuals in this way, the book claims, is by recognizing and protecting a set of animal rights. Thus far, this book is in agreement with the majority of proponents of animal rights. However, it is this book's contention that many advocates of animal rights have misread what the interests of animals actually are. These advocates have noted the importance of liberty both to human well-being and to human rights and have claimed that liberty holds the same importance for animal well-being and animal rights. This is a mistake: animals are not autonomous, self-governing agents with the power to frame, revise, and pursue their own conceptions of the good and so do not have a fundamental interest in liberty. As such, animals have compelling rights that impose strict limitations on what we may permissibly do to them in a range of contexts. However, animals have no general right never to be used, owned, or exploited by human beings.

Notes

1. Introduction

1. For examples of this position, see Peter Carruthers, *The Animals Issue: Moral Theory in Practice* (Cambridge: Cambridge University Press, 1992); Roger Scruton, *Animal Rights and Wrongs*, 3rd ed. (London: Metro Books, 2000); and Tibor R. Machan, *Putting Humans First: Why We Are Nature's Favorite* (Oxford: Rowman & Littlefield, 2004).

2. For examples of this position, see Tom Regan, *The Case for Animal Rights*, 2nd ed. (Berkeley: University of California Press, 2004); Gary L. Francione, *Animals, Property, and the Law* (Philadelphia: Temple University Press, 1995); and Steven M. Wise, *Unlocking the Cage: Science and the Case for Animal Rights* (Oxford: Perseus Press, 2002).

3. By exploitation I simply mean using them for profit.

4. Gary L. Francione is the best example of someone who makes this argument. See Francione, *Animals, Property, and the Law*; *Rain Without Thunder: The Ideology of the Animal Rights Movement* (Philadelphia: Temple University Press, 1996); *Introduction to Animal Rights: Your Child or the Dog?* (Philadelphia: Temple University Press, 2000); and *Animals as Persons: Essays on the Abolition of Animal Exploitation* (New York: Columbia University Press, 2008). But also see David Sztybel, "Distinguishing Animal Rights from Animal Welfare," in *Encyclopedia of Animal Rights and Animal Welfare*, ed. M. Bekoff (Westport: Greenwood, 1998), 130–2. For one voice that rejects this understanding of animal rights, see Robert Garner's contribution in Gary L. Francione and Robert Garner, *The Animal Rights Debate: Abolition or Regulation?* (New York: Columbia University Press, 2010).

5. Francione, *Rain Without Thunder*, 2.

6. Peter Singer, *Animal Liberation*, 2nd ed. (London: Pimlico, 1995).

7. See also Peter Singer, "All Animals Are Equal," in *Applied Ethics*, ed. P. Singer (Oxford: Oxford University Press, 1986).

8. While Peter Singer popularized the term "speciesism" in *Animal Liberation*, it was actually coined by the British psychologist and animal protection campaigner Richard Ryder.

9. Regan, *The Case for Animal Rights*.

10. Ibid., 249.

11. Ibid., 243.
12. Ibid., 395 (emphasis in original).
13. Francione, *Rain Without Thunder*, 18.
14. For some examples of books that introduce such nontraditional approaches to animal ethics, see Matthew Calarco and Peter Atterton, eds., *Animal Philosophy: Essential Readings in Continental Thought* (New York: Continuum, 2004); Peter H. Steeves, ed., *Animal Others: On Ethics, Ontology, and Animal Life* (Albany: State University of New York Press, 1999); and Josephine Donovan and Carol J. Adams, eds., *The Feminist Care Tradition in Animal Ethics* (New York: Columbia University Press, 2007).
15. Immanuel Kant, *Lectures on Ethics*, trans. Louis Infield (New York: Harper and Row, 1963), 239.
16. Joel Feinberg, "The Rights of Animals and Unborn Generations," in *Philosophy and Environmental Crisis*, ed. W. T. Blackstone (Athens: University of Georgia Press, 1974); Bernard E. Rollin, *Animal Rights and Human Morality*, 3rd ed. (New York: Prometheus Books, 2006), 115; James Rachels, *Created from Animals: The Moral Implications of Darwinism* (Oxford: Oxford University Press, 1990), 207.
17. Joseph Raz, *The Morality of Freedom* (Oxford: Clarendon Press, 1988), 166.
18. Joseph Raz, "Liberating Duties," *Law and Philosophy* 8, no. 1 (April 1989): 3–4.
19. Francione, *Animals, Property, and the Law*.
20. For a full defense of this argument, see Alasdair Cochrane, "Do Animals Have an Interest in Liberty?," *Political Studies* 57, no. 3 (December 2009). I have since discovered that this claim is also made, in a completely different context, in David Miller, "Political Philosophy for Earthlings," in *Political Theory: Methods and Approaches,* ed. D. Leopold and M. Stears (Oxford: Oxford University Press, 2008), 35.
21. This understanding of autonomy comes originally from John Rawls, *Political Liberalism* (New York: Columbia University Press, 1993), 72.
22. Peter Singer and Paola Cavalieri, eds., *The Great Ape Project: Equality Beyond Humanity* (London: Fourth Estate, 1993); and Thomas I. White, *In Defense of Dolphins: A New Moral Frontier* (Malden: Blackwell, 2007).
23. This example is discussed further in Cochrane, "Do Animals Have an Interest in Liberty?," 664.
24. See Hillel Steiner, "Moral Rights," in *The Oxford Handbook of Ethical Theory,* ed. D. Copp (Oxford: Oxford University Press, 2005), 460; and Cécile Fabre, *Whose Body Is It Anyway?* (Oxford: Oxford University Press, 2006), 16.
25. This point is also made in Fabre, *Whose Body Is It Anyway?*, 19–20.
26. Ibid.
27. For a useful discussion of this issue, see Ronald Dworkin, *Freedom's Law: The Moral Reading of the American Constitution* (New York: Oxford University Press, 1996), 15–35; and Jeremy Waldron, "The Core of the Case Against Judicial Review," *Yale Law Journal* 115, no. 6 (April 2006).
28. Adam Swift and Stuart White, "Political Theory, Social Science and Real Politics," in Leopold and Stears, *Political Theory*, 54.
29. Ibid.

2. Animals, Interests, and Rights

1. Mary Anne Warren, *Moral Status: Obligations to Persons and Other Living Things* (Oxford: Oxford University Press, 1997), 9.

2. Indeed, the animal welfare laws of most states seem to reflect this. Take, for example, the EU's 1997 Treaty of Amsterdam, which includes a legally binding protocol on animal welfare, recognizing animals as sentient beings whose welfare must be considered when formulating and implementing policies relating to agriculture, transport, research, and the internal market.

3. Colin Allen, "Animal Consciousness," in *The Stanford Encyclopedia of Philosophy*, ed. E. N. Zalta (Summer 2003), http://plato.stanford.edu/archives/summer2003/entries/consciousness-animal/.

4. These three reasons can be found in Mark Rowlands, *Animals Like Us* (London: Verso, 2002), 5–9; Robert Garner, *Animal Ethics* (Cambridge: Polity, 2005), 28–9; David DeGrazia, *Animal Rights: A Very Short Introduction* (Oxford: Oxford University Press, 2002), 42–3; and David DeGrazia, *Taking Animals Seriously: Mental Life and Moral Status* (Cambridge: Cambridge University Press, 1996), 108–12.

5. Donald R. Griffin, *The Question of Animal Awareness: Evolutionary Continuity of Mental Experience* (New York: Rockefeller University Press, 1976), 70.

6. For more on animal experimentation, see chapter 3.

7. "Crippled Chickens Choose Pain Relief," *BBC News*, March 26, 2000, http://news.bbc.co.uk/1/hi/uk/691129.stm.

8. "Anglers Are Finally Off the Hook: Fish Feel No Pain," *Daily Telegraph*, February 9, 2003.

9. Alex Kirby, "Fish Do Feel Pain, Scientists Say," *BBC News*, April 30, 2003, http://news.bbc.co.uk/1/hi/sci/tech/2983045.stm.

10. Peter H. Raven and George B. Johnson, *Biology*, 4th ed. (London: WCB Publishers, 1996), 896.

11. Douglas Fox, "Do Fruit Flies Dream of Electric Bananas?," *New Scientist*, February 14, 2004.

12. DeGrazia, *Taking Animals Seriously*, 111.

13. David Adam, "Scientists Say Lobsters Feel No Pain," *Guardian,* February 8, 2005.

14. Colin Barras, "Lobster Pain May Prick Diners' Consciences," *New Scientist*, November 9, 2007.

15. From here on the book will predominantly focus on sentient nonhuman animals. Hence when I use the convenient term "animal," I usually mean "sentient nonhuman animal."

16. For a Christian approach to animal rights, see Andrew Linzey, *Animal Theology* (London: SCM Press, 1994).

17. For example, see Carl Cohen, "The Case for the Use of Animals in Biomedical Research," *New England Journal of Medicine* 315 (October 1986): 866; and Michael Fox, "'Animal Liberation': A Critique," *Ethics* 88, no. 2 (January 1978): 112.

18. Kant, *Lectures on Ethics*.

19. The following discussion can also be found in Cochrane, "Do Animals Have an Interest in Liberty?," 667–8.

20. Peter Singer, *Practical Ethics*, 2nd ed. (Cambridge: Cambridge University Press, 1993), 111.

21. DeGrazia, *Taking Animals Seriously*, 208.

22. Marc Hauser, *Wild Minds: What Animals Really Think* (London: Penguin, 2001), 309–14.

23. Cohen, "The Case for the Use of Animals in Biomedical Research," 866; Fox, "Animal Liberation," 110.

24. Nathan Nobis, "Carl Cohen's 'Kind' Arguments for Animal Rights and Against Human Rights," *Journal of Applied Philosophy* 21, no. 1 (January 2004): 50–1.

25. Feinberg, "The Rights of Animals and Unborn Generations."

26. See, for example, Scruton, *Animal Rights and Wrongs*, 80.

27. Of course, it is possible to hold a contractarian account of rights without also holding a reciprocity-based account of rights. For example, one might want to assign rights based on what parties would choose in a contract because the contract models what is fair, rather than because each party will themselves be advantaged by the process. If the contracting process is constructed in the former way, it is possible that parties could assign rights to animals, children, people with mental disabilities, and so on, despite the fact that they will get nothing in return. Obviously such accounts do not see moral agency as necessary for the possession of rights. For contractarian accounts of this kind in relation to animals, see Donald VanDeVeer, "Of Beasts, Persons and the Original Position," *Monist* 62, no. 3 (July 1979); Mark Rowlands, "Contractarianism and Animal Rights," *Journal of Applied Philosophy* 14, no. 3 (November 1997); and Andrew I. Cohen, "Contractarianism, Other-Regarding Attitudes and the Moral Standing of Nonhuman Animals," *Journal of Applied Philosophy* 24, no. 2 (May 2007).

28. For some examples of the will theory, see H.L.A. Hart, "Are There Any Natural Rights?," in *Political Philosophy*, ed. A. Quinton (Oxford: Oxford University Press, 1967); L. W. Sumner, *The Moral Foundation of Rights* (Oxford: Clarendon Press, 1987); N. E. Simmonds, "Rights at the Cutting Edge," in *A Debate Over Rights*, ed. Matthew H. Kramer et al. (Oxford: Clarendon Press, 1998); and Hillel Steiner, "Working Rights," in Kramer et al., *A Debate Over Rights.*

29. Steiner, "Working Rights," 259–61.

30. Elizabeth Anderson, "Animal Rights and the Values of Nonhuman Life," in *Animal Rights: Current Debates and New Directions*, ed. M. C. Nussbaum and C. R. Sunstein (New York: Oxford University Press, 2004), 283.

31. Ibid., 284.

32. Ibid., 288.

33. Ibid., 289.

34. For just one example of an argument along these lines, see Henry Shue, *Basic Rights: Subsistence, Affluence and US Foreign Policy*, 2nd ed. (Princeton: Princeton University Press, 1996).

35. H. J. McCloskey, "Rights," *Philosophical Quarterly* 15, no. 5 (April 1965); and R. G. Frey, *Interests and Rights* (Oxford: Clarendon Press, 1980).

36. McCloskey, "Rights," 126.

37. Tom Regan, "McCloskey on Why Animals Cannot Have Rights," *Philosophical Quarterly* 26, no. 104 (July 1976): 255.

38. Frey, *Interests and Rights*, 82–6.

39. Many environmental ethicists have claimed that plants possess interests. They are usually more reluctant than Matthew Kramer to assign interests to inanimate objects. For examples, see Paul W. Taylor, *Respect for Nature: A Theory of Environmental Ethics* (Princeton: Princeton University Press, 1986); Gary E. Varner, *In Nature's Interests? Interests, Animal Rights, and Environmental Ethics* (Oxford: Oxford University Press, 1998); Lawrence E. Johnson, *A Morally Deep World: An Essay on Moral Significance and Environmental Ethics* (Cambridge: Cambridge University Press, 1991); and Robin Attfield, "The Good of Trees," *Journal of Value Inquiry* 15, no. 1 (March 1981).

40. Matthew H. Kramer, "Do Animals and Dead People Have Legal Rights," *Canadian Journal of Law and Jurisprudence* 14, no. 1 (January 2001): 33.

41. Interestingly, despite being an interest-theorist, Kramer himself thinks that not all those entities with interests are potential right-holders. He thinks a further requirement is needed: that one's interests are sufficiently close in morally relevant ways to mentally competent human adults.

42. Roger Crisp, "Well-Being," in *The Stanford Encyclopedia of Philosophy*, ed. E. N. Zalta (Summer 2003), http://plato.stanford.edu/archives/sum2003/entries/well-being; L. W. Sumner, *Welfare, Happiness and Ethics* (Oxford: Clarendon Press, 1996), 20; and T. Scanlon, "Value, Desire and Quality of Life," in *The Quality of Life*, ed. M. C. Nussbaum and A. Sen (Oxford: Clarendon Press, 1993), 185.

43. Singer, *Animal Liberation*.

44. Regan, *The Case for Animal Rights*, 205.

45. For examples, see Robert Nozick, *Anarchy, State and Utopia* (New York: Basic Books, 1974), 28–9; and Ronald Dworkin, "Rights as Trumps," in *Theories of Rights*, ed. J. Waldron (Oxford: Oxford University Press, 1984).

46. Mark Rowlands, *Animal Rights: Moral Theory and Practice*, 2nd ed. (Basingstoke: Palgrave Macmillan, 2009), 86–9; and Warren, *Moral Status*, 167–8.

47. The classic statement of skepticism about moral rights is undoubtedly Jeremy Bentham, "Anarchical Fallacies: Being an Examination of the Declaration of Rights Issued During the French Revolution," in *Nonsense upon Stilts: Bentham, Burke and Marx on the Rights of Man*, ed. J. Waldron (London: Methuen, 1987).

48. Raz, *The Morality of Freedom*, 166.

49. Swift and White, "Political Theory, Social Science and Real Politics," 54.

50. Tibor B. Machan, "Why Human Beings May Use Animals," *Journal of Value Inquiry* 36, no. 1 (March 2002): 12–13; Simmonds, "Rights at the Cutting Edge," 197; and Steiner, "Working Rights," 289–91.

51. Machan, "Why Human Beings May Use Animals," 13.

52. Raz, *The Morality of Freedom*, 192.

53. See also Dworkin, "Rights as Trumps."

54. On the notion of prima facie rights, see Gregory Vlastos, "Justice and Equality," in *Social Justice*, ed. R. Brandt (Englewood Cliffs: Prentice-Hall,

1962), 31. On the notion of concrete rights, see Dworkin, *Taking Rights Seriously*, 93–4.

55. Marti Kheel, "The Liberation of Nature: A Circular Affair," in *The Feminist Care Tradition in Animal Ethics*, ed. J. Donovan and C. Adams (New York: Columbia University Press, 2007), 51.

56. Charles Taylor, "Atomism," in Charles Taylor, *Philosophy and the Human Sciences: Philosophical Papers 2* (Cambridge: Cambridge University Press, 1985).

57. Deborah Slicer, "Your Daughter or Your Dog? A Feminist Assessment of the Animal Research Issue," in Donovan and Adams, *The Feminist Care Tradition in Animal Ethics*, 108–9.

58. Ibid., 110.

59. For a useful critical review of such arguments in relation to animal ethics, see Elisa Aaltola, "'Other Animal Ethics' and the Demand for Difference," *Environmental Values* 11, no. 2 (May 2002).

3. Animal Experimentation

1. I borrow this distinction from Robert Garner, *Animals, Politics and Morality* (Manchester: Manchester University Press, 1993), 121.

2. The testing of cosmetics on animals has been banned in the UK since 1998 and in the EU since 2009. By 2013 it will be illegal to sell within the EU those cosmetics that have been tested on animals elsewhere in the world. Whether the EU will meet this deadline is the source of some debate. See Bibi Van Der Zi, "Cosmetics Industry Criticised as EU Set to Admit Delay in Animal Testing Ban," *Guardian*, December 31, 2010.

3. Quoted in Sholto Byrnes, "Animal Rights, Human Wrongs," *New Statesman*, February 28, 2008.

4. See, for example, Alistair Currie, "Abusing the Weak," *New Statesman*, March 4, 2008.

5. This account of the strength of an interest is greatly influenced by Jeff McMahan's account of the strength of what he calls "time-relative interests." See Jeff McMahan, *The Ethics of Killing* (Oxford: Oxford University Press, 2002), 80. As I make clear later in the chapter, however, my account differs in one important regard.

6. Ibid., 233.

7. Ibid., 39.

8. Ibid., 198.

9. DeGrazia, *Animal Rights*, 103.

10. For a philosophical example of such an argument, see Hugh LaFollette and Niall Shanks, *Brute Science: Dilemmas of Animal Experimentation* (London: Routledge, 1996).

11. The Nuremburg Code and Helsinki Declaration can be found at the Office of Human Subjects Research, http://ohsr.od.nih.gov/guidelines/index.html. The Universal Declaration of Bioethics and Human Rights can be found at http://www.unesco.org.

12. Another important advocate of this relationship-based approach is Mary Midgley. See Mary Midgley, *Animals and Why They Matter* (Athens: University of Georgia Press, 1984), 98–111.

13. Lewis Petrinovich, *Darwinian Dominion: Animal Welfare and Human Interests* (London: MIT Press, 1999), 217.

14. Ibid., 220–2.

15. Ibid., 3–4.

16. Ibid., 238.

17. See LaFollette and Shanks, *Brute Science*, 229.

18. This argument follows the distinction between first- and second-order impartiality made in Brian Barry, *Justice as Impartiality* (Oxford: Oxford University Press, 1995), 194.

19. Bonnie Steinbock, "Speciesism and the Idea of Equality," *Philosophy* 53, no. 204 (April 1978): 253–4.

20. The assertion that we should consider the claims of nonhumans and humans with similar capacities on an equal footing is often called the "argument from marginal cases." See Daniel Dombrowski, *Babies and Beasts: The Argument from Marginal Cases* (Urbana: Illinois University Press, 1997).

21. Steinbock, "Speciesism and the Idea of Equality," 255.

22. Angus Taylor, *Animals and Ethics* (Ontario: Broadview Press, 2003), 127.

23. Steinbock, "Speciesism and the Idea of Equality," 255.

24. I say "ordinarily" because an animal might have a disease that means it will necessarily have painful experiences for the rest of his life. In such cases, there seems little reason to attribute to the animal an interest in continued life.

25. This view is put forward by DeGrazia, *Animal Rights*, 59–64; Rollin, *Animal Rights and Human Morality*, 113; and S. F. Sapontzis, *Morals, Reason and Animals* (Philadelphia: Temple University Press, 1987), 169.

26. Once again, I say "ordinarily" because in some cases individuals will have no prospect for future valuable experiences or projects: consider individuals with debilitating illnesses that cause severe and relentless pain, for example. Under my account, such individuals will naturally have a much weaker interest in continued life.

27. R. G. Frey has faced up to the possibility of using human (and animal) nonpersons in medical experiments based on the potential benefits to human persons. See his contribution in R. G. Frey and Sir William Paton, "Vivisection, Morals and Medicine: An Exchange," in *Bioethics: An Anthology*, ed. H. Kushe and P. Singer (Oxford: Blackwell, 2002). However, he categorically rejects the use of humans in R. G Frey, "Animals," in *The Oxford Handbook of Practical Ethics*, ed. H. LaFollette (Oxford: Oxford University Press, 2005).

28. McMahan, *The Ethics of Killing*, 233.

29. Ibid., 195.

30. The notion that animals have an interest in freedom—however it is construed—is pervasive in the animal rights literature. For examples, see Taylor, *Respect for Nature*, 106–8; Bernard E. Rollin, *The Unheeded Cry: Animal Consciousness, Animal Pain and Science* (Oxford: Oxford University Press, 1989), 173, 203; Rollin, *Animal Rights and Human Morality*, 90; Evelyn B. Pluhar, *The*

Moral Significance of Human and Nonhuman Animals (Durham, N.C.: Duke University Press, 1995), 248–9; Paola Cavalieri, *The Animal Question: Why Nonhuman Animals Deserve Human Rights* (Oxford: Oxford University Press, 2001), 88, 138; Dale Jamieson, "Against Zoos," in Dale Jamieson, *Morality's Progress: Essays on Humans, Other Animals, and the Rest of Nature* (Oxford: Oxford University Press, 2002), 167; Dale Jamieson, "Zoos Revisited," in *Morality's Progress*, 179–80; Regan, *The Case for Animal Rights*, 92, 97–8; Anderson, "Animal Rights and the Values of Nonhuman Life," 283–4; and Martha C. Nussbaum, *Frontiers of Justice: Disability, Nationality, Species Membership* (London: Belknap Press of Harvard University Press, 2006), 345. David DeGrazia also recognizes this interest, but, in my view, in a more qualified way. See DeGrazia, *Taking Animals Seriously*, 233–4. Peter Singer claims that animals' interests are exhausted by their preferences—hence liberty may or may not be in their interests. See Singer, *Practical Ethics*, 13. I claim that animals have no intrinsic interest in liberty. See Cochrane, "Do Animals Have an Interest in Liberty?"

31. I say "almost certain" because it is conceivable that an experiment could be conducted that simply involved observing the animal in its natural environment without interference. Whether such fieldwork should properly be referred to as an experiment, I do not know.

32. For the classic exposition of the distinction between negative and positive liberty, see Isaiah Berlin, "Two Concepts of Liberty," in *Political Philosophy*, ed. A. Quinton (Oxford: Oxford University Press, 1967).

33. Once again, I say "most animals" to leave open the possibility that some animals are in fact autonomous creatures with capacities to reflect on, choose, and pursue their own goals.

34. Taylor, *Respect for Nature*, 106–9.

35. Such policies are pursued in many zoos and wildlife parks around the world. Rare species are taken into captivity and bred, in the hope that the resultant offspring will have a better chance of survival.

36. Regan, *The Case for Animal Rights*, 84. Similar arguments emphasizing the importance of this kind of agency are put forward by Pluhar, *The Moral Significance of Human and Nonhuman Animals*, 248–9; Cavalieri, *The Animal Question*, 137–8; and Steven M. Wise, *Unlocking the Cage: Science and the Case for Animal Rights* (Oxford: The Perseus Press, 2002), 32–3.

37. Gerald Dworkin, *The Theory and Practice of Autonomy* (Cambridge: Cambridge University Press, 1988), 108.

38. This argument can be found in Cochrane, "Do Animals Have an Interest in Liberty?," 670.

39. This example is inspired by a similar one given in DeGrazia, *Animal Rights*, 55.

40. I owe this objection to Cécile Fabre.

4. Animal Agriculture

1. *Statistics of Scientific Procedures on Living Animals: Great Britain 2005* (London: HMSO, 2006), 6.

2. This figure comes from combining the statistics from two sources: for slaughtered poultry, National Statistics, "Poultry and Poultrymeat Statistics Notice," November 30, 2006; and for other slaughtered animals, "Slaughterhouse Surveys, Defra, SEERAD, DARD (NI)," November 23, 2006. Both datasets are available from http://www.defra.gov.uk.

3. Mark Bittman, "Rethinking the Meat-Guzzler," *New York Times,* January 27, 2008.

4. These stalls are banned in the UK and Sweden for animal welfare reasons. A ban will be imposed across the EU in 2013.

5. This account is informed by Timothy E. Blackwell, "Production Practices and Well-Being: Swine," in *The Well-Being of Farm Animals: Challenges and Solutions*, ed. G. J. Benson and B. E. Rollin (Ames: Blackwell, 2004).

6. David Benatar, "Why the Naïve Argument Against Moral Vegetarianism Really Is Naïve," *Environmental Values* 10, no. 1 (February 2001): 106.

7. There might be extremely good reasons not to eat animals who have died of natural causes: they might be disease-ridden and, if they have lived to old age, their flesh might be intolerably tough. However, the point still stands that we are under no obligation not to eat animals who have died of natural causes.

8. For example, see, Feinberg, "The Rights of Animals and Unborn Generations," 58–60.

9. See Ernest Partridge, "Posthumous Interests and Posthumous Respect," *Ethics* 91, no. 2 (January 1981): 253.

10. Jeff McMahan makes the same point in "Eating Animals the Nice Way," *Dædalus* 137, no. 1 (Winter 2008): 71.

11. This example borrows a little from Kazuo Ishiguro's novel *Never Let Me Go* (London: Faber and Faber, 2006).

12. McMahan, "Eating Animals the Nice Way," 71.

13. For this argument, see Regan, *The Case for Animal Rights*, 357.

14. S. F. Sapontzis, *Morals, Reason, and Animals* (Philadelphia: Temple University Press, 1987), 230; and Peter Alward, "The Naïve Argument Against Moral Vegetarianism," *Environmental Values* 9, no. 1 (February 2000): 83.

15. Alward, "The Naïve Argument Against Moral Vegetarianism," 83.

16. Dale Jamieson, "Rights, Justice, and Duties to Provide Assistance: A Critique of Regan's Theory of Rights," *Ethics* 100, no. 2 (January 1990): 354.

17. Sapontzis makes this same point in *Morals, Reason, and Animals*, 232.

18. Alison McIntyre, "Doctrine of Double Effect," in *The Stanford Encyclopedia of Philosophy*, ed. E. N. Zalta (Fall 2009), http://plato.stanford.edu/archives/fall2009/entries/double-effect/.

19. Andy Lamey, "Food Fight! Davis Versus Regan on the Ethics of Eating Beef," *Journal of Social Philosophy* 38, no. 2 (Summer 2007): 343.

20. Richard Hull, "Deconstructing the Doctrine of Double Effect," *Ethical Theory and Moral Practice* 3, no. 2 (June 2000): 198.

21. Peter Singer, "Review: Do Consequences Count? Rethinking the Doctrine of Double Effect," *Hastings Center Report* 10, no. 1 (February 1980): 43.

22. Steven L. Davis has attributed this argument to Tom Regan following personal correspondence. See Steven L. Davis, "The Least Harm Principle May

Require That Humans Consume a Diet Containing Large Herbivores, Not a Vegan Diet," *Journal of Agricultural and Environmental Ethics* 16, no. 4 (July 2003): 388.

23. Ibid.

24. Ibid., 390.

25. Lamey, "Food Fight!," 335–8.

26. Gaverick Matheny, "Least Harm: A Defense of Vegetarianism from Steven Davis's Omnivorous Proposal," *Journal of Agricultural and Environmental Ethics* 16, no. 5 (September 2003): 506.

27. Ibid., 507.

5. Animals and Genetic Engineering

1. These examples are taken from a useful summary given in Michael J. Reiss and Roger Straughan, *Improving Nature? The Science and Ethics of Genetic Engineering* (Cambridge: Cambridge University Press, 1996), 166–74.

2. For more on such killings, see Kevin R. Smith, "Animal Genetic Manipulation: A Utilitarian Response," in *The Animal Ethics Reader*, ed. S. J. Armstrong and R. G. Botzler, 2nd ed. (Abingdon: Routledge, 2008), 391.

3. These examples are discussed in David Boonin, *A Defense of Abortion* (Cambridge: Cambridge University Press, 2003), 45–9.

4. This line of reasoning is influenced by the argument found in Allen Buchanan et al., *From Chance to Choice: Genetics and Justice* (New York: Cambridge University Press, 2000), 236.

5. This summary is taken from Ben Mepham, "'Würde der Kreatur' and the Common Morality," *Journal of Agricultural and Environmental Ethics* 13, no. 1 (March 2000): 67.

6. I cannot find out whether Alba did have similar opportunities for well-being compared to other rabbits. However, we can at least assume that the creation of a glow-in-the-dark animal with such opportunities is possible, making the example a useful one. For more on Alba and some recently engineered glow-in-the-dark pigs, see "Glow-in-the-Dark Pigs Make Debut," *ABC News,* January 12, 2006, http://abcnews.go.com/Technology/Health/story?id=1498324.

7. Leon R. Kass, "The Wisdom of Repugnance: Why We Should Ban the Cloning of Humans," *New Republic* 216, no. 22 (June 1997).

8. I appreciate that Kass claims that repugnance is not an argument. But then what is it? Something to be invoked simply to end debate and analysis? To engage with it and evaluate it, I am treating it as an argument for the purposes of this section.

9. This point is also made in Peter Singer, "Heavy Petting," *Nerve.com* (2001), http://www.nerve.com/Opinions/Singer/heavyPetting/main.asp.

10. On the so-called unnatural is unethical argument, see D. R. Cooley and G. A. Goreham, "Are Transgenic Organisms Unnatural?," *Ethics and the Environment* 9, no. 1 (Spring 2004).

11. David Cooper, "Intervention, Humility and Animal Integrity," in *Animal Biotechnology and Ethics*, ed. A. Holland and A. Johnson (London: Chapman and Hall, 1998), 155.

12. Mary Midgley, "Biotechnology and Monstrosity: Why We Should Pay Attention to the 'Yuk Factor'," *Hastings Center Report* 30, no. 5 (September–October 2000): 12.

13. Philipp Balzer, Klaus Rippe, and Peter Schaber, "Two Concepts of Dignity for Humans and Non-human Organisms in the Context of Genetic Engineering," *Journal of Agricultural and Environmental Ethics* 13, nos. 1–2 (March 2000): 23.

14. Sara Elizabeth Gavrell Ortiz, "Beyond Welfare: Animal Integrity, Animal Dignity, and Genetic Engineering," *Ethics and the Environment* 9, no. 1 (Spring 2004): 114.

15. Nussbaum, *Frontiers of Justice*, 325.

16. For use of this term, see, for example, Buchanan et al., *From Chance to Choice*, 225.

17. Bernard E. Rollin, *Science and Ethics* (New York: Cambridge University Press, 2006), 169.

18. Ibid.

19. Derek Parfit, *Reasons and Persons* (Oxford: Clarendon Press, 1984), chap. 16.

20. For an excellent example of such an argument, see Dan W. Brock, "Preventing Genetically Transmitted Disabilities While Respecting Persons with Disabilities," in *Quality of Life and Human Difference: Genetic Testing, Health Care and Disability*, ed. D. Wasserman et al. (New York: Cambridge University Press, 2005).

21. Jeff McMahan, "Preventing the Existence of People with Disabilities," in Wasserman et al., *Quality of Life and Human Difference*, 145.

22. Robin Attfield, "Intrinsic Value and Transgenic Animals," in Holland and Johnson, *Animal Biotechnology and Ethics*, 187.

23. James Woodward, "The Non-Identity Problem," *Ethics* 96, no. 4 (July 1986): 810.

24. This objection has been leveled at Bernard Rollin, but it also applies to the proposals outlined in this chapter. Rollin judges the permissibility of genetic engineering by reference to a "Principle of Conservation of Welfare." In other words, to be permissible, the engineered animals must be no worse off in terms of suffering than their parent stock. While this principle is similar to the proposal of this book because of its use of well-being as the final determinant of the permissibility of engineering, Rollin uses *achieved* well-being, while this book uses *opportunities* for well-being. See Bernard E. Rollin, *The Frankenstein Syndrome: Ethical and Social Issues in the Genetic Engineering of Animals* (Cambridge: Cambridge University Press, 1995), 179.

25. This example and objection can be found in Bernice Bovenkerk et al., "Brave New Birds: The Use of 'Animal Integrity' in Animal Ethics," *Hastings Center Report* 32, no. 1 (January–February 2002): 16–17; and Ortiz, "Beyond Welfare," 95.

6. Animal Entertainment

1. For two notable examples, see John Bryant, *Fettered Kingdoms*, rev. ed. (Winchester: Fox Press, 1990), 9; and Francione, *Introduction to Animal Rights*,

169–70. These two authors should be commended for facing up to the implications of their theory. In my view, too many other proponents of animal rights propose an animal interest in liberty and yet ignore the implications of this claim for the practice of pet keeping. This inconsistency is also pointed out by Stuart Spencer et al., "History and Ethics of Keeping Pets: Comparison with Farm Animals," *Journal of Agricultural and Environmental Ethics* 19, no. 1 (February 2006): 21.

2. Two examples of such a view can be found in Jamieson, "Against Zoos"; and Rowlands, *Animals Like Us*, 152–9.

3. "RSPCA Reports Year of Shocking Animal Abuse," *Guardian*, July 26, 2006.

4. Roger A. Mugford, "Canine Behavioural Therapy," in *The Domestic Dog: Its Evolution, Behaviour and Interventions with People*, ed. J. Serpell (Cambridge: Cambridge University Press, 1995), 150.

5. M. Engebretson, "The Welfare and Suitability of Parrots as Companion Animals: A Review," *Animal Welfare* 15, no. 3 (August 2006): 272–3.

6. Michael W. Fox, *The Dog: Its Domestication and Behaviour* (London: Garland STMP Press, 1978), 258–9.

7. Figures from the "Stray Dog Survey 2006" conducted by GfK NOP on behalf of Dogs Trust, http://www.dogstrust.org.uk/press_office/stray_dog_survey_2006/.

8. In the UK it used to be necessary to have a license to own a dog. However, this was phased out in 1987.

9. We ordinarily refer to the killing of sick animals as "putting them down." Presumably this phrase is used (just as the term "culling" is used) because it is easier to stomach than "killing." I will mainly stick with the term "killing" in this discussion to avoid the bias inherent in these softer terms.

10. Frans De Waal, "Bonobo Sex and Society," *Scientific American* (March 1995): 82.

11. Jonathan Balcombe, *Pleasurable Kingdom: Animals and the Nature of Feeling Good* (Basingstoke: Palgrave Macmillan, 2006), 107–24 .

12. C. Victor Spain, Janet M. Scarlett, and Katherine A. Houpt, "Long-Term Risks and Benefits of Early-Age Gonadectomy in Dogs," *Journal of the American Veterinary Medical Association* 224, no. 3 (February 2004).

13. This same argument can be found in Keith Burgess-Jackson, "Doing Right by Our Animal Companions," *Journal of Ethics* 2, no. 2 (June 1998): 183–4.

14. "Pedigree Dogs Plagued by Disease," *BBC News*, August 19, 2008, http://news.bbc.co.uk/go/pr/fr/-/1/hi/uk/7569064.stm.

15. This issue has become an interesting topic of debate in the UK in recent years, with the RSPCA criticizing the Kennel Club for maintaining "breed-standards" that inevitably lead to health problems and suffering within dogs. See ibid.

16. For just one recent example, note the reports on Bangkok's Pata zoo. See Ben Doherty, "Plight of Animals at Bangkok's Rooftop Zoo Above Department Store," *Guardian*, September 10, 2010.

17. One of the most notorious examples in the UK relates to the circus owner Mary Chipperfield, who was convicted of twelve counts of animal cruelty in rela-

tion to her beating of a young chimpanzee. See Helen Carter, "Circus Trainer Guilty of Cruelty to Chimpanzee," *Guardian,* January 28, 1999.

18. Brian Bertram, "Misconceptions About Zoos," *Biologist* 51, no. 4 (2004): 205 (my emphasis).

19. The interest that humans have in performing such activities might be argued to be more compelling if those activities are based on a cultural practice. In chapter 8 I consider cultural practices that harm animals.

20. Chapter 2 argued that fish are very likely to be sentient. For more evidence, see Quirin Schiermeier, "New Evidence That Fish Feel Pain," *Nature News,* April 30, 2003, http://www.nature.com/news/2003/030430/full/news030428-9 .html; and James Randerson, "Does a Hook Hurt a Fish? The Evidence Is Reeling In," *New Scientist,* May 3, 2003.

21. Daniel Foggo, "Revealed: The Man Who Killed 10,000 Dogs," *Sunday Times,* July 16, 2006.

22. "The Slaughtered Horses That Shame Our Racing," *Observer,* October 1, 2006.

23. See Monty Roberts, *The Man Who Listens to Horses* (London: Arrow Books, 1997).

24. "The Slaughtered Horses That Shame Our Racing."

25. Suzanne Laba Cataldi, "Animals and the Concept of Dignity: Critical Reflections on a Circus Performance," *Ethics and the Environment* 7, no. 2 (Autumn 2002): 106.

26. Ibid, 107, 109.

27. Ibid., 117–18.

28. Ibid., 116.

29. Dita Wickins-Dražilová, "Zoo Animal Welfare," *Journal of Agricultural and Environmental Ethics* 19, no. 1 (February 2006): 32.

30. Ibid.

31. Ibid., 34.

32. David DeGrazia, "Animal Ethics Around the Turn of the Twenty-First Century," *Journal of Agricultural and Environmental Ethics* 11, no. 2 (May 1998): 128.

33. Ibid., 128–9.

34. Ibid., 128.

35. This case is rather like farmers who choose to spray their sheep with nontoxic paint to help identify them, or even to amuse passing motorists. See "Sheep Turning Blue for St Andrew," *BBC News,* November 27, 2008, http:// news.bbc.co.uk/go/pr/fr/-/1/hi/scotland/7751243.stm.

36. Regan, *The Case for Animal Rights*, 243.

37. Ibid., 248.

38. Ibid., 249.

39. Gary L. Francione, "Animals—Property or Persons?" in Nussbaum and Sunstein, *Animal Rights*, 124. Steven M. Wise is another important writer who argues that animals' property status necessarily renders them being treated as a "thing." See Steven M. Wise, *Rattling the Cage: Towards Legal Rights for Animals* (London: Profile Books, 2000), 4. Since Wise's argument claims to be more concerned with legal rather than moral rights, my discussion focuses on Francione.

40. Francione, *Introduction to Animal Rights*, 79.

41. A. M. Honoré, "Ownership," in *Oxford Essays in Jurisprudence,* ed. A. G. Guest (Oxford: Oxford University Press, 1961).

42. Jeremy Waldron, *The Right to Private Property* (Oxford: Clarendon Press, 1988), 49–50.

43. For more on this point, and the issue of animal ownership generally, see Alasdair Cochrane, "Ownership and Justice for Animals," *Utilitas* 21, no. 4 (December 2009).

44. Francione, *Rain Without Thunder*, 127.

45. Cass R. Sunstein, "Introduction: What Are Animal Rights?" in Nussbaum and Sunstein, *Animal Rights*, 11.

46. This kind of domination is often referred to in republican thought. See, for example, Philip Pettit, *Republicanism* (Oxford: Clarendon Press, 1997), chap. 2.

7. Animals and the Environment

1. For the classic statements of such a claim, see J. Baird Callicott, "Animal Liberation: A Triangular Affair," in *Environmental Ethics*, ed. R. Elliot (Oxford: Oxford University Press, 1995); and Mark Sagoff, "Animal Liberation and Environmental Ethics: Bad Marriage: Quick Divorce," in *Environmental Ethics: What Really Matters, What Really Works*, ed. D. Schmidtz and E. Willott (Oxford: Oxford University Press, 2002).

2. For the initial distinction between "deep" and "shallow"' environmental ethics, see Arne Naess, "The Shallow and the Deep, Long-Range Ecology Movement. A Summary," *Inquiry* 16, no. 1 (1973).

3. Varner, *In Nature's Interests?* 58; and Johnson, *A Morally Deep World,* 101.

4. Varner, *In Nature's Interests?*, 60.

5. Aldo Leopold, *A Sand County Almanac: And Sketches Here and There*, commemorative ed. (Oxford: Oxford University Press, 1989), 218–25.

6. J. Baird Callicott, "The Conceptual Foundations of the Land Ethic," in *Environmental Philosophy: From Animal Rights to Radical Ecology*, ed. M. E. Zimmerman et al., 2nd ed. (Englewood Cliffs: Prentice Hall, 1998), 107.

7. For two prominent examples, see James Nickel, "The Human Right to a Safe Environment: Philosophical Perspectives on Its Scope and Justification," *Yale Journal of International Law* 18, no. 1 (Winter 1993); and Tim Hayward, *Constitutional Environmental Rights* (Oxford: Oxford University Press, 2005).

8. This kind of welfare-centric environmental ethic has been proposed by other thinkers. One similar theory—but without a rights-based framework—is Peter Singer's. See Singer, *Practical Ethics*, chap. 10; and Singer, "Not for Humans Only: The Place of Nonhumans in Environmental Issues," in *Ethics and Problems of the 21st Century*, ed. K. E. Goodpaster and K. M. Sayre (Notre Dame: University of Notre Dame Press, 1979).

9. Bryan G. Norton, "Environmental Ethics and Nonhuman Rights," in *The Animal Rights / Environmental Ethics Debate: The Environmental Perspective*, ed. E. C. Hargrove (Albany: State University of New York Press, 1992), 83.

10. See Cheryl S. Asa and Ingrid J. Porton, "Introduction: The Need for Wildlife Contraception: Problems Related to Unrestricted Population Growth," in *Wildlife Contraception: Issues, Methods and Applications*, ed. C. S. Asa and I. J. Porton (Baltimore: John Hopkins University Press, 2005), xxvii.

11. John Hadley, "Nonhuman Animal Property: Reconciling Environmentalism and Animal Rights," *Journal of Social Philosophy* 36, no. 3 (Fall 2005).

12. Ibid., 308.

13. The obligation to limit our release of greenhouse gases also gives us another reason to dismantle the meat industry. After all, the Intergovernmental Panel on Climate Change (IPCC) calculates that meat production puts more greenhouse gases into the atmosphere than transport. See Richard Black, "Shun Meat Says UN Climate Chief," *BBC News,* September 7, 2008, http://news.bbc.co.uk/1/hi/sci/tech/7600005.stm.

14. Nicholas Stern, *The Economics of Climate Change: The Stern Review* (Cambridge: Cambridge University Press, 2007), 105.

15. See also Rollin, *Science and Ethics*, 144.

16. Holmes Rolston III, "Duties to Endangered Species," in Elliot, *Environmental Ethics*, 67.

17. Ibid., 72.

18. Ibid., 68.

19. Ibid., 72.

20. This argument is made in Mark A. Michael, "Is It Natural to Drive Species to Extinction?," *Ethics and the Environment* 10, no. 1 (Spring 2005).

21. Regan, *The Case for Animal Rights*, 359.

22. Ibid., xl.

23. This point is made in a different context in Simon Caney, "Environmental Degradation, Reparations, and the Moral Significance of History," *Journal of Social Philosophy* 37, no. 3 (Fall 2006): 467–76.

24. For more on the relationship between human health and biodiversity, see Eric Chivian and Aaron Bernstein, eds., *Sustaining Life: How Human Health Depends on Biodiversity* (Oxford: Oxford University Press, 2008).

25. Fred Pearce, "Birds Do It, Bees Do It: Pollinators Are Vital for Crop Yields. But They Are Dying Out," *New Scientist*, February 14, 1998.

26. For example, see Holmes Rolston III, "Challenges in Environmental Ethics," in Zimmerman et al., *Environmental Philosophy*, 142.

27. For this analogy with works of art—and a refutation of it—see Singer, "Not for Humans Only," 203–4.

28. Lilly-Marlene Russow, "Why Do Species Matter?," in *Planet in Peril: Essays in Environmental Ethics*, ed. D. Westphal and F. Westphal (Orlando: Harcourt Brace College Publishers, 1994), 260–1.

29. Deer Commission for Scotland "Annual Report: 2006–7: Cull Data," http://www.dcs.gov.uk/info_documents.aspx#annual.

30. Varner, *In Nature's Interests*, 114.

31. Ibid., 115.

32. For example, see Regan, *The Case for Animal Rights*, 357. But also see Pluhar, *Beyond Prejudice*, 276.

33. Asa and Porton, "Introduction," xxvii.

34. Jay F. Kirkpatrick, "Measuring the Effects of Wildlife Contraception: The Argument for Comparing Apples with Oranges," *Reproduction, Fertility and Development* 19, no. 4 (2007): 548.

35. Jay F. Kirkpatrick and Kimberley M. Frank, "Contraception in Free-Ranging Wildlife," in Asa and Porton, *Wildlife Contraception*, 201–10.

36. Ibid., 215.

37. Zhibon Zhang, "Mathematical Models of Wildlife Management by Contraception," *Ecological Modelling* 132, nos. 1–2 (July 2000): 106.

38. For one important skeptic, see Mark Sagoff, "Do Non-Native Species Threaten the Natural Environment?," *Journal of Agricultural and Environmental Ethics* 18, no. 3 (May 2005). For a response to this view that claims that nonnative species do cause extinctions, see Daniel Simberloff, "Non-native Species *Do* Threaten the Natural Environment," *Journal of Agricultural and Environmental Ethics* 18, no. 7 (December 2005).

39. Jessica Gurevitch and Dianna F. Padilla, "Are Invasive Species a Major Cause of Extinctions?," *Trends in Ecology and Evolution* 19, no. 9 (September 2004): 473.

40. Miguel Clavero and Emil Garcia-Berthou, "Invasive Species Are a Leading Cause of Animal Extinctions," *Trends in Ecology and Evolution* 20, no. 3 (March 2005): 110.

8. Animals and Cultural Practices

1. It might be claimed that foxhunters do not constitute a cultural group. Perhaps instead they are a group who share a common source of enjoyment, much like football supporters. There is not the room in this chapter to discuss the extremely difficult issue of the necessary and sufficient conditions of a "culture." For this reason, I will simply assume that all the groups mentioned in this chapter can justifiably be referred to as cultural groups.

2. Giles Tremlett, "Bullfight Reform Plan Is Red Rag to Aficionados," *Guardian*, December 21, 2006.

3. DEFRA, *Government's Final Response to the Farm Animal Welfare Council Report*, March 8, 2005, http://www.defra.gov.uk/animalh/welfare/farmed/final_response.pdf.

4. Quotation taken from DEFRA website, "Hunting with Dogs—Questions and Answers," http://www.defra.gov.uk/rural/hunting/hunting_qa.htm.

5. See, for example, Susan Moller Okin et al., *Is Multiculturalism Bad for Women?* (Princeton: Princeton University Press, 1999).

6. Anne Phillips, *Multiculturalism Without Culture* (Princeton: Princeton University Press, 2007), 8.

7. Chandran Kukathas, "Are There Any Cultural Rights?," in *The Rights of Minority Cultures*, ed. W. Kymlicka (Oxford: Oxford University Press, 1995).

8. Chandran Kukathas, "Cultural Toleration," in *NOMOS XXIX: Ethnicity and Group Rights*, ed. I. Shapiro and W. Kymlicka (New York: New York University Press, 1997), 87.

9. Kukathas, "Are There Any Cultural Rights?," 251; and Chandran Kukathas, *The Liberal Archipelago* (Oxford: Oxford University Press, 2003), 141–5.

10. Sampath Kumar, "Dangers of Taming the Bull," *BBC News*, January 21, 2005, http://news.bbc.co.uk/1/hi/world/south_asia/4188611.stm.

11. Alex Kirby, "Harpooned Whales 'Seldom Die Instantly'," *BBC News*, March 14, 2001, http://news.bbc.co.uk/1/hi/sci/tech/1218720.stm.

12. This point is made in Will Kymlicka, *Multicultural Citizenship: A Liberal Theory of Minority Rights* (Oxford: Oxford University Press, 1995), 107.

13. Brian Barry, *Culture and Equality* (Cambridge: Polity Press, 2001), 256–7.

14. Janet Williams, "US Judge Blocks Tribal Whaling," *BBC News*, May 4, 2002, http://news.bbc.co.uk/1/hi/world/americas/1967677.stm. This point is also made in Alasdair Cochrane, *An Introduction to Animals and Political Theory* (Basingstoke: Palgrave Macmillan, 2010), p. 89.

15. Once again, I should point out that I am extremely skeptical that there is any such community.

16. Michael Hartney, "Some Confusions Concerning Collective Rights," in Kymlicka, *The Rights of Minority Cultures*, 206.

17. This same point is made in Barry, *Culture and Equality*, 45. See also Cochrane, *An Introduction to Animals and Political Theory*, 89.

18. Paula Casal, "Is Multiculturalism Bad for Animals?," *Journal of Political Philosophy* 11, no. 1 (March 2003): 6.

19. F. Barbara Orlans et al., *The Human Use of Animals: Case Studies in Ethical Choice* (Oxford: Oxford University Press, 1998), 307–11.

20. I have taken these candidates from four main sources: Paul Bou-Habib, "A Theory of Religious Accommodation," *Journal of Applied Philosophy* 23, no. 1 (January 2006): 114–21; Kent Greenawalt, "Freedom of Association and Religious Association," in *Freedom of Association,* ed. A. Gutmann (Princeton: Princeton University Press, 1998), 121–2; Martha C. Nussbaum, "A Plea for Difficulty," in Okin et al., *Is Multiculturalism Bad for Women?*, 106; and Casal, "Is Multiculturalism Bad for Animals?," 14–15.

21. Bou-Habib, "A Theory of Religious Accommodation," 117.

22. Kukathas, *The Liberal Archipelago*, 55.

23. Basing minority rights on the value of equality is proposed in Kymlicka, *Multicultural Citizenship*, 108–15. Basing them specifically on equality of opportunity is advanced by Jonathan Quong, "Cultural Exemptions, Expensive Tastes and Equal Opportunities," *Journal of Applied Philosophy* 23, no. 1 (January 2006).

24. For more on equal opportunity and the chance-choice distinction, see Sue Mendus, "Choice, Chance and Multiculturalism," in *Multiculturalism Reconsidered: 'Culture and Equality' and Its Critics*, ed. P. Kelly (Cambridge: Polity Press, 2002); and David Miller, "Liberalism, Equal Opportunities and Cultural Commitments," in Kelly, *Multiculturalism Reconsidered*.

25. Quong, "Cultural Exemptions, Expensive Tastes and Equal Opportunities," 58.

26. Bou-Habib, "A Theory of Religious Accommodation," 123.

27. Undoubtedly, other religions and nonreligious cultural groups might also make this claim.

28. Casal, "Is Multiculturalism Bad for Animals?," 17.

29. I make this same claim in Cochrane, *An Introduction to Animals and Political Theory*, 91.

9. Conclusion

1. Adam Swift and Stuart White, "Political Theory, Social Science and Real Politics," in Leopold and Stears, *Political Theory*, 54.

2. Ibid.

Bibliography

Aaltola, Elisa. "'Other Animal Ethics' and the Demand for Difference." *Environmental Values* 11, no. 2 (May 2002): 193–209.

Adam, David. "Scientists Say Lobsters Feel No Pain." *Guardian*, February 8, 2005.

Allen, Colin. "Animal Consciousness." In *The Stanford Encyclopedia of Philosophy*, edited by E. N. Zalta (Summer 2003). http://plato.stanford.edu/archives/summer2003/entries/consciousness-animal/.

Alward, Peter. "The Naïve Argument Against Moral Vegetarianism." *Environmental Values* 9, no. 1 (February 2000): 81–9.

Anderson, Elizabeth. "Animal Rights and the Values of Nonhuman Life." In *Animal Rights: Current Debates and New Directions*, edited by M. C. Nussbaum and C. R. Sunstein, 277–98. New York: Oxford University Press, 2004.

"Anglers Are Finally Off the Hook: Fish Feel No Pain." *Daily Telegraph*, February 9, 2003.

Asa, Cheryl S., and Ingrid J. Porton. "Introduction: The Need for Wildlife Contraception: Problems Related to Unrestricted Population Growth." In *Wildlife Contraception: Issues, Methods and Applications*, edited by C. S. Asa and I. J. Porton, xxv–xxxii. Baltimore: Johns Hopkins University Press, 2005.

Attfield, Robin. "The Good of Trees." *Journal of Value Inquiry* 15, no. 1 (March 1981): 35–51.

——. "Intrinsic Value and Transgenic Animals." In *Animal Biotechnology and Ethics*, edited by A. Holland and A. Johnson, 172–89. London: Chapman and Hall, 1998.

Balcombe, Jonathan. *Pleasurable Kingdom: Animals and the Nature of Feeling Good*. Basingstoke: Palgrave Macmillan, 2006.

Balzer, Philipp, Klaus Rippe, and Peter Schaber. "Two Concepts of Dignity for Humans and Non-human Organisms in the Context of Genetic Engineering." *Journal of Agricultural and Environmental Ethics* 13, nos. 1–2 (March 2000): 7–27.

Barras, Colin. "Lobster Pain May Prick Diners' Consciences." *New Scientist*, November 9, 2007.

Barry, Brian. *Justice as Impartiality*. Oxford: Oxford University Press, 1995.

——. *Culture and Equality*. Cambridge: Polity Press, 2001.

Benatar, David. "Why the Naïve Argument Against Moral Vegetarianism Really Is Naïve." *Environmental Values* 10, no. 1 (February 2001): 103–12.

Bentham, Jeremy. "Anarchical Fallacies: Being an Examination of the Declaration of Rights Issued During the French Revolution." In *Nonsense upon Stilts: Bentham, Burke and Marx on the Rights of Man*, edited by J. Waldron, 46–76. London: Methuen, 1987.

Berlin, Isaiah. "Two Concepts of Liberty." In *Political Philosophy*, edited by A. Quinton, 141–52. Oxford: Oxford University Press, 1967.

Bertram, Brian. "Misconceptions About Zoos." *Biologist* 51, no. 4 (2004): 199–206.

Black, Richard. "Shun Meat Says UN Climate Chief." *BBC News*, September 7, 2008. http://news.bbc.co.uk/1/hi/sci/tech/7600005.stm.

Blackwell, Timothy E. "Production Practices and Well-Being: Swine." In *The Well-Being of Farm Animals: Challenges and Solutions*, edited by G. J. Benson and B. E. Rollin, 241–69. Ames: Blackwell, 2004.

Boonin, David. *A Defense of Abortion*. Cambridge: Cambridge University Press, 2003.

Bou-Habib, Paul. "A Theory of Religious Accommodation." *Journal of Applied Philosophy* 23, no. 1 (January 2006): 109–26.

Bovenkerk, Bernice, Frans W. A. Brom, and Babs J. van den Bergh. "Brave New Birds: The Use of 'Animal Integrity' in Animal Ethics." *Hastings Center Report* 32, no. 1 (January–February 2002): 16–22.

Brock, Dan W. "Preventing Genetically Transmitted Disabilities While Respecting Persons with Disabilities." In *Quality of Life and Human Difference: Genetic Testing, Health Care and Disability*, edited by D. Wasserman, J. Bickenbach, and R. Wachbroit, 67–100. New York: Cambridge University Press, 2005.

Bryant, John. *Fettered Kingdoms*. Rev. ed. Winchester: Fox Press, 1990.

Buchanan, Allen, Dan W. Brock, Norman Daniels, and Daniel Wikler. *From Chance to Choice: Genetics and Justice*. New York: Cambridge University Press, 2000.

Burgess-Jackson, Keith. "Doing Right by Our Animal Companions." *Journal of Ethics* 2, no. 2 (June 1998): 159–85.

Byrnes, Sholto. "Animal Rights, Human Wrongs." *New Statesman*, February 28, 2008.

Calarco, Matthew, and Peter Atterton, eds. *Animal Philosophy: Essential Readings in Continental Thought*. New York: Continuum, 2004.

Callicott, J. Baird. "Animal Liberation: A Triangular Affair." In *Environmental Ethics*, edited by R. Elliot, 29–59. Oxford: Oxford University Press, 1995.

———. "The Conceptual Foundations of the Land Ethic." In *Environmental Philosophy: From Animal Rights to Radical Ecology*, edited by M. E. Zimmerman, J. Baird Callicott, G. Sessions, K. J. Warren, and J. Clark, 101–23. 2nd ed. Englewood Cliffs: Prentice Hall, 1998.

Caney, Simon. "Environmental Degradation, Reparations, and the Moral Significance of History." *Journal of Social Philosophy* 37, no. 3 (Fall 2006): 464–82.

Carruthers, Peter. *The Animals Issue: Moral Theory in Practice.* Cambridge: Cambridge University Press, 1992.

Carter, Helen. "Circus Trainer Guilty of Cruelty to Chimpanzee." *Guardian,* January 28, 1999.

Casal, Paula. "Is Multiculturalism Bad for Animals?" *Journal of Political Philosophy* 11, no. 1 (March 2003): 1–22.

Cataldi, Suzanne Laba. "Animals and the Concept of Dignity: Critical Reflections on a Circus Performance." *Ethics and the Environment* 7, no. 2 (Autumn 2002): 104–26.

Cavalieri, Paola. *The Animal Question: Why Nonhuman Animals Deserve Human Rights.* Oxford: Oxford University Press, 2001.

Chivian, Eric, and Aaron Bernstein, eds. *Sustaining Life: How Human Health Depends on Biodiversity.* Oxford: Oxford University Press, 2008.

Clavero, Miguel, and Emil Garcia-Berthou. "Invasive Species Are a Leading Cause of Animal Extinctions." *Trends in Ecology and Evolution* 20, no. 3 (March 2005): 110.

Cochrane, Alasdair. "Do Animals Have an Interest in Liberty?" *Political Studies* 57, no. 3 (December 2009): 660–79.

———. *An Introduction to Animals and Political Theory.* Basingstoke: Palgrave Macmillan, 2010.

———. "Ownership and Justice for Animals." *Utilitas* 21, no. 4 (December 2009): 424–42.

Cohen, Andrew I. "Contractarianism, Other-Regarding Attitudes and the Moral Standing of Nonhuman Animals." *Journal of Applied Philosophy* 24, no. 2 (May 2007): 188–201.

Cohen, Carl. "The Case for the Use of Animals in Biomedical Research." *New England Journal of Medicine* 315 (October 1986): 865–70.

Cooley, D. R., and G. A. Goreham. "Are Transgenic Organisms Unnatural?" *Ethics and the Environment* 9, no. 1 (Spring 2004): 46–55.

Cooper, David. "Intervention, Humility and Animal Integrity." In *Animal Biotechnology and Ethics,* edited by. A. Holland and A. Johnson, 145–55. London: Chapman and Hall, 1998.

"Crippled Chickens Choose Pain Relief." *BBC News,* March 26, 2000. http://news.bbc.co.uk/1/hi/uk/691129.stm.

Crisp, Roger. "Well-Being." In *The Stanford Encyclopedia of Philosophy,* edited by. E. N. Zalta (Summer 2003). http://plato.stanford.edu/archives/sum2003/entries/well-being.

Currie, Alistair. "Abusing the Weak." *New Statesman,* March 4, 2008.

Davis, Steven L. "The Least Harm Principle May Require That Humans Consume a Diet Containing Large Herbivores, Not a Vegan Diet." *Journal of Agricultural and Environmental Ethics* 16, no. 4 (July 2003): 387–97.

Deer Commission for Scotland. "Annual Report: 2006–7: Cull Data." http://www.dcs.gov.uk/info_documents.aspx#annual.

DEFRA. *Government's Final Response to the Farm Animal Welfare Council Report.* March 8, 2005. http://www.defra.gov.uk/animalh/welfare/farmed/final_response.pdf.

———. "Hunting with Dogs—Questions and Answers." http://www.defra.gov.uk/rural/hunting/hunting_qa.htm.

DeGrazia, David. "Animal Ethics Around the Turn of the Twenty-First Century." *Journal of Agricultural and Environmental Ethics* 11, no. 2 (May 1998): 111–29.

———. *Animal Rights: A Very Short Introduction.* Oxford: Oxford University Press, 2002.

———. *Taking Animals Seriously: Mental Life and Moral Status.* Cambridge: Cambridge University Press, 1996.

De Waal, Frans. "Bonobo Sex and Society." *Scientific American* (March 1995): 82–6.

Doherty, Ben. "Plight of Animals at Bangkok's Rooftop Zoo Above Department Store." *Guardian,* September 10, 2010.

Dombrowski, Daniel. *Babies and Beasts: The Argument from Marginal Cases.* Urbana: Illinois University Press, 1997.

Donovan, Josephine, and Carol J. Adams, eds. *The Feminist Care Tradition in Animal Ethics.* New York: Columbia University Press, 2007.

Dworkin, Gerald. *The Theory and Practice of Autonomy.* Cambridge: Cambridge University Press, 1988.

Dworkin, Ronald. *Freedom's Law: The Moral Reading of the American Constitution.* New York: Oxford University Press, 1996.

———. "Rights as Trumps." In *Theories of Rights,* edited by J. Waldron, 153–67. Oxford: Oxford University Press, 1984.

Engebretson, M. "The Welfare and Suitability of Parrots as Companion Animals: A Review." *Animal Welfare* 15, no. 3 (August 2006): 263–76.

Fabre, Cécile. *Whose Body Is It Anyway?* Oxford: Oxford University Press, 2006.

Feinberg, Joel. "The Rights of Animals and Unborn Generations." In *Philosophy and Environmental Crisis,* edited by W. T. Blackstone, 43–68. Athens: University of Georgia Press, 1974.

Foggo, Daniel. "Revealed: The Man Who Killed 10,000 Dogs." *Sunday Times,* July 16, 2006.

Fox, Douglas. "Do Fruit Flies Dream of Electric Bananas?" *New Scientist,* February 14, 2004.

Fox, Michael A. "'Animal Liberation': A Critique." *Ethics* 88, no. 2 (January 1978): 106–18.

Fox, Michael W. *The Dog: Its Domestication and Behaviour.* London: Garland STMP Press, 1978.

Francione, Gary L. *Animals as Persons: Essays on the Abolition of Animal Exploitation.* New York: Columbia University Press, 2008.

———. *Animals, Property, and the Law.* Philadelphia: Temple University Press, 1995.

———. "Animals—Property or Persons?" In *Animal Rights: Current Debates and New Directions,* edited by M. C. Nussbaum and C. R. Sunstein, 108–42. Oxford: Oxford University Press, 2004.

———. *Introduction to Animal Rights: Your Child or the Dog?* Philadelphia: Temple University Press, 2000.

———. *Rain Without Thunder: The Ideology of the Animal Rights Movement.* Philadelphia: Temple University Press, 1996.

Frey, R. G. "Animals." In *The Oxford Handbook of Practical Ethics,* edited by H. LaFollette, 161–87. Oxford: Oxford University Press, 2005.

―――. *Interests and Rights.* Oxford: Clarendon Press, 1980.

Frey, R. G., and Sir William Paton. "Vivisection, Morals and Medicine: An Exchange." In *Bioethics: An Anthology*, edited by. H. Kushe and P. Singer, 471–9. Oxford: Blackwell, 2002.

Garner, Robert. *Animal Ethics.* Cambridge: Polity, 2005.

―――. *Animals, Politics and Morality.* Manchester: Manchester University Press, 1993.

"Glow-in-the-Dark Pigs Make Debut." *ABC News*, January 12, 2006. http://abc news.go.com/Technology/Health/story?id=1498324.

Greenawalt, Kent. "Freedom of Association and Religious Association." In *Freedom of Association*, edited by A. Gutmann, 109–44. Princeton: Princeton University Press, 1998.

Griffin, Donald R. *The Question of Animal Awareness: Evolutionary Continuity of Mental Experience.* New York: Rockefeller University Press, 1976.

Gurevitch, Jessica, and Dianna F. Padilla. "Are Invasive Species a Major Cause of Extinctions?" *Trends in Ecology and Evolution* 19, no. 9 (September 2004): 470–4.

Hadley, John. "Nonhuman Animal Property: Reconciling Environmentalism and Animal Rights." *Journal of Social Philosophy* 36, no. 3 (Fall 2005): 305–15.

Hart, H.L.A. "Are There Any Natural Rights?" In *Political Philosophy*, edited by A. Quinton, 53–66. Oxford: Oxford University Press, 1967.

Hartney, Michael. "Some Confusions Concerning Collective Rights." In *The Rights of Minority Cultures*, edited by W. Kymlicka, 202–27. Oxford: Oxford University Press, 1995.

Hauser, Marc. *Wild Minds: What Animals Really Think.* London: Penguin, 2001.

Hayward, Tim. *Constitutional Environmental Rights.* Oxford: Oxford University Press, 2005.

Home Office. *Statistics of Scientific Procedures on Living Animals: Great Britain 2005.* London: HMSO, 2006.

Honoré, A.M. "Ownership." In *Oxford Essays in Jurisprudence*, edited by A. G. Guest, 107–47. Oxford: Oxford University Press, 1961.

Hull, Richard. "Deconstructing the Doctrine of Double Effect." *Ethical Theory and Moral Practice* 3, no. 2 (June 2000): 195–207.

Ishiguro, Kazuo. *Never Let Me Go.* London: Faber and Faber, 2006.

Jamieson, Dale. "Against Zoos." In *Morality's Progress: Essays on Humans, Other Animals, and the Rest of Nature*, edited by Dale Jamieson, 166–75. Oxford: Oxford University Press, 2002.

―――. "Rights, Justice, and Duties to Provide Assistance: A Critique of Regan's Theory of Rights." *Ethics* 100, no. 2 (January 1990): 349–62.

―――. "Zoos Revisited." In *Morality's Progress: Essays on Humans, Other Animals, and the Rest of Nature*, edited by Dale Jamieson, 176–89. Oxford: Oxford University Press, 2002.

Johnson, Lawrence E. *A Morally Deep World: An Essay on Moral Significance and Environmental Ethics.* Cambridge: Cambridge University Press, 1991.

Kant, Immanuel. *Lectures on Ethics*, translated by Louis Infield. New York: Harper and Row, 1963.

Kass, Leon R. "The Wisdom of Repugnance: Why We Should Ban the Cloning of Humans." *New Republic* 216, no. 22 (June 1997).

Kheel, Marti. "The Liberation of Nature: A Circular Affair." In *The Feminist Care Tradition in Animal Ethics*, edited by J. Donovan and C. Adams, 39–57. New York: Columbia University Press, 2007.

Kirby, Alex. "Fish Do Feel Pain, Scientists Say." *BBC News*, April 30, 2003. http://news.bbc.co.uk/1/hi/sci/tech/2983045.stm.

———. "Harpooned Whales 'Seldom Die Instantly'." *BBC News,* March 14, 2001. http://news.bbc.co.uk/1/hi/sci/tech/1218720.stm.

Kirkpatrick, Jay F. "Measuring the Effects of Wildlife Contraception: The Argument for Comparing Apples with Oranges." *Reproduction, Fertility and Development* 19, no. 4 (2007): 548–52.

Kirkpatrick, Jay F., and Kimberley M. Frank. "Contraception in Free-Ranging Wildlife." In *Wildlife Contraception*, edited by C. Asa and I. J. Porton, 195–221. Baltimore: Johns Hopkins University Press, 2005.

Kramer, Matthew H. "Do Animals and Dead People Have Legal Rights." *Canadian Journal of Law and Jurisprudence* 14, no. 1 (January 2001): 29–54.

Kukathas, Chandran. "Are There Any Cultural Rights?" In *The Rights of Minority Cultures*, edited by W. Kymlicka, 228–55. Oxford: Oxford University Press, 1995.

———. "Cultural Toleration." In *NOMOS XXIX: Ethnicity and Group Rights*, edited by I. Shapiro and W. Kymlicka, 69–104. New York: New York University Press, 1997.

———. *The Liberal Archipelago*. Oxford: Oxford University Press, 2003.

Kumar, Sampath. "Dangers of Taming the Bull." *BBC News*, January 21, 2005. http://news.bbc.co.uk/1/hi/world/south_asia/4188611.stm.

Kymlicka, William. *Multicultural Citizenship: A Liberal Theory of Minority Rights*. Oxford: Oxford University Press, 1995.

LaFollette, Hugh, and Niall Shanks. *Brute Science: Dilemmas of Animal Experimentation*. London: Routledge, 1996.

Lamey, Andy. "Food Fight! Davis versus Regan on the Ethics of Eating Beef." *Journal of Social Philosophy* 38, no. 2 (Summer 2007): 331–48.

Leopold, Aldo. *A Sand County Almanac: And Sketches Here and There*. Commemorative ed. Oxford: Oxford University Press, 1989.

Linzey, Andrew. *Animal Theology*. London: SCM Press, 1994.

Machan, Tibor R. "Why Human Beings May Use Animals." *Journal of Value Inquiry* 36, no. 1 (March 2002): 9-16.

Machan, Tibor R. *Putting Humans First: Why We Are Nature's Favorite*. Oxford: Rowman & Littlefield, 2004.

Matheny, Gaverick. "Least Harm: A Defense of Vegetarianism from Steven Davis's Omnivorous Proposal." *Journal of Agricultural and Environmental Ethics* 16, no. 5 (September 2003): 505–11.

McCloskey, H. J. "Rights." *Philosophical Quarterly* 15, no. 5 (April 1965): 115–27.

McIntyre, Alison. "Doctrine of Double Effect." In *The Stanford Encyclopedia of Philosophy*, edited by E. N. Zalta (Fall 2009). http://plato.stanford.edu/archives/fall2009/entries/double-effect/.

McMahan, Jeff. "Eating Animals the Nice Way." *Dœdalus* 137, no. 1 (Winter 2008): 66–76.

————. *The Ethics of Killing*. Oxford: Oxford University Press, 2002.

————. "Preventing the Existence of People with Disabilities." In *Quality of Life and Human Difference: Genetic Testing, Health Care and Disability*, edited by D. Wasserman, J. Bickenbach, and R. Wachbroit, 142–71. New York: Cambridge University Press, 2005.

Mendus, Sue. "Choice, Chance and Multiculturalism." In *Multiculturalism Reconsidered: 'Culture and Equality' and Its Critics*, edited by P. Kelly, 31–44. Cambridge: Polity Press, 2002.

Mepham, Ben. "'Würde der Kreatur' and the Common Morality." *Journal of Agricultural and Environmental Ethics* 13, no. 1 (March 2000): 65–78.

Michael, Mark A. "Is It Natural to Drive Species to Extinction?" *Ethics and the Environment* 10, no. 1 (Spring 2005): 49–66.

Midgley, Mary. *Animals and Why They Matter*. Athens: University of Georgia Press, 1984.

————. "Biotechnology and Monstrosity: Why We Should Pay Attention to the 'Yuk Factor'." *Hastings Center Report* 30, no. 5 (September–October 2000): 7–15.

Miller, David. "Liberalism, Equal Opportunities and Cultural Commitments." In *Multiculturalism Reconsidered: 'Culture and Equality' and its Critics*, edited by P. Kelly, 45–61. Cambridge: Polity Press, 2002.

————. "Political Philosophy for Earthlings." In *Political Theory: Methods and Approaches*, edited by. D. Leopold and M. Stears, 29–48. Oxford: Oxford University Press, 2008.

Mugford, Roger A. "Canine Behavioural Therapy." In *The Domestic Dog: Its Evolution, Behaviour and Interventions with People*, edited by J. Serpell, 139–52. Cambridge: Cambridge University Press, 1995.

Naess, Arne. "The Shallow and the Deep, Long-Range Ecology Movement: A Summary." *Inquiry* 16, no. 1 (1973): 95–100.

National Statistics. "Poultry and Poultrymeat Statistics Notice," November 30, 2006. http://www.defra.gov.uk.

————. "Slaughterhouse surveys, Defra, SEERAD, DARD (NI)," November 23, 2006. http://www.defra.gov.uk.

Nickel, James. "The Human Right to a Safe Environment: Philosophical Perspectives on Its Scope and Justification." *Yale Journal of International Law* 18, no. 1 (Winter 1993): 281–95.

Nobis, Nathan. "Carl Cohen's 'Kind' Arguments for Animal Rights and Against Human Rights." *Journal of Applied Philosophy* 21, no. 1 (January 2004): 43–59.

Norton, Bryan G. "Environmental Ethics and Nonhuman Rights." In *The Animal Rights / Environmental Ethics Debate: The Environmental Perspective*, edited by E. C. Hargrove, 71–94. Albany: State University of New York Press, 1992.

Nozick, Robert. *Anarchy, State and Utopia*. New York: Basic Books, 1974.

Nussbaum, Martha C. *Frontiers of Justice: Disability, Nationality, Species Membership*. London: Belknap Press of Harvard University Press, 2006.

————. "A Plea for Difficulty." In Susan Moller Okin with respondents, *Is Multiculturalism Bad for Women?* edited by J. Cohen, M. Howard, and M. C. Nussbaum, 105–14. Princeton: Princeton University Press, 1999.

Okin, Susan Moller, with respondents. *Is Multiculturalism Bad for Women?* edited by J. Cohen, M. Howard, and M. C. Nussbaum. Princeton: Princeton University Press, 1999.

Orlans, F. Barbara, T. Beauchamp, R. Dresser, F. Morton, and J. Gluck. *The Human Use of Animals: Case Studies in Ethical Choice.* Oxford: Oxford University Press, 1998.

Ortiz, Sara Elizabeth Gavrell. "Beyond Welfare: Animal Integrity, Animal Dignity, and Genetic Engineering." *Ethics and the Environment* 9, no. 1 (Spring 2004): 94–120.

Parfit, Derek. *Reasons and Persons.* Oxford: Clarendon Press, 1984.

Partridge, Ernest. "Posthumous Interests and Posthumous Respect." *Ethics* 91, no. 2 (January 1981): 243–64.

Pearce, Fred. "Birds Do It, Bees Do It: Pollinators Are Vital for Crop Yields. But They Are Dying Out." *New Scientist*, February 14, 1998.

"Pedigree Dogs Plagued by Disease." *BBC News*, August 19, 2008. http://news .bbc.co.uk/go/pr/fr/-/1/hi/uk/7569064.stm.

Petrinovich, Lewis. *Darwinian Dominion: Animal Welfare and Human Interests.* London: MIT Press, 1999.

Pettit, Philip. *Republicanism.* Oxford: Clarendon Press, 1997.

Phillips, Anne. *Multiculturalism Without Culture.* Princeton: Princeton University Press, 2007.

Pluhar, Evelyn B. *The Moral Significance of Human and Nonhuman Animals.* Durham, N.C.: Duke University Press, 1995.

Quong, Jonathan. "Cultural Exemptions, Expensive Tastes and Equal Opportunities." *Journal of Applied Philosophy* 23, no. 1 (January 2006): 53–71.

Rachels, James. *Created from Animals: The Moral Implications of Darwinism.* Oxford: Oxford University Press, 1990.

Randerson, James. "Does a Hook Hurt a Fish? The Evidence Is Reeling In." *New Scientist*, May 3, 2003.

Raven, Peter H., and George B. Johnson. *Biology.* 4th ed. London: WCB Publishers, 1996.

Rawls, John. *Political Liberalism.* New York: Columbia University Press, 1993.

Raz, Joseph. "Liberating Duties." *Law and Philosophy* 8, no. 1 (April 1989): 3–21.

——. *The Morality of Freedom.* Oxford: Clarendon Press, 1988.

Regan, Tom. *The Case for Animal Rights.* 2nd ed. Berkeley: University of California Press, 2004.

——. "McCloskey on Why Animals Cannot Have Rights." *The Philosophical Quarterly* 26, no. 104 (July 1976): 251–7.

Reiss, Michael J., and Roger Straughan. *Improving Nature? The Science and Ethics of Genetic Engineering.* Cambridge: Cambridge University Press, 1996.

Roberts, Monty. *The Man Who Listens to Horses.* London: Arrow Books, 1997.

Rollin, Bernard E. *Animal Rights and Human Morality.* 3rd ed. New York: Prometheus Books, 2006.

——. *The Frankenstein Syndrome: Ethical and Social Issues in the Genetic Engineering of Animals.* Cambridge: Cambridge University Press, 1995.

——. *Science and Ethics.* New York: Cambridge University Press, 2006.

————. *The Unheeded Cry: Animal Consciousness, Animal Pain and Science.* Oxford: Oxford University Press, 1989.

Rolston III, Homes. "Challenges in Environmental Ethics." In *Environmental Philosophy: From Animal Rights to Radical Ecology,* edited by M. E. Zimmerman, J. Baird Callicott, G. Sessions, K. J. Warren, and J. Clark, 124–44. 2nd ed. Englewood Cliffs: Prentice Hall, 1998.

————. "Duties to Endangered Species." In *Environmental Ethics,* edited by R. Elliot, 60–75. Oxford: Oxford University Press, 1995.

Rowlands, Mark. *Animals Like Us.* London: Verso, 2002.

————. *Animal Rights: Moral Theory and Practice.* 2nd ed. Basingstoke: Palgrave Macmillan, 2009.

————. "Contractarianism and Animal Rights." *Journal of Applied Philosophy* 14, no. 3 (November 1997): 235–47.

"RSPCA Reports Year of Shocking Animal Abuse." *Guardian,* July 26, 2006.

Russow, Lilly-Marlene. "Why Do Species Matter?" In *Planet in Peril: Essays in Environmental Ethics,* edited by D. Westphal and F. Westphal, 251–62. Orlando: Harcourt Brace College Publishers, 1994.

Sagoff, Mark. "Animal Liberation and Environmental Ethics: Bad Marriage: Quick Divorce." In *Environmental Ethics: What Really Matters, What Really Works,* edited by D. Schmidtz and E. Willott, 38–44. Oxford: Oxford University Press, 2002.

————. "Do Non-Native Species Threaten the Natural Environment?" *Journal of Agricultural and Environmental Ethics* 18, no. 3 (May 2005): 215–36.

Sapontzis, S. F. *Morals, Reason and Animals.* Philadelphia: Temple University Press, 1987.

Scanlon, T. "Value, Desire and Quality of Life." In *The Quality of Life,* edited by M. C. Nussbaum and A. Sen, 185–200. Oxford: Clarendon Press, 1993.

Schiermeier, Quirin. "New Evidence That Fish Feel Pain." *Nature News,* April 30, 2003. http://www.nature.com/news/2003/030430/full/news030428-9.html.

Scruton, Roger. *Animal Rights and Wrongs.* 3rd ed. London: Metro Books, 2000.

"Sheep Turning Blue for St Andrew." *BBC News,* November 27, 2008. http://news.bbc.co.uk/go/pr/fr/-/1/hi/scotland/7751243.stm.

Shue, Henry. *Basic Rights: Subsistence, Affluence and US Foreign Policy.* 2nd ed. Princeton: Princeton University Press, 1996.

Simberloff, Daniel. "Non-native Species *Do* Threaten the Natural Environment." *Journal of Agricultural and Environmental Ethics* 18, no. 7 (December 2005): 595–607.

Simmonds, N. E. "Rights at the Cutting Edge." In *A Debate over Rights,* edited by Matthew H. Kramer, N. E. Simmonds, and Hillel Steiner, 113–232. Oxford: Clarendon Press, 1998.

Singer, Peter. "All Animals Are Equal." In *Applied Ethics,* edited by P. Singer, 215–28. Oxford: Oxford University Press, 1986.

————. *Animal Liberation.* 2nd ed. London: Pimlico, 1995.

————. "Heavy Petting." *Nerve.com* (2001). http://www.nerve.com/Opinions/Singer/heavyPetting/main.asp.

————. "Not for Humans Only: The Place of Nonhumans in Environmental Issues." In *Ethics and Problems of the 21ˢᵗ Century,* edited by K. E. Goodpaster and K. M. Sayre, 191–206. Notre Dame: University of Notre Dame Press, 1979.

―――. *Practical Ethics.* 2nd ed. Cambridge: Cambridge University Press, 1993.

―――. "Review: Do Consequences Count? Rethinking the Doctrine of Double Effect." *Hastings Center Report* 10, no. 1 (February 1980): 42–4.

Singer, Peter, and Paola Cavalieri eds. *The Great Ape Project: Equality Beyond Humanity.* London: Fourth Estate, 1993.

Slicer, Deborah. "Your Daughter or Your Dog? A Feminist Assessment of the Animal Research Issue." In *The Feminist Care Tradition in Animal Ethics*, edited by J. Donovan and C. Adams, 105–24. New York: Columbia University Press, 2007.

Smith, Kevin R. "Animal Genetic Manipulation: A Utilitarian Response." In *The Animal Ethics Reader*, edited by S. J. Armstrong and R.G. Botzler, 390–7. 2nd ed. Abingdon: Routledge, 2008.

Spain, C. Victor, Janet M. Scarlett, and Katherine A. Houpt. "Long-Term Risks and Benefits of Early-Age Gonadectomy in Dogs." *Journal of the American Veterinary Medical Association* 224, no. 3 (February 2004): 380–7.

Spencer, Stuart, Eddy DeCuypere, Stefan Aerts, and Johan De Tavernier. "History and Ethics of Keeping Pets: Comparison with Farm Animals." *Journal of Agricultural and Environmental Ethics* 19, no. 1 (February 2006): 17–25.

Steeves, Peter H. ed. *Animal Others: On Ethics, Ontology, and Animal Life.* Albany: State University of New York Press, 1999.

Steinbock, Bonnie. "Speciesism and the Idea of Equality." *Philosophy* 53, no. 204 (April 1978): 247–56.

Steiner, Hillel. "Moral Rights." In *The Oxford Handbook of Ethical Theory*, edited by D. Copp, 459–80. Oxford: Oxford University Press, 2005.

―――. "Working Rights." In *A Debate over Rights*, edited by Matthew H. Kramer, N. E. Simmonds, and Hillel Steiner, 283–300. Oxford: Clarendon Press, 1998.

Stern, Nicholas. *The Economics of Climate Change: The Stern Review.* Cambridge: Cambridge University Press, 2007.

"Stray Dog Survey 2006," conducted by GfK NOP on behalf of Dogs Trust. http://www.dogstrust.org.uk/press_office/stray_dog_survey_2006/.

Sumner, L. W. *The Moral Foundation of Rights.* Oxford: Clarendon Press, 1987.

―――. *Welfare, Happiness and Ethics.* Oxford: Clarendon Press, 1996.

Sunstein, Cass R. "Introduction: What Are Animal Rights?" In *Animal Rights: Current Debates and New Directions*, edited by C. R. Sunstein and M. C. Nussbaum, 3–15. Oxford: Oxford University Press, 2004.

Swift, Adam, and Stuart White. "Political Theory, Social Science and Real Politics." In *Political Theory: Methods and Approaches*, edited by D. Leopold and M. Stears, 49–69. Oxford: Oxford University Press, 2008.

Sztybel, David. "Distinguishing Animal Rights from Animal Welfare." In *Encyclopedia of Animal Rights and Animal Welfare*, edited by M. Bekoff, 130–2. Westport: Greenwood Publishing, 1998.

Taylor, Angus. *Animals and Ethics.* Ontario: Broadview Press, 2003.

Taylor, Charles. "Atomism." In *Philosophy and the Human Sciences: Philosophical Papers 2*, 187–210. Cambridge: Cambridge University Press, 1985.

Taylor, Paul W. *Respect for Nature: A Theory of Environmental Ethics.* Princeton: Princeton University Press, 1986.

"The Slaughtered Horses That Shame Our Racing." *Observer*, October 1, 2006.

Tremlett, Giles. "Bullfight Reform Plan Is Red Rag to Aficionados." *Guardian*, December 21, 2006.

VanDeVeer, Donald. "Of Beasts, Persons and the Original Position." *The Monist* 62, no. 3 (July 1979): 368–77.

Van Der Zi, Bibi. "Cosmetics Industry Criticised as EU Set to Admit Delay in Animal Testing Ban." *Guardian*, December 31, 2010.

Varner, Gary. *In Nature's Interests? Interests, Animal Rights and Environmental Ethics*. Oxford: Oxford University Press, 1998.

Vlastos, Gregory. "Justice and Equality." In *Social Justice*, edited by R. Brandt, 31–72. Englewood Cliffs, N.J.: Prentice-Hall, 1962.

Waldron, Jeremy. "The Core of the Case Against Judicial Review." *Yale Law Journal* 115, no. 6 (April 2006): 1346–1406.

———. *The Right to Private Property*. Oxford: Clarendon Press, 1988.

Warren, Mary Anne. *Moral Status: Obligations to Persons and Other Living Things*. Oxford: Oxford University Press, 1997.

White, Thomas I. *In Defense of Dolphins: A New Moral Frontier*. Malden: Blackwell, 2007.

Wickins-Dražilová, Dita. "Zoo Animal Welfare." *Journal of Agricultural and Environmental Ethics* 19, no. 1 (February 2006): 27–36.

Williams, Janet. "US Judge Blocks Tribal Whaling." *BBC News*, May 4, 2002. http://news.bbc.co.uk/1/hi/world/americas/1967677.stm.

Wise, Steven M. *Rattling the Cage: Towards Legal Rights for Animals*. London: Profile Books, 2000.

———. *Unlocking the Cage: Science and the Case for Animal Rights*. Oxford: Perseus Press, 2002.

Woodward, James. "The Non-Identity Problem." *Ethics* 96, no. 4 (July 1986): 804–31.

Zhang, Zhibon. "Mathematical Models of Wildlife Management by Contraception." *Ecological Modelling* 132, nos. 1–2 (July 2000): 105–13.

Index

abolitionism, 3, 7, 80, 204
adoption, 131
aesthetic value, 74–75, 173
agency, 2, 8, 11, 26–32, 63, 75, 91–92, 108, 132, 214n27, 218n36. *See also* autonomy; conception of the good; dignity; ends-in-themselves; personhood; self-government
agriculture, use of animals in, 17, 79–102 . *See also* farming; meat, industry
AIDS virus, 58, 171
Alba, the rabbit, 109
alien species. *See* nonnative species
Alward, Peter, 92, 219nn14–15
Anderson, Elizabeth, 32–33, 214n30, 218n30
Animal Liberation, 3–6, 39, 203, 211n6, 215n43
anthropocentrism, 49, 156–57, 162
Aquinas, Thomas, 96
arrogance. *See* humility
arthritis, interest in not contracting, 56
ascorbic acid, interest in, 158
asylums, for the mentally ill, 145–47
Attfield, Robin, 120, 158, 215n39, 221n22
autonomy, 8–13, 16, 26, 31, 63, 66, 69, 72–78, 108, 115, 132, 138, 142, 193, 204–206, 210, 212n21, 218n33; preference autonomy, 75–76. *See also* agency; conception of the good; dignity; ends-in-themselves; personhood; self-government

babies, 36, 68–70, 76, 77, 120. *See also* young infants
Balcombe, Jonathan, 133, 222n11
Balzer, Philipp, 115, 221n13
Barry, Brian, 191, 217n18, 227nn13&17
bears, 128, 138–40, 143–47
Bedlam, 146
bestiality, 109–111

biocentrism, 156–57. *See also* ecocentrism
biodiversity loss, 156
biological ends, 74–75, 124. *See also* functions, species-typical
biotic community. *See* land ethic
birds: as messengers, 107; on whether are sentient, 23
Blakemore, Colin, 51–52
blameworthiness, 92–93
bonobos, 26, 133. *See also* great apes
Bou-Habib, Paul, 199, 227nn20–21, 227n26
breeding, of animals, 60, 74, 103, 120, 131–36
buffalo, water, 175, 177
bullfighting, 139, 181, 186–89, 191. *See also* jallikattu
burdens, of duties, 10, 30, 42–43, 62, 83, 87, 94–96, 191, 194, 20, 205

Callicott, James Baird, 160–61, 224n1, 224n6
cancer, 58, 119, 122, 134–35
cannibalism, 87–88, 109–111
capture and relocation. *See* wild animals
Casal, Paula, 194, 200, 227nn18&20, 228n28
cascade effects, 93, 173
castration, of piglets, 82
Cataldi, Suzanne Laba, 143–45, 223n25
cats, 35, 68, 94–95, 128, 133–35, 150; Manx, 135
cattle. *See* cows
cephalods, on whether are sentient, 24
cetaceans, 11–12, 26, 138. *See also* dolphins; hunting, of whales; killer whales; ocean parks
chickens, 23; battery, 79–80; nonconscious, 124–26
circus, 3, 128–29, 136–39, 142–46, 153, 206, 222n17